Conflict and Stability
in Fifteenth-Century England

J. R. Lander

J. R. Lander was born in the Midlands, and became the first member of[1] his family to consider a career outside industry or commerce. He was encouraged in this by a brilliant and inspiring history master, H. E. Howard. He won a scholarship to Pembroke College, Cambridge, where he was much influenced as an undergraduate by the economic historian H. J. Habakkuk, and later as a graduate student by the late Helen Maud Cam, one of the most brilliant English medievalists of her generation. After a few years as a civil servant in the Board of Trade he returned to Cambridge to research and produce his thesis on 'The Administration of the Yorkist Kings 1461–1485'. From 1950 to 1963 Professor Lander taught at the University College of the Gold Coast, later the University of Ghana. In 1963 he moved to Dalhousie University in Nova Scotia, and in 1965 to the University of Western Ontario.

Conflict and Stability in Fifteenth-Century England

J. R. Lander
J. B. Smallman Professor of History
in the University of Western Ontario

Hutchinson of London

Hutchinson & Co (Publishers) Ltd
3 Fitzroy Square, London w1

London Melbourne Sydney Auckland
Wellington Johannesburg and agencies
throughout the world

First published 1969
Reprinted 1971
Second edition 1974
Third edition 1977
© J. R. Lander 1969, 1974, 1977 and 1979

Set in Monotype Times

Printed in Great Britain by The Anchor Press Ltd
and bound by Wm Brendon & Son Ltd
both of Tiptree, Essex

ISBN 0 09 129190 9 (cased)
ISBN 0 09 129191 7 (paper)

To Paul

Contents

Preface to third edition

Since this book was first published in 1969 new research has considerably modified opinions on several important aspects of fifteenth-century English history. I have, therefore, taken the opportunity of a new edition both to change points of emphasis and detail which seem desirable after more mature reflection upon them; and following the results of recent researches (both those of other scholars and my own) to rewrite sections of the chapters on economic history (particularly on wool production and the causes of enclosures), on the character of King Henry VI, on the role of the nobility in the Wars of the Roses and on the background to Lollardy.

Preface to first edition

After long neglect, many scholars, over the last two decades, have turned to investigate the history of fifteenth-century England. From their labours many technical, and in some cases controversial, studies of high quality have appeared. No general consensus of opinion upon the century's development has yet emerged from these modern studies, if, indeed, considering the type of evidence available, such agreement will ever be possible. Anyone who, in a short book, rushes to give a general picture of the period may well expect outraged specialists to scatter his rash bones to whiten by the wayside. I, therefore, offer these pages only as one man's reflection upon the century after many years of study, in the hope that those who disagree may riposte with their own.

This book is not intended to replace basic textbooks on the later Middle Ages. In so few pages I cannot hope to deal with everything significant in English development. I am well aware that it would have been possible to write a completely different kind of book, and that some readers may well deplore many omissions, in particular any analysis of the technical development of institutions, especially of parliament. However, such topics, to be made convincing, require accumulations of detail beyond the scope of any work of this kind. I have therefore tried to concentrate upon the broader developments of society.

I should like to thank Professor J. Hurstfield who first suggested that I should write this book and who made many valuable suggestions after reading my draft; Mr P. Hyslop who read my manuscript at various stages and made many pertinent criticisms; Dr W. K. Ferguson, Dr W. H. Stockdale, and Dr J. G. Rowe, who read the typescript and suggested many improvements; and Margaret Ferguson, who so painstakingly went through the typescript, revising its spelling, punctuation and layout, and also read the proofs. Lastly my thanks go to Mrs L. Weyerman for her careful typing from a difficult manuscript.

1 The dark glass of the fifteenth century

The fifteenth century north of the Alps was once described as the age of 'the *devotio moderna*, Our Lady of Sorrows, and the *danse macabre*'; an epoch running to such turbulent and motley extremes, 'that it bore the mixed smell of blood and roses', 'oscillating between the fear of hell and the most naïve joy, between cruelty and tenderness, between harsh asceticism and insane attachment to the delights of this world'.[1] Historians better informed about the high Middle Ages and the sixteenth century dismissed it as either a dreary or a wildly picturesque waste land between two greater and more constructive epochs. 'The Waning of the Middle Ages' is a mesmeric concept which has for long dominated the prose of historians so fascinated by an imagined morphology of decay that one of them has even endowed the century with a collective death wish. At best, amid its supposed violent chaos, feeble institutions, economic decline and the macabre details of its *momento mori* art[2] some few hopeful signs could be detected of transition to the modern world and the modern state.

The concept of the swift sixteenth-century growth of the national state and of modern institutions from the débris of a decaying medievalism was, until lately, an almost universal commonplace of European historical writing. It assumed its own peculiar, insular form in England – the image (now, like the wider concept, somewhat tarnished) of a renewed and powerful Tudor monarchy emotionally based on a growing nationalism, suppressing the remains of a turbulent nobility and supported by a middle class increasing in wealth and political pretensions.

Modern studies of the fifteenth, and of the sixteenth, century are

1. J. Huizinga, *The Waning of the Middle Ages* (London, 1924), p. 18.
2. The symbols of death, the corpse, the skeleton, are, after all, prominent enough in certain types of baroque art, but no one has therefore called the seventeenth century decadent. Mr A. R. Myers (*England in the Later Middle Ages*, p. 162) has convincingly suggested that in the fifteenth century it was 'the increasing attraction of this world, which made death seem the more terrible'.

producing a mass of evidence which is quietly obliterating these traditional speculations. Before commenting on the results of such studies it is, however, desirable to say something of the materials upon which they are based.

Since professional schools of history were first organized in the English universities during the mid-nineteenth century, until very recently, academic historians flocked to the more tractable sources of earlier and later periods. In the process they abandoned the fifteenth century to the romancers and the novelists, who wrote of it in cloak and dagger, blood and thunder terms which derived mainly (though they were quite unaware of it) from political propaganda first put out by the Yorkists and developed by the early Tudors.

In 1461, when a small and far from representative group of magnates seized the throne by force for Edward IV, they justified their action in terms which assumed that no right-minded man could possibly deny the validity of his right to occupy it. They then pointed out to parliament in words ringing with a vehement righteousness that their deeds in restoring its true inheritance to the new king's family would result in the restoration of social peace and good government. God had visited the land with punishment and tribulation the like of which had never been seen or heard in any other Christian land, and the troubles and bloodshed (which we call the Wars of the Roses) had been the divine retribution for the wicked murder of King Richard II and the usurpation of Henry IV and his son and grandson.

Henry VII's official historian, Polydore Vergil of Urbino, who listened to the somewhat distant reminiscences of men who had lived through these events, and those of their descendants, was well aware of such opinions. This propagandist, exculpatory theme of divine retribution, inflicted upon usurpers and their subjects through bloody and calamitous civil wars, dominates the section of his *Anglica Historia* devoted to the fifteenth century. Once the Tudor historians, Edward Hall and Ralph Holinshed, hallowed and embellished this moral theme and William Shakespeare transformed it for the stage, necessarily dropping its more prosaic qualifications in the process, the blood-curdling horrors of fatal strife, dynastic tragedy and extreme aristocratic mortality reigned supreme in the popular mind.

No careful modern historian with any respect for truth can even hope to depict the century in terms so forceful or dramatic. This is not because contemporary materials are lacking. They have come down to us in terrifying abundance, and they are, to say the least, unalluring. Miles of parchment and occasional scraps of paper unroll the humdrum operations of Chancery, Exchequer, royal household, and law courts, in the prosaic Latin, prolix French, and repetitive English which the clerks of these institutions habitually used. Such documents reveal the essential continuity of the forms of administration behind semi-collapse into unusual violence caused mainly by weak government and to a lesser degree by dynastic ambition. They enable the patient investigator, with considerable drudgery, to re-create the social structure of the period against which he may interpret political events perhaps a little more certainly than before. Yet, when all is said in its favour, evidence of this kind can never wholly compensate the lack of more consciously intelligent and communicative material. The fifteenth century, though one of the great creative periods of English architecture and music, produced very little readable literature, and no single political writer of first-rate talent. The great series of monastic chronicles which so memorably depict, though inevitably in a biased clerical way, the conflicts and personalities of earlier centuries, come to an end in 1422 with the death of Thomas Walsingham of St Albans. His only successor in the monastic scriptorium, Abbot John Whethampstede, with his naïve strivings for a high-flown euphuistic style (*verborum florida venustas*, as he called it), was too conceited a literary craftsman, for other than odd passages of his works to be taken as satisfactory evidence of the politics of the day. The English chronicles, national and local, which took the place of the monastic writers, although they mark the beginnings of a new type of popular literature, are naïve, myopic, and meagre. Their poverty-stricken vocabulary, limited vision, credulous reproduction of rumour and slander, long and immensely detailed descriptions of ceremonies and pageants combined with the most exiguous political information, leave the critical middle years of the century in a shroud of darkness. Towards its end the Italians, Dominic Mancini and Polydore Vergil, and that most accomplished Englishman, Sir Thomas More (the only author ever to write drafts of a book simultaneously in Latin and English) enter a new world of sophisticated observation. Yet although their accounts are based on oral evidence and oral tradition, their works were written too much under the influence of humanist ideas of history to provide the detailed veracities which a modern reader expects. Above all, we lack the series of state papers and personal correspondence which bring to life the motives and inner thoughts of Tudor statesmen. Research workers can accumulate a vast amount of comparatively insignificant detail about the lives and the possessions – particularly the possessions – of fifteenth-century statesmen, nobles, and gentry; only rarely any statements which throw a sure light upon their motives. With rare exceptions their thoughts may be inferred only from their actions, and such inferences, without knowledge of the evasions and compromises which so often precede momentous political decisions are, at best, an equivocal, and may be a completely misleading, guide to the springs of action.

In days before rapid and easy communications, rumour always flourished. Historians, desperate for facts and faced by such comparative dearth, have fed lavishly on the exceptionally rich undergrowth of history which the fifteenth century produced: dubious legends propagated by contemporary writers and those of the next generation, smears, slanders, false accusations, the unstinted exaggerations of criminal indictments, deliberate fabrications placed on official records to conceal inconvenient or discreditable facts, partisan literature taken at its face value have all contributed to a rich mélange in which it is difficult to distinguish truth from fiction – and, until recently, very few indeed have even tried to do so. Generations of historians have repeated the fable of the Shepherd Lord, invented or somehow picked up by Edward Hall seventy or eighty years later. The story runs that Lord Clifford brutally murdered Edward IV's twelve-year-old[1] brother, Edmund of Rutland, after the battle of Wakefield (1460). After her husband's death in battle a few weeks later Clifford's timorous widow, for dread of Yorkist revenge, concealed their son and brought him up in obscurity amongst the hills and flocks of Yorkshire and Cumberland, to come out of hiding an uncouth, illiterate rustic only after Henry VII's accession. In fact he was living openly and unmolested in England as early as 1472.

Another atrocity story of even later origin is that of the so-called 'battle of Nibley Green' between Viscount Lisle and Lord Berkeley, the two main claimants to the long-disputed Berkeley inheritance, in which Viscount Berkeley was killed. The story of this battle, from which all modern accounts derive, was written by James Smyth, the Berkeleys' family steward, in the early seventeenth century. The two parties to the quarrel exchanged insulting letters of defiance on 19 March 1469 and agreed to fight between eight and nine o'clock the following morning. Overnight Lord Berkeley hastily procured men from Thornbury and from the Forest of Dean (which, at this period, according to William Camden, writing a century or more

1. He was, in fact, seventeen.

later, harboured a population of desperadoes always ready for outrage). Smyth also added Bristol, though he honestly admitted that he had seen the records of an enquiry made by the mayor of Bristol on 2 May which exonerated twenty people questioned of all suspicion of sending armed men to sustain Lord Berkeley. Yet he darkly remarked that he knew from 'other notes and memorials of a stronger dye' that many men did in fact turn up from Bristol. And, to clinch the matter, added that 'if traditions be here allowed' he had heard in Nibley, Wotton, and other nearby villages from William Longe, John Cole, Mother Burton, Mother Pernell, Mother Peter and many others, 'some of them one hundred and ten years old, divers an hundred and none under four score', how their parents and relations, boys of twelve and sixteen, after carrying victuals and weapons to the combatants had climbed into trees to watch the fight and they knew that Lord Berkeley had led a thousand men.

If this be true, the population of Nibley and the surrounding villages would be a unique geriatric phenomenon! It is, after all, hardly credible that Lord Berkeley could have assembled so many men upon such short notice. James Smyth himself, in fact, within two pages dignifies this particular brawl with the hardly synonymous titles of 'riot', 'battle', and 'skirmish'. Readers of a credulity even greater than his own have turned into a pitched battle a not uncommon, but unusually magnificent, riot.

Deliberate falsification adds difficulties even greater than the accretions of legend. Neither consistency nor excessive regard for truth were conspicuously medieval virtues. Contemporary writers changed their views to laud the successful and to denigrate the fallen and in their partisan zeal often piled the muck-heap of scandal exceedingly high. After Henry IV seized the throne Thomas Walsingham cut out of his *Chronica Majora* a number of bitterly disparaging references to the king's father, John of Gaunt. John Hardyng wrote two different accounts of the revolution of 1399, the first for Lancastrian, the second for Yorkist, readers, and after Henry VII's accession, John Rous, the Warwickshire antiquary, made a new Latin version of his English *Roll of the Earls of Warwick*, changing a laudatory account of Richard III into one quite hostile. Accusations of bastardy became almost a political convention. Towards the end of the king's life hostile rumours alleged that a French canon in the Black Prince's household had fathered Richard II, and added for good measure that he was born without a skin and nourished in the skins of goats. Yorkist propaganda at one point claimed that Margaret of Anjou was illegitimate, and when the same faction also claimed that she had conceived her son, Edward, Prince of Wales, in adultery, Sir John Fortescue and others riposted with a story that Edward IV's ancestress, Philippa of Clarence, through whom he claimed his throne, had never been acknowledged by her father. The tale that Edward IV was the son of a French archer was well known by the early 1470s and Richard III not only impugned the validity of his brother's marriage with Elizabeth Wydeville, but, seizing upon the now old story of the French archer, publicly accused his own mother of adultery.

Men always expected to make a substantial profit, if not substantial fortune, out of the royal service. Such expectations were amongst the principal factors which held government and society together. At the same time low standards of conduct, particularly in matters financial, combined with a normal condition of confusion and arrears in the royal accounts, made plausible enough almost any accusation of corruption against political opponents. Even Henry V, as Prince of Wales, was forced to clear himself of accusations that he had made away with funds intended for the Calais garrison.

Confusion is even worse confounded by the deliberate fabrications of triumphant factions, by those who practised the art of forgery to gain immediate political ends, or took care to place on official records their own mendacious *ex parte* interpretations of events. There is a distinct possibility that Richard II tampered with the Parliament Roll of 1397, and he certainly forged that of January 1398. The victorious Lancastrians of 1399 set out on the roll an account, to say the least disingenuous, of their actions against Richard II, while Richard of York and his friends wrote for the record their own version of the events which led to the first battle of St Albans in 1455.

The more formal partisan literature of the times adds its share to the delusions of venerable fable and political calculation. The popular views of both Henry V and Edward IV originated, one in a eulogy, the other in a calculated smear: Henry's transformation from a conventional, if exceptionally successful, warrior and dispenser of justice into the splendid hero-king, the very paragon of piety, justice and valour, derived in great measure from an 'official life' commissioned in the late 1430s by his brother, Humphrey of Gloucester, from the Italian humanist, Tito Livio da Forli, though it remained for the imagination of William Shakespeare to transform him into a nationalist leader.

The reputation of Edward IV suffered from the opposite process of denigration. At the end of his life, and for two centuries and more later, his reputation stood high amongst the writers of his own country. It was only in the early eighteenth century that Rapin de Thoyras, in a best-selling work, fixed for the future the standard account of Edward as a handsome but politically immature prince given over in his later years to lust and luxury, neglecting affairs of state except when roused to momentary bursts of energy and cruelty by a political crisis or a fit of avarice: opinions which he took from Philippe de Commynes' *Mémoires*, a book written by a royal councillor so anxious to show that his employer, King Louis XI (d. 1483), stood so far above any other prince of his time in shrewdness and statecraft that he consistently wrote down the abilities of other contemporary rulers to serve as foils for the king of France.

The fifteenth century is still, and will probably always remain, one of the most obscure centuries of English history. The decline of contemporary political writing into naïve English chronicles means that our knowledge of even its most elementary political events is woefully incomplete. The recent discovery of a short, jejune Latin chronicle in the library of Trinity College, Dublin, provides new information even on such elementary details as the dates of the sessions of parliament. Any political narrative – of the mid-century in particular – inevitably made up from shreds and tatters and wisps of information, is bound to give a false impression of certainty unless the reader is occasionally reminded to treat it with the scepticism which it deserves. On the other hand, events and characters can now, to some extent, be stripped of their deceiving veils of contemporary perjury, forgery, adulation, or slander and the accretions of a long-hallowed romantic tradition – what Edward Hall, himself a guilty enough projector of legend, called 'conjectures, which as often deceive the imaginations of fantastical folk'. Future accounts of fifteenth-century England may now become more plausible than those of the past: they will also be more prosaic.

2 The country's economy

Though hardly one of the 'last enchantments of the Middle Ages' the economic condition of fifteenth-century England is certainly one of their darker mysteries. Most generalizations about it are still controversial, and the remarks which follow can be offered as no more than hypotheses deduced from intricate and intractable evidence.

Even in the days of the Roman Empire, with its well-constructed aqueducts, ample water supplies and high standards of sanitation, the expectation of life even amongst the rich was as low as that of the degraded masses crowded into a Victorian slum. Conditions were certainly no better at any time during the Middle Ages. Life in England was more akin to that of under-developed countries than to anything we know in Europe today: a medley of the extremes of riches and bitter poverty, splendour and squalor, untreated and un-treatable disease and the expectation of an early death. Life was short: its standards for most of the population unbelievably low. Although the fortunate who survived their middle or late twenties could expect perhaps another twenty years of life, child mortality was appallingly high. Dean Colet's nineteen brothers and sisters (to quote an extreme example) all died one after another in childhood. The Dean's parents had been abnormally fertile for, contrary to popular ideas, large families were exceptional in the pre-industrial world. Peasants, artisans and merchants married later than nineteenth-century factory workers. Peasants had to wait until they inherited the family holding, artisans and merchants served a long apprenticeship. The combination of late marriage and low expectation of life kept down the number of children to about four or five per marriage. It also bred a population less fitted to bear the burden of life than that of today. As in present-day India, Ceylon, and West Africa, probably few people came to maturity with both parents still living, and two-fifths of the population were children under fourteen, as compared with about one-quarter in England today. Moreover, physical deterioration came upon the adult far earlier than it comes in the later twentieth century. Most men and women endured chronic bad health by the age of forty. Such a population, with so short a life span when their working capacity was at its maximum, must have been, by modern standards, terribly unproductive.

In spite of this gloomy assessment, the people of fifteenth-century England were fortunate as compared with earlier and later generations. In pre-industrial societies in which it was impossible to import any considerable supplies of cheap foodstuffs the standard of life depended upon a crude equation between the acreage of land available for agriculture and the number of mouths dependent upon it. Once the population rose above a certain level (as, once again, is still the case in the more backward parts of the world) it began to press dangerously upon its food supplies. The standard of life deteriorated to the point of chronic malnutrition, and inevitable disaster followed.

It may, at first sight, seem incredible that, in the early fourteenth century, England, with a population of only three and three-quarter millions, or thereabout, could have reached this point of 'critical population density'. Its population, however, forced a far greater segment of their needs from the soil than their descendants do today. Imported cotton and artificial fibres have now released wide acres of the countryside from flax production and the hunger of the wool-producing sheep. Coal, oil, natural gas, and steel have reduced the need for vast forests formerly essential to provide fuel and to meet the needs of the building trades. Petrol has reduced the horse population to a level necessary only to satisfy the well-to-do who regard obsolete forms of traction as one of their major sports. A horse had been an expensive animal to keep, for the medieval horse ate quite as much as its modern descendant, which meant that a much larger area was needed for its maintenance, and for that of its rider himself. With grain yields standing at about threefold the quantity of seed sown as compared with twenty today and each acre of wheat producing nine or ten bushels as compared with today's fifty-eight or sixty, it took a far larger acreage of land to sustain a comparable population. Even these low figures are unduly complimentary to medieval agriculture, for the modern bushel is slightly greater in size and the specific gravity of modern grains is higher – which may well involve an increase of more than one-fifth. Moreover, under late medieval conditions much land and man-power were wasted. At least one-third of the arable area lay fallow every year, and in the days before mechanization agriculture depended to a far greater extent than it does today upon casual labour to deal with its seasonal rushes. It could function only if there was a considerable pool of casual labour, a pool necessarily unemployed, or at least under-employed, for a great part of the year, and therefore poverty-stricken and degraded. In 1960 in the United States of America every farm worker produced enough food to feed twelve people. The figure for fifteenth-century England was probably nearer to that for Ghana, where a single worker on the land can still feed no more than one and a half people.

During the fourteenth century a cycle of agrarian disasters developed in Europe. As early as the eleventh century, if not earlier in some areas, population had begun to rise. Although the amount of land under the plough was vastly extended, and extended to the point of cultivating really marginal soils, the balance between population and food supplies had reached danger point by the early fourteenth century. During its second decade a frightful famine, the result of disastrous harvests over three consecutive years caused by unheard-of torrential rains, afflicted the peoples of Europe. According to the Annals of Bermondsey the poor ate dogs, cats, the dung of doves and their own children and John Trokelowe relates that starving men and women haunted the London streets, that filthy corpses lay everywhere in the wards and in the lanes, that famished thieves in the gaols ferociously fell upon new prisoners and devoured them half-alive. A generation later the Black Death of 1349, the hardly less mortal Grey Death of 1361, and continuing but gradually less virulent outbreaks of bubonic plague and other obscure epidemic diseases, were so lethal (if historians interpret the circumstantial evidence correctly) because they struck a population whose resistance to epidemic disease had been seriously lowered by chronic under-nourishment.

The frightful mortality of the plague – the population declined by about two-fifths between 1348 and the end of the century – was a blessing in disguise for the survivors, for it restored a more favourable balance between food supplies and population. Marginal lands, forced under plough and harrow at the peak of the thirteenth-century economic boom, now reverted to scrub and waste. Historians have too readily assumed that these widening acres of uncultivated land meant declining prosperity for the country as a whole. This assumption is quite unwarranted. There is nothing at this point theoretically incompatible between diminished total production and the maintenance or even the advancement of general prosperity. The reduction in population and the contraction of the cultivated area must be set against each other. Although total agricultural production was less in 1400 than it had been a century earlier, and probably still remained so in 1500, production per head of the population was certainly greater.

The visual evidence of the countryside shows that throughout the fifteenth century there was money and to spare above the level of immediate need in most parts of England. The extent of building bears ample witness to its prosperity. Although in the Midlands, in Leicestershire and Northamptonshire, the fourteenth century had been the great age of church building, in many other districts, particularly Lincolnshire, East Anglia, and the south-west, parish churches now rose to a new magnificence. Between the Black Death and the accession of King Henry VIII the inhabitants of hundreds of towns and villages rebuilt or enlarged their churches. In the south-western counties and in Lancashire hundreds of little private oratories and chapels appeared during the fifteenth century, the greater number of them attached to remote and lonely houses, some built at cross roads to serve districts far distant from parish churches. Great monasteries made extensive improvements to their buildings. Secular lords erected magnificent castles and lesser men comfortable country houses.

A new and marked development of the off-shore fishing industry resulted in the growth of new fishing villages where it paid enterprising local landowners or other people to build stone quays and breakwaters to form man-made harbours on dangerous coasts. Staithes (the very name means 'landing place') is first heard of on the north Yorkshire coast in 1415. In Cornwall Mevagissey appeared in 1410, New Quay and Bude later in the century. Some of the handsomest stone bridges of the Middle Ages were either built or rebuilt at this time. Important bridges, first erected in the twelfth and thirteenth centuries, proving unsafe or too narrow for an apparently great increase in road traffic, were now replaced by new stone structures. Those over the River Ouse at Huntingdon and St Ives still attract the comments of travellers; so does that at East Farley over the Medway. At Twizel in Northumberland one magnificent stone span leapt over the River Till, and in 1603 Richard Carew still described the bridge at Wadebridge in Cornwall, built in 1468–70, as 'the longest, strongest and fairest that the shire can muster'.

Recent writers, by comparing the yield of taxation in 1334 and that of the new Tudor subsidy evolved between 1512 and 1515, have swung to extremes in trying to depict the fifteenth century as an age of considerable economic growth. At first sight a comparison of these taxation returns more than confirms the increase in wealth suggested by extensive building. It shows something like a threefold increase in the country's riches and their redistribution over different regions. As, however, there was little, if any, improvement in either agricultural or industrial techniques, so vast an increase in wealth would seem to be, on *a priori* grounds alone, a statistical delusion. In fact we may immediately rule out of court the product of these particular taxes as evidence of any remarkable growth in the country's resources. Over the centuries tax evasion has been a favourite avocation of Englishmen, and until recently it has seldom taken them more than a generation or so after the introduction of a new tax to devise the means of bilking their government in a big way.

The so-called Tudor subsidy was an innovation, tapping new sources of wealth and based on new criteria of assessment. Although for a short time highly productive, it took only thirty years before its yield began to show a calamitous decline, and long before the end of Elizabeth I's reign evasion had become a national scandal, notorious to all, but a scandal which the queen and her advisers found it necessary to tolerate for political reasons. On the other hand by 1334 the existing taxation system had already hardened into this fossil stage. Edward I had introduced the standard late medieval tax on personal property in 1275. By 1334 it was already half submerged in the usual swamps of evasion and corruption. In just over forty years a combination of conventional valuations and fraudulent under-assessment had reduced its yield by about two-thirds: all this at a time when it is most unlikely that either the population or the wealth of the country had declined. A disillusioned government now tacitly admitted failure by abandoning the established practice of directly assessing individuals, and allocated lump sums to be raised by each county. The yield thereupon became fixed at a figure merely derisory when compared with that of forty years earlier. In 1334 the system of taxation on personal property hardly began to tap the country's wealth.

The extent of the country's increased wealth is, therefore, an open question. Some increase there was, yet the prosperity of the period was due less to any total increase in production (which, indeed, declined) than to the division of the comparatively static product of a rigid agrarian economy between a far smaller number of people.

On the other hand, assuming that the inefficiency of the tax collectors varied but little from district to district, these same tax figures can be used fairly safely to compare relative changes in prosperity in different parts of the country. In the early fourteenth century the twelve richest counties were those of the grain-producing areas of the Midland belt, the area of champaign country, of the so-called classical manor, bounded on the north-west by a line drawn from Gloucester to Lincoln and on the south-east by a line from Reading to Yarmouth. By the early sixteenth century the area of greatest prosperity lay south of a line drawn from the Wash to the Severn estuary. By the 1520s two well-defined wealthy areas had emerged in southern England – a south-western group of counties, Gloucestershire, Somerset, and Wiltshire, roughly linked by Berkshire to a south-eastern block grouped round London and made up of Kent, Surrey, Middlesex, Hertfordshire, Essex and Suffolk: a remarkable transformation which suggests that by this time prosperity may have become more associated with wool, cloth, and other commodities than with the production of wheat.

The generations following the Black Death saw remarkable changes which greatly improved the lot of the working population. The plague had wiped out a large part of the pool of surplus labour, and in spite of attempts at rigid enforcement of legislation to keep wages at their traditional levels real wages doubled in the generations between the Black Death (1349) and the battle of Agincourt (1415). With such an increase labourers and artisans enjoyed remarkable prosperity as compared with earlier times.

At the same time the small landowners, the peasant farmers, and the increasing numbers of modest tradesmen who served their needs enjoyed a prosperity which forcibly, though not always favourably, impressed contemporary observers of this changing scene. The aristocratically minded French chronicler, Jean Froissart, with a sense of conservative outrage in a topsy-turvy world, excoriated the Peasants' Revolt of 1381 as the insolent result of the great prosperity which the common people enjoyed. Eighty years or so later Chief Justice Fortescue (d. 1479?), writing when in exile at Margaret of Anjou's poverty-stricken little court, rapturously praised the comfort and well-being of the English peasantry as compared with the French – and there is no occasion, as some have done, to dismiss his opinions as the mistaken nostalgic dreams of an émigré.

Peasant farming as it existed in most parts of England had always been mixed farming, partly arable, partly pasture, and so it remained during the fifteenth century. It is doubtful if the Black Death began any new trends in the history of the English farm house and its occupants, but it certainly quickened those already in being. There had been an active peasant land market in various parts of England, certainly from the thirteenth century if not earlier. Its activity gradually, but inexorably, destroyed the unity and cohesion of the peasant class; a process which quickened in the post-plague years. Poorer villeins fled the manor or sold out to become landless wage-earners. The more fortunate and the more able, by adding strip to strip and lease to lease, became prosperous, substantial farmers, their upper ranks beginning to form a peasant aristocracy, the Franklin of Chaucer's day, in whose house it 'snowed of meat and drink', or the yeoman of early Tudor times like Bishop Latimer's father. The good bishop's mother milked forty kine, his father was able to relieve the poor, provide his daughters with dowries and put his son to the university. The process stands out with remarkable clarity in the manor of Apsley Guise. There in 1275 the peasantry held more or less equal tenements of fifteen acres. By 1542 three only remained with this erstwhile standard tenement, while one prosperous tenant held sixty acres and three had accumulated as many as seventy-five.

When in the late fourteenth century great landlords began to let their manorial demesnes extensively they added considerably to the opportunities of the smaller landowner, whether peasant or gentleman of modest estate. Former estate officials often set up farming on their own account or added demesne acres to their existing holdings. Nicholas Stake, who was sergeant of Mertsham in 1389, ran the demesne on behalf of the monks of Christchurch, Canterbury, in return for a yearly wage. In 1395 he took up the lease of the manor for a term of ten years, paying an annual rent of £38, a considerable sum of money. Many a man who called himself a gentleman possessed a cash income of less than half that amount.

During the fifteenth century the English peasantry were 'in quiet and prosperous estate'. Villeinage was dying, and even if land was being absorbed on one particular manor by peasants consolidating two or more tenements, it was often available for others elsewhere. Depopulation meant that many people could now obtain holdings who would have envied them in vain before the Black Death. The prosperity of labourer and artisan was, however, dangerously flawed. Time would run against it. Already by the later decades of the century their time was slowly, perhaps almost imperceptibly, running out. The first proclamation against that notorious Tudor horror, the sturdy beggar, dates from as early as 1473. The prosperity of the labourer and artisan crashed during the sixteenth century when rapidly rising population drove the landless once again into the deepening misery inevitable to any large increase in numbers before industrialization could sustain them upon new sources of wealth.

A large section of the peasantry was almost equally vulnerable. Their prosperity rested on dangerously insecure legal foundations. Tenurially there were three types of peasant farmer – the freeholder, the copyholder, and the leaseholder. The freeholder enjoyed a security of tenure well-nigh absolute. As long as he performed certain minor services demanded by the custom of the manor he stood firm in his rights and could be neither financially oppressed nor evicted. By contrast his neighbour, holding a tenement under a lease, was at the mercy of a lord who could rackrent, otherwise alter terms, or evict him as the conditions of the local land market allowed. Copyholders, who occupied an intermediate position, came in the course of the fifteenth century to be the most numerous part of the landholding classes, in some Midland counties over sixty per cent and in Northumberland over ninety. Many, if not most, copyhold tenures developed from villein tenures. As labour services were commuted most ex-villeins came to pay money rents for their tenements, acquiring in the process copies (the very origin of the term) of the entries on the manorial rolls where their obligations were set out. Roughly speaking the copyholder paid a stipulated rent, and his rent could not be raised. Unfortunately even now, from time to time, the copyholder became vulnerable to pressure from his landlord. A peasant family held a tenement by copyhold for a number of lives, generally three. On the death of the sitting tenant the heir was compelled to pay a fine to the lord before he was allowed to take possession. In some copyhold tenures these fines were fixed, but in most they stood at the will of the lord who would naturally demand a sum as high as the current traffic in land would bear. The phrase 'for three lives' is apt to convey an excessive impression of immutability, however. Late sixteenth-century estate managers (and there is no reason to think that their predecessors calculated differently) reckoned three lives as the equivalent of no more than a twenty-one year lease. So every two decades the accident of death and succession left many peasant families helpless before their landlords. Moreover, as time went on, by the late sixteenth century, inflation made even small freehold farms less viable in some areas and lesser members of all the peasant groups gave way before the more prosperous.

Thus, during the fifteenth century, as the result of a fall in the level of the population in comparison with the extent of land available, the greater part of the peasant population had improved its economic position. As Thorold Rogers averred a century ago, this was the English peasant's golden age. Unfortunately, though strong economically, his vulnerable legal position left the peasant dangerously weak once economic conditions began to change. The process of improvement was uneven and the cohesion of village society, which had begun to crack long before, was now shattered. Less uniform in condition, split into richer and poorer sections, the peasantry ceased to exist as a group with much will to resist landlord pressure. This increasing diversity, together with their vulnerable position before the law, which was of little consequence during the fifteenth century, proved disastrous to them during the sixteenth. As population increased (already slowly rising from the mid-fifteenth century, it seems to have doubled between 1500 and 1600) its relentless pressure on the land once again forced up prices, and tenants, helpless before the law, found themselves, in many cases to the detriment of their standard of life, bidding against each other in offering higher and higher rents to their lords. It is true that from the reign of Henry VII the copyholder, unlike his villein forebears, could protect himself by appeals to the court of Chancery and by the middle of the sixteenth century to the much more conservative courts of common law. Such protection for copyhold tenants, however, was due to no peculiar, novel tenderness towards the peasantry, and its scope was distinctly limited, for the courts could give decisions only on the agreements set out on the manorial rolls. By this time economic and legal status had become much more distinct than they had formerly been. Owing to the operations of a fluid, and rising, land market all sorts and conditions of men above the mere yokel ploughing a few acres came to rent copyhold land, and access to the royal courts for its protection became essential for men, even gentlemen, who held the bulk of their estates in freehold.

Many writers, falsely assuming that no man can profit without another's loss, have asserted that the golden age of the peasantry was a nightmare for the landlord. This neat and tidy package, however, is hardly acceptable on the evidence available, tenuous, complicated, and conflicting as that evidence is. During the previous two centuries great landlords had obtained a considerable proportion of their income (in some cases nearly one-half) from the direct exploitation of their estates. Plague and population decline certainly brought crisis to these estates: crisis which led their owners to revert to a more complete system of leasing which had been customary before the mid-twelfth century. Owing to the customary dishonesty of estate officials, then and later, it may well have been possible to exploit large estates by direct demesne farming and show a profit only in times of rising prices and of a flooded, and therefore brutally exploitable, labour market – conditions which vanished with the Black Death.[1] Whatever the truth of this contention may be, the same decades, those between the Black Death and the battle of Agincourt which saw the greatest rise in costs and wages, also saw most great landlords abandoning direct exploitation for a system of leasehold and tenantry. Although some did indeed suffer loss of income as declining population reduced pressure on the land, it is unsafe to assume anything like a direct correlation between these two things. Besides existing tenants, there were men formerly condemned to labouring status eager to take over farms. The almost pathological desire of those of peasant status to farm for themselves may have served to keep up rents.

It is impossible to make generalizations covering the whole country. England was not, in the fifteenth century, the close economic unity which modern industry and modern transport have made it. Regional variations were still immense, and even villages a few miles apart could vary greatly in their social structure. Transport by land was exceedingly expensive. Although they are only fifty-odd miles apart, in the 1450s the price of wheat was nearly half as much again in London than it was in Oxford. Comparatively short distances could isolate a particular area from potentially valuable markets if it lacked water transport or if its roads passed over heavy clay soils which were miry and water-logged for a good part of the year.

The income of some estates, particularly those in the corn-growing districts of the Midlands and East Anglia, were acutely depressed during the first three or four decades of the century. The monastic houses of Leicestershire and Ramsey Abbey in Huntingdonshire suffered a severe decline in income. The yield of the Percy estates in all parts of England fell by about a quarter between 1416 and 1461 – but other than purely economic factors may account for part of this. The greater part of the decline occurred before 1437 – at a time when, owing to the political folly of Earl Henry Percy I, the estates were confiscated by the crown under an Act of Attainder, dispersed

1. In spite of violent short-term fluctuations, the basic price index of foodstuffs remained remarkably stable over two centuries. In 1332–4 and 1514–15 it stood at the index numbers of 117 and 113 respectively. (The base compiled from an average for the years 1451–75.)

amongst several holders, and restored to the family only in a rather piecemeal and long-drawn-out fashion. (In this area in particular houses and tenements decayed, arable land fell out of cultivation and many landlords were desperate to find tenants.) Continuity of administration was always an important factor in maintaining agrarian profits. Some estates in Wales and the Marches endured prolonged depression after Owen Glendw̄r's revolt and ran into even graver difficulties in the 1450s, though their declining income during this later period may have been due, in part at least, to inadequate supervision and to the corruption of the local officials of absentee magnate landlords.

Other estates can hardly be termed depressed. Those of Tavistock Abbey in Devon and some of the south-western estates of the duchy of Cornwall show an economic life more buoyant than in earlier centuries. Rents on the abbot of Westminster's estates showed a tendency to sag in the early fifteenth century but thereafter remained stable over a long period of time. The Greys of Ruthin, with estates scattered through eight English counties as well as North Wales, contrived by careful, effective management to keep their income remarkably constant over most of the century – it began to rise before the end – and even to buy more land. The income of Christchurch Priory, Canterbury, reached the record figure of £4100 1*s.* 9*d.* in 1411 and, although it is impossible to calculate their total income in later years, between 1449 and 1472 the monks finally completed, at the very considerable cost of £1500, the reclamation of Appledore Marsh which they had begun about 1400. Nor was their titular abbot, the archbishop of Canterbury, any worse off. His net income from land rose by something like thirty-two per cent between 1391 and 1432, and although it sagged slightly in the forties it began to rise again after 1480.

Conditions varied widely. The Black Death, therefore, hardly produced over the entire country (as some historians have rashly assumed) 'a landlord's purgatory'[1] of declining incomes, negligent, unsatisfactory tenants and decaying farm buildings. The term 'rentier' usually applied, with distinctly pejorative overtones, to landlords who were now leasing their estates, is distinctly misleading.[2] One of the most naïve blunders of historians has been to condemn such

1. The phrase is Professor F. R. H. Du Boulay's – who argues convincingly against the concept.
2. *The Shorter Oxford Dictionary* (1963) gives the definition 'one whose income is derived from investments'.

people as a type, a species of lumpen-aristocracy devoted to brutal warfare and conspicuous waste. In fact, they had become estate managers rather than rentiers, and they were, after all, individuals, and like any other generation, the generations of the fifteenth century boasted both their competent and their incompetent members. Many of them, no less than their notorious Tudor descendants, seem to have been grasping landlords, their harsh, avaricious activities much resented by both their tenants and their estate officials. Moreover, as estate managers they were now far better equipped to control their estates than their predecessors had been in the earlier medieval period of leasing. Techniques of management had grown much more sophisticated during the thirteenth and fourteenth centuries, and great lords now controlled their estates with the assistance of the best legal and professional talent of the day, that of the growing class of 'gentlemen bureaucrats', one of the most significant developments of the later Middle Ages; often minor, or even middling, landowners themselves, trained in law at the Inns of Court or even in what passed in those days for courses in business and estate management at Oxford.

Whatever staff he employed, the individual lord set the tone. Dishonesty and corruption were normal in this society, and however competent and well chosen a great landlord's council and officials were (as the dukes of Buckingham, the earls of Warwick, the Lords Grey of Ruthin, even kings themselves found), the yield of his estates depended in the last resort on his own industry and vigilance. No landlord could afford to sit back and merely wait for his rents to come in. When Richard Beauchamp, earl of Warwick returned to England in 1423, after six years' more or less continuous absence in the French wars, the state of his finances so disturbed him that he engaged John Thorlthorpe, one of the auditors of the royal exchequer, to investigate his estate accounts. Thorlthorpe's report accused the earl's receiver of making away with over £3000. This the receiver naturally denied, and after prolonged squabbles the earl grudgingly allowed over £1180 of the sum disputed, which, however, still left his coffers short of more than £1860 which the receiver had fraudulently made away with. A prominent and trusted but hopelessly dishonest official had obviously taken advantage of his employer's long absence to cook the books on a really grand scale. The undetected results of such corruption could easily lead the modern historian to assume declining income.

Other landlords were more fortunate because in a position to be more vigilant. The Greys of Ruthin are a good example. After suffering badly in their quarrel with Owen Glyndŵr, in the first decade of the century, thereafter they avoided all the hazards which could damage the prosperity of a noble house. No ransom was ever paid out during the Hundred Years War, no minority for a whole century, and no attainder or forfeiture during the civil wars interrupted the vigilance of their estate management. Lord Edmund, who succeeded to his lands in 1440, became earl of Kent in 1465, lived to a ripe old age, quietly attentive to his estates until he died in 1490.

The Greys of Ruthin were amongst the richest of the barons, their thirty-four manors producing, in the 1460s, a gross income of about £1200 – and all but about £15 of it came from rent. Lord Edmund devoted himself to the minutiae of estate management, even abolishing the office of receiver-general so that he or his personal secretary took in the revenues from the local receivers. Careful, detailed entries in the estate accounts show sales of cow-hides, sheep pelts and wax, the receipt of royal licences to export oxen, the exploitation of dairies, the encouragement of the cloth industry on the Ruthin lordship in North Wales and considerable investment on enclosures in at least five manors. All through the century the income from the estates was well maintained and during the last thirty years showed an increase of at least £100 – no mean proportion.

The same is true of carefully run monastic and episcopal estates. Between 1391 and 1517 Christchurch, Canterbury, saw amongst its priors five men of remarkable ability in temporal affairs. Prior Thomas Chillenden in only five years (1391–6) carried through a sweeping reorganization of the estates by switching from demesne farming to leasing. In the following years, in spite of the immense cost of rebuilding the nave of the cathedral, the community's debts never became oppressively large, and at the end of the century they found enough money to rebuild the great tower, Bell Harry. The archbishop was equally successful in running his own estates, finding no difficulty in letting the former manorial demesnes on leases which allowed for adequate maintenance and strict control of the tenants. The tenants themselves came from all sections of society, but prominent amongst them were a number of substantial gentry whose intimate knowledge of, and capacity to exploit, local conditions enabled them to pay their landlord a substantial rent and at the same time make a good profit for themselves.

As in any other age, the incompetent landlord suffered. The Greys of Ruthin came to ruin under Lord Edmund's feckless grandson, but the most telling contrast of success and failure in estate management comes from two districts in Wiltshire and Gloucestershire, only a few miles apart, Castle Combe and Stroudwater. The development of cloth weaving and its auxiliary crafts in the first half of the century at Castle Combe (in north-western Wiltshire) added to a secluded agricultural settlement at Overcome, on the upland, a thriving industrial community concentrated in the river valley below at Nethercombe. By the 1430s, if not earlier, Castle Combe men were selling their cloth at Blackwell Hall in London. A quarter of a century later the manorial steward, William Worcester, wrote of fifty new houses, mostly of stone, built since 1409, besides older tenements rebuilt and enlarged. The new clothier tenants at Lower Combe who had built these houses were far richer men than the traditional small farmers at Upper Combe – one was rich enough for his widow to pay fines totalling the enormous sum of £140 for the necessary licence allowing her to take possession of his property. The development of its new prosperity was not lost on Castle Combe's landlord, the great war captain, Sir John Fastolf, an immensely shrewd, hard-headed businessman, one of the few war captains of the age who began life with a comparatively small fortune and ended as a great landed proprietor. Although for a quarter of a century he took an active part in the war in Normandy, he somehow contrived to keep a very tight hand on his English estates. Sir John's annual purchases over a period of twenty years of £100 of red and white cloth with which to clothe the retinues he led to France may indeed have stimulated Castle Combe's development. In turn its warrior landlord greatly increased the income which he drew from the district, charging a *chevage* or capitation tax of twopence a year, for permission to remain there, on the sixty or seventy workmen employed by the master clothiers, letting the holdings to a succession of new tenants who would pay the highest entry fines, and even demanding agreements from them that if within a year a prospective tenant appeared offering a higher rent, the first must make up his payment to the larger sum or get out. Although it is now impossible to calculate Fastolf's increasing profits, they must have been considerable, for, over a period of seventy years in the late fourteenth and the early fifteenth century, some of the entry fines for tenements doubled, one nearly quadrupled.

If Castle Combe shows the possibilities open to an alert landlord, the nearby area known as Stroudwater reveals a remarkable failure in estate management. Stroudwater is best described as a new industrial district possessing no legal existence as either a manor or a borough. It was made up of a number of new and interdependent settlements on either side of the rivers in the Stroud valley and one or two adjacent valleys, which, legally, were divided between the manor of Minchinhampton to the south of the river and that of Bisley to the north, the properties respectively of Syon Abbey and the duke of York. In each of these manors, as at Castle Combe, there was an ancient agricultural settlement on a plateau high above the streams and a new industrial development in the valleys below. During the fifteenth century the old upland settlement at Minchinhampton was practically worthless. Its cottages had been abandoned, most probably after the Black Death, and so they remained tenantless over the years. If the settlement at Minchinhampton was ruined, that at Bisley seems to have been to the last degree ill-run. From 1448 onwards the manorial accounts became completely fossilized. The names in the entries remained the same through the whole century. They were still the same at the death of King Henry VIII.

Official accounts convey the impression that Stroudwater was passing through a dire period of poverty and depression. Other, incidental, evidence, however, makes clear that what they really demonstrate is the appalling incompetence and lost control of the manorial lords of Minchinhampton and Bisley, for Stroudwater was passing through an industrial development similar to, though somewhat later than, that of Castle Combe. Land values were rising, new men eagerly sought tenements, the demand for water power was increasing, and the land along the river banks was being rapidly developed, but little, if any, of this growing wealth flowed into the coffers of the landlord. At Bisley, the principal tenants of the manor, not its lord, the duke of York, creamed off the profits from rising values, by sub-letting their holdings. In the 1450s the tenants of Longford's mill, then a fulling mill and still a well-known cloth factory today, paid the duke an annual rent of 15s. 4½d. and sub-let for 66s. 8d. There may, in the 1440s, have been an attempt to obtain for the duke some financial advantage from these developments. If so, the attempt was unsuccessful. From the reign of Henry V to that of Henry VIII the income which its lord drew from the manor of Bisley remained more or less static.

Bisley, though it may have been an extreme case, suggests that Richard, duke of York (d. 1460), was an uncommonly incompetent landlord. A recent investigation of his income seems to confirm this impression, though the fragmentary and disjointed nature of his surviving estate accounts forbids more than a tentative suggestion at this point. Leaving aside his Irish lands and certain hereditary annuities to which he was entitled at the royal exchequer, the gross value of his English estates stood at £8800 or more. Their net value, or his cash income after all the administrative expenses had been deducted, was about £4500. What he actually collected in cash may have been little more than £3500. Not only were the administrative expenses unusually high, there was (if the figures be correct) a leakage of revenue of nineteen or twenty per cent on the returns – a leakage of something like £650 a year. In other words, York, though on paper the richest man in England, was either so poor an administrator, or so badly served or cheated by his officials, or both, that the proceeds of his two hundred and seventy or so manors in England and Wales brought him in cash no more than four times what his prudent contemporary, Edmund Grey of Ruthin, extracted from his well-controlled estate of only thirty-four manors and lordships.

As we have noted, at the beginning of the century the country was passing through a phase of economic crisis and readjustment which led to widespread prosperity. The middle of the century saw the beginning of other changes which, although they greatly increased England's total wealth, in the long run once again depressed a large section of the population into poverty. The key factors in this process were increasing population and the expansion of the cloth trade.

There are signs, though no more than signs, that the changes resulting from the Black Death had petered out by about 1440, and that a new economic equilibrium then became established. It was until recently assumed that the thirty new outbreaks of plague recorded over the century were widespread enough and acute enough to keep down the level of the population until Tudor times. The habits of the plague, however, seem to have changed with the passing years. It became so predominantly an urban phenomenon that by the mid-1420s the habit of fleeing to the country to avoid contagion was already well established. From now onwards many of the epidemics were no more than local outbreaks. Only twelve swept over the whole country and another eight appear to have been confined to London. Between 1400 and 1485 only five plagues affected the whole country as compared with seven which hit the capital. There were no 'national' outbreaks between 1413 and 1435 nor again between 1439 and 1467, and even the country-wide attacks, with the exception of one in 1467, do not seem to have been severe enough to affect working life to any great extent. Moreover, it is now known that a significant increase in the birth rate often follows a high death rate. Everything argues against

B

any continuous decline of the population. Evidence recently collected from the registry of wills in the archdeaconry of St Albans suggests a small but significant rise in the replacement rate of the population from *c.* 1430, a rise which gathered considerable strength about thirty years later and which, by the late 1520s, had once again begun to exert acute pressure on the available arable land.

In the areas of agrarian depression in the Midlands and the south sheep farming to a notorious extent replaced arable or mixed farming. Economic historians have traditionally maintained that wool production was far more profitable than grain farming: a most attractive crop to the farmer whose land was equally suitable for grass and corn, for despite the risk of murrain, scab and other sheep diseases, wool was the safer crop, less affected by the vagaries of the weather, produced with the minimum of labour (a single shepherd replaced many labourers in husbandry) and its prices in the long term remained steady from year to year as against the more violent fluctuations in the price of grain. Many landlords – the Berkeleys, the Howards, the Hungerfords, the Stonors, Sir John Fastolf and the abbots of Gloucester, Dorchester, Oseney and Winchcombe amongst others – who abandoned direct arable farming on their demesnes therefore, found it profitable to continue their demesne flocks. Others, however, abandoned both methods of direct exploitation in favour of letting their demesnes to tenants. In either case, however, attracted by the high price of wool as compared with grain, and the higher profits or rents therefore obtained they ruthlessly depopulated scores of villages to make sheep-runs.

John Rous, the Warwickshire antiquary (d. 1491) claimed that he had presented a petition to parliament against enclosures as early as 1459 and in his *Historia Regum Angliae* he left a list of fifty-eight depopulated places in his native county alone. In bitterly indignant words he denounced the greed of those who made the change:

What shall be said of the modern destruction of villages which brings Dearth to the Commonwealth. The root of this evil is greed. The plague of avarice infects these times and it blinds men. They are not the sons of God but of Mammon. . . . As Christ wept over Jerusalem so do we over the destruction of our own times.[1]

At about the same time the bishop of Lincoln denounced the same developments. John Rous, in spite of his rhetorical tone, may not have exaggerated. His Warwickshire list, which historians once regarded

1. Quoted from M. Beresford, *The Lost Villages of England* (1954), p. 81.

with the gravest suspicion as an almost impossible fabrication, is now known to be incomplete. There are, in fact, over one hundred deserted villages and hamlets in Warwickshire and ninety of them were depopulated between 1400 and 1485.

Yet the assumption that 'the plague of avarice', the greed of the sons of Mammon evicted a once thriving peasantry from these settlements was less a statement of fact than of bewildered speculation. Neither Rous nor the bishop of Lincoln ever mentioned sheep in their denunciations and Sir Thomas More's notorious statement in *Utopia* about the solitary shepherd wildly underestimated the overhead expenses of running a large sheep flock – and he wrote it in 1516 when conditions had considerably changed.[1] Whatever they may have been later, before 1500 the profits of sheep farming were hardly of sufficient magnitude to propel landlords into a drastic reorganization of land usage. Even during the mid-1460s and the early 1480s, when wool prices were high by fifteenth-century standards over most parts of the country, they never approached those prevailing during the peak periods of the fourteenth century. They probably returned no more than half the rent from acres of wheat or rye barley, drage or maslin. After 1440 the annual export of raw wool rarely reached an annual average of more than 9000 sacks in any decade, and after 1520 declined to an average of 5000 sacks by the 1530s. At the same time a great expansion in the export of woollen cloth, begun before, and only temporarily interrupted by, the Black Death, reached a peak in the 1390s. It slumped disastrously by 1411, was booming once again by 1440, at more than thirty per cent above the record figures of the nineties, fell into acute depression during the third quarter of the century, but from *c.* 1470 expansion continued steadily and almost unbroken until the 1540s.[2] Impressive as the increased exports were, total production probably rose even more than these figures

---

1. I. Blanchard, *Ec. H. R.*, 2 ser., xxiii (1970), 438, n. 1, points out that Sir Thomas More seems to have been the only contemporary writer who ever systematically pointed out a connection between eviction and enclosing landlords and that most other writers relate the destruction of villages to a generally avaricious and greedy society.

2. Average annual figures of cloth exports:

1392–5	43 072	1462–5	25 855
1410–15	26 958	1479–82	62 586
1437–40	56 317	1509–23	84 789
1448–51	35 000	1534–9	102 647
1456–9	30 059		

The standard cloth for customs purposes was 24 yards long × 1½–2 yards broad.

would indicate. It has been plausibly suggested that the more prosperous lower ranks of the population which survived the Black Death were able to spend a greater proportion of their incomes on textiles, with the result that the diminished population of 1400 were able to buy at least twice as many cloths as their predecessors a century earlier. Consequently in spite of diminished exports of raw material the combination of rising exports and rising home consumption of cloth sustained the level of demand for wool and from the late fourteenth century even increased it.

The hypothesis (it is no more) is highly dubious. By the mid-fifteenth century the differential in export prices between the finest wool, produced in the Herefordshire area, and those of the medium and lower grades was far wider than it had been a century earlier – a differential which may indicate a brisk demand for, even a shortage of, the superior grades. On the other hand, although the domestic consumption of cloth had risen considerably, the prices of the medium and lower grades of wool (those made into cloth for the wear of the majority of the population) had fallen considerably below their mid-fourteenth-century levels,[1] indicating excessively large flocks and something of a glut of raw material. The sheep flock had become the last resort of the more depressed agrarian districts. Most landlords, handicapped by heavy administrative costs, ultimately abandoned sheep farming to peasants, who, like their modern counterparts in under-developed countries, counted their wealth in the visible grandeur of their flocks and herds rather than in the calculation of a profit and loss account. In general, the prospect of high profits could hardly have dictated the movement to sheep farming. Landlords both practised it and allowed their tenants to practise it as a counsel of despair – a couple of sheep to the acre at least avoided the deterioration of their land into scrub. There may, in the fifteenth century, have been some enclosures in the hope of high profits, but in most cases en-

1. T. H. Lloyd, 'The Movement of Wool Prices in Medieval England', *Economic History Review* Supplements, No. 6 (1973), pp. 10–11. In a price list (somewhat on the high side) of 1343 the best wool, that of Shropshire and Lincolnshire, was rated at fourteen marks, while in 1454 that of Herefordshire was rated at nineteen-and-a-half marks. This latter figure may be somewhat artificially high for it occurs in a petition to parliament to attempt to prevent the export of the finest wools, desired by both English and foreign manufacturers. By fixing a minimum price for the export of such wools the petitioners hoped to give some relief to the home manufacturer. On the other hand in 1343 only three counties had a minimum price of less than seven-and-a-half marks, whereas in 1454 the suggested minimum export price for the greater part of England was below that figure.

closures, far from being the vicious wholesale evictions of tradition were the result of the previous decay of village communities rather than their sudden enforced end. They affected only the remnant of the arable tenants. The depopulators who nominally destroyed such villages generally did no more than remove the survivors. A village with only two or three surviving tenants could yield the lord neither rents from tenanted holdings nor the rent of unified grazings.

At this period the cost of labour accounted for at least half the price of any manufactured article. The change from the export of raw wool to the export of cloth therefore added even more than it would today to the country's wealth. Moreover, a far greater proportion of cloth was dyed and finished before export than was the case a century later. Twenty-four thousand bales of woad besides madder, the rarer dyes and the essential mordant, alum, came into the country every year. The extent of the change should not, however, be exaggerated. In 1400, when the change was already well under way, all the cloth made in England could hardly have kept more than 15 000 people (or considerably less than one per cent of the population) fully employed, though it is true that spinning provided a by-occupation for a good many more. England was far from becoming an industrial nation.

Nor did this modest industrial progress turn the English into an urban people. It is easy to gain an exaggerated idea of the importance of the English towns. Standard accounts, which describe at length their distinctive institutions, are apt, unwittingly, to leave an unduly strong impression of their economic significance. Foreign observers saw England as almost unbelievably rural. Their impressions were undoubtedly correct, for nine-tenths of the population still lived by agriculture, and the proportion of urban to rural population was probably still no greater than it had been in late Anglo-Saxon times. Even the growth of the cloth industry, especially upon its cheaper side, took place to a considerable extent in the country districts. By modern standards, or even by the standards of fifteenth-century Italy, most English towns were no more than prosperous villages.

An English market town at this period could vary in population from as few as two or three hundred people to as many as a thousand, or even two thousand, if it were a county town or the site of a great church. Some twenty provincial towns boasted more than three thousand people and only a few 'giants' like Bristol, York, Norwich and Coventry passed the four thousand mark. In the second quarter of the sixteenth century the antiquary, John Leland, called Uppingham, which boasted all of three hundred inhabitants, the best town in Rutland, and in 1545 a chantry certificate described Oakham, the county town, as 'a great town', although its population was little more than five hundred.

In Oakham thirty-four tradesmen, engaged in over twenty crafts, served the modest needs of the local country folk for clothing and for metal goods. Their fellow townsmen were two yeomen, thirty-three husbandmen and seventy-five labourers and servants. At most the craftsmen made up something like a quarter of the male population. Agriculture, still the town's main occupation, still overshadowed them. Indeed, in two different lists of the townsmen made in the 1520s, all, except a single draper, were classed as craftsmen in one list and yeomen or husbandmen in the other. Many of Oakham's so-called artisans were nothing more than part-time craftsmen who, whenever the needs of agriculture called them forth, put up their shutters and went out to work on their farms. Except for places like High Wycombe which, owing to its geographical position, became the leading corn market of the Chilterns, driving a substantial trade in grain with London, and towns with a specialized cloth manufacture, the majority, though somewhat bigger, were still of the same type as Oakham, centres of a merely local commerce – minute metropolises for villages from six to twelve miles around them.

Towards the end of the fifteenth century and the beginning of the sixteenth, local trade in some areas tended to become more concentrated in a few of the greater centres, with other village fairs and markets decaying. High Wycombe was even, as Dr Cornwall has pointed out, showing 'the beginning of the change from the transient conditions of the fair ground to the permanence of the shopping street'; its periodical fair was declining because (it was said) the burgesses preferred to keep 'their shops and their stalls at home' rather than move them at intervals to a temporary site.[1]

The condition of various towns once again shows both the growth and redistribution of wealth already described. Until recently many historians were convinced that, with few exceptions, the English towns were going through a stage of sad decline during the fifteenth and early sixteenth centuries. John Russell, bishop of Lincoln, in a sermon drafted for the opening of parliament in 1483, even wrote of the desolation of well-nigh all the cities and boroughs of England. Although he exaggerated grossly he could, had he chosen to do so, have cited some extreme examples. By the mid-fifteenth century (and

1. *Ec. H. R.*, 2 ser., xv (1962–3), 68.

earlier in many cases) some of the older and more famous English towns were petitioning, with piteous allegations of their desperate poverty, for the reduction of the annual fee-farms which they paid to the Exchequer. Such petitions alone cannot be accepted as proof of poverty, for the town authorities were certainly not backward in prevarication and chicanery in a society where financial dealings were accompanied wherever plausible by unblushing perjury. Other evidence is more convincing. Owing to the decline of the export trade in raw wool and the silting up of the River Witham, the city of Lincoln had long been in a slow, agonized decline. It was given exemption from half its tax in 1434, total exemption in 1437 and 1440, and on numerous later occasions. The number of its parish churches (they must always have exceeded its needs even by the lavish ecclesiastical standards of the high Middle Ages) fell from forty-six in the fourteenth century to only nine in 1549. As early as 1428 seventeen parishes were described as having no more than ten inhabitants each. The suburbs and the back streets were quietly abandoned and, apart from the Bail and the Close, Lincoln became a single-street city which it remained until modern times. In 1442 a petition from Winchester claimed that eleven streets, seventeen parish churches and eighty-seven messuages had decayed within the previous fifty years. Though its details may be somewhat exaggerated, an incident related in *Gregory's Chronicle* testifies to the complaint's essential truth. When the Lombards fled from London after the anti-alien riots of 1456 and 1457, they decided to settle in Winchester where there were many old and unoccupied mansions which could be taken over immediately.

Other towns which had long been prosperous flourished; some as they had never flourished in earlier centuries. Bristol, Salisbury, Norwich, and King's Lynn were anything but stagnant, and if York slumped after 1430 owing to the decline of its cloth exports, Leeds, Bradford, Halifax, and Wakefield, which produced for the home market, were expanding fast. Exeter grew rich on the proceeds of the cloth trade. Ludlow in the 1480s and Saffron Walden a decade later began to rebuild their parish churches on the most magnificent scale. The ribbon trade flourished in Coventry, where the splendour of St Mary's Guildhall, St John's Church, St Michael's and the buildings of several charitable and educational foundations bear witness to the riches of the town's more prosperous burgesses in the decades on either side of the year 1500. Even after the frightful destruction of the second world war the late medieval buildings of Coventry are some of the most impressive in the country.

Many historians have created a false impression of urban decay in the later Middle Ages by an undue concentration upon one easily accessible, but also one-sided, type of evidence, the records of the long-established chartered boroughs, and through an excessively narrow definition of what makes a town. Chartered boroughs kept formal records and, no matter what the extent of their decline, they continued to be classed as boroughs and duly continued to keep their records. From the fourteenth century until the nineteenth a kind of legal inertia prevented the promotion of rapidly growing settlements to borough status, and left new industrial areas governed through the less full and less privileged structure of the manorial court. Such was the legal status of Castle Combe whose not inconsiderable industrial expansion has already been described. Stroudwater, also legally non-existent, being divided between two manorial lords, was too scattered along its water-courses to be considered or even to look like a town, yet the industrial interdependence between its various sections and the output of its looms made it at least as much of a town in the economic sense as minute but legally enfranchised Oakham. Lavenham, different again in that it was a closely concentrated settlement, also, like Leeds, Bradford, Halifax, and Wakefield remained legally a village, but its one thousand or so inhabitants made it larger than many a formally chartered borough, and by 1515 its cloth industry was in so flourishing a condition that there were only twelve richer communities in the whole kingdom.

The towns cannot be fitted into any rigid, tidy definition. Forms of government and legal status by this time were no longer, as they had once been, a sure indication of a community's significance in the life of its district. From an economic point of view it is better to abandon any narrow juristic definition, and to class as a town any community in which more than a small minority of the inhabitants earned their living by trade and manufacturing. Such a definition, somewhat vague though it may be, even perhaps a little tendentious, at least avoids the curious anomaly of writing off some of the most prosperous communities of late medieval England, like the cloth towns of Wakefield, Halifax and Lavenham, as mere villages because they lacked certain legal privileges. Amongst the enfranchised communities themselves many prospered and expanded, and if to these are added the legally insignificant but newly prosperous districts, we at least obtain a more realistic (and less depressing) picture of urban life. As in most ages, decay and expansion were found together in different places.

With towns so small, genuine urban life was nowhere intensified except in London. To the Scottish poet, Dunbar, accustomed to the even smaller towns of his own country, London was 'the flower of cities all'. Though the figures, like all medieval population figures, are controversial, its population may have risen from about 35 000 to 50 000 in the century and a half before 1500. London – with its ninety-nine parish churches within the walls and another ten outside, over fifty of them rebuilt or enlarged during the fifteenth century, twenty-three religious houses, the great town 'inns' of the bishops, the higher nobility and the richer merchants, built according to an Italian envoy in 'the French style', that is of brick with timber framing – could stand comparison with most European towns, except the very greatest. It had, indeed, the advantage, unique in the Europe of the day, of being at the same time its country's political capital, its principal port, and its financial centre, in particular the centre of its major export trade in cloth which was becoming more and more concentrated in London as the foreign trade of the provincial outports, with the exception of Bristol and Southampton, declined, and its society of Merchant Venturers outstripped those of other towns.

London, owing to the presence of the court at the Tower or Westminster Palace, its size and the wealth of its principal merchants, possessed, by contrast with the semi-rural atmosphere of most other English towns, what even the inhabitants of the great Italian and south German cities would have recognized as a genuine urban quality. Most of its glories have long since vanished, the victims of Protestant iconoclasm, the Great Fire of 1666 and the destructive activities of modern vandals. Although its walls by the 1470s were crumbling and dilapidated, a series of magnificent battlemented buildings, including Baynard's Castle, the town residence of the dukes of York, lined the north bank of the Thames. The remains of St Bartholomew the Great give some idea of the monumental scale of its greater ecclesiastical buildings – the existing edifice formed only the choir of the original monastic church. Within the walls, many pleasant open spaces, mainly in the franchises like St Martin-le-Grand and in the precincts of the greater convents, survived in spite of the city's increasing population, and open country for the recreation of the citizens still lay immediately outside the walls on the northern and eastern sides. Although William Morris's vision of

> London small and white and clean,
> The clear Thames bordered by its gardens green

must be dismissed as a poetic fantasy, for Londoners over a century and more had been complaining of the pollution of the atmosphere by coal smoke, flocks of kites, which were encouraged for scavenging and which it was an offence to kill, could be seen snatching slices of bread and butter out of children's hands, and a game of a thousand or so mute swans still floated upon the unpolluted stream. London possessed the amenities of a great city. Between 1460 and 1483 John Howard, his family and servants, at various times, slept, dined, and drank in at least forty-four inns and taverns in the city, Westminster, and Southwark, and there must have been many more to which the single East Anglian family did not take their custom. The quality of the accommodation which London could provide probably did not compare at all badly with that of the two hundred and thirty-six hotels and inns of Rome before its sack in 1527 by the Emperor's German troops when the pilgrim traffic had already made it the greatest tourist centre in Europe, and hotel touts already waited at the Porta del Popolo to catch travellers from the north. The London inns were far from being mere dens. They were centres of social life, and even great ladies went to take their cup of wine at some of the London and Westminster taverns. The bishop of Winchester's baths, the 'stews' as they were called, provided for the casual sexual pleasures of the town – public baths were, as often as not, brothels by this time. A few years later the fifty-two goldsmiths' shops in Cheapside astounded the Venetian ambassador into remarking upon the extraordinary quantity of wrought plate in the country. The court and the rich (as only royalty still does nowadays) exhibited row upon row of gold and silver cups and dishes upon cupboards at their banquets besides what they used on the tables. Even comparatively mean innkeepers possessed their collections of silver goblets, and it has been suggested that the system of hallmarking, first introduced about 1300 as a protection for growing numbers of casual and somewhat uninstructed customers, was improved and more stringently enforced under the Yorkists, just as the sale of secular plate became more important for the goldsmiths than the provision of plate for churches – English churches which, according to the same Venetian ambassador, already possessed it on a scale unknown in his experience elsewhere.

English trade in the fifteenth century covered wide though changing markets. At the beginning of the century English merchants themselves had traded in Normandy, Brittany, Gascony, Scandinavia and the Baltic lands, Iceland, the Netherlands, and the Western coasts of the Iberian peninsula (the Mediterranean itself they began to penetrate successfully only towards the end of the century). Merchants imported iron, pitch, tar, and wax from the Baltic, wine from Gascony, salt from Bourgneuf, iron, oil, fruit, and leather from the Iberian peninsula, and Genoese, Florentine, and Venetian galleys bore into London and Southampton, besides their famous oriental spices, silks, satins, cloths of gold, damasks, fruit, sugar, and gems – the expensive luxury goods the rich desired, which moralizing statesmen already condemned as a dangerous drain on the country's bullion supplies. The century opened in a phase of prosperity for foreign commerce, it slumped to less than half its former value during the middle years of the century, then rose to new heights during the last thirty years. Although the depression partially coincided with the Wars of the Roses, it had already set in slightly earlier, and civil disturbances in England were only to a very small extent responsible. Cross Channel trade with Normandy and Brittany almost vanished for a time with the fall of Normandy in 1450, and after the loss of Gascony in 1453 the Anglo-Gascon wine trade slumped to just over forty per cent of its former value, with a consequent decline in Bristol's cloth exports which the Gascons had largely taken in exchange. At the same period bitter dissensions with the Hanseatic League, unsettled conditions in Scandinavia and civil war in Prussia led to serious decline. Foreign trade, and in particular the export trade in cloth, continued depressed from 1448 until the mid-1470s. Then more settled conditions in the main export markets, the commercial clauses of the Treaty of Pécquigny (1475) with France and that of Utrecht (1476) with the Hanseatic League led to a remarkable expansion of cloth exports.[1] The growth in the export trade may, in fact, have been even greater than the customs figures show, for towards the end of the century some manufacturers were producing 'long cloths', as much as forty yards in length as compared with the twenty-four of the standard 'cloth of assize' – a development which until 1536 seems to have escaped the vigilance of the customs officials.

In the mid-fourteenth century English merchants themselves had pioneered the sale of English cloth abroad. By the mid-fifteenth century, however, as more and more cloth went to the Baltic countries, to eastern and central Europe and the Mediterranean, at least fifty per cent of this export trade fell into the hands of foreigners; only in Bristol was it handled almost exclusively by English merchants. Later

1. See above, p. 35.

in the century the share of English merchants steadily increased; unfortunately in a peculiar and dangerous way, becoming perilously confined to a single area. The famous company of Merchant Adventurers paradoxically became prominent as they ceased to be adventurous. At the beginning of the century at least three English chartered companies traded in Scandinavia, Prussia, and the Netherlands. Chronic conflict with Denmark and the Hanseatic League in the end, however, served only to expel them from their trading posts in Scandinavia, Prussia, and eastern Europe. By the end of the eighties English merchants had almost vanished from these areas. The export trade of the east coast ports very much diminished (though expanding coasting fleets seem to have maintained their prosperity) and Hanseatics rather than English merchants now imported Baltic products. From this time forward the bulk of the growing production of cloth came to be exported through London to the Netherlands, whence it was redistributed to Central Europe and elsewhere. The single company trading to the Netherlands, the Merchant Adventurers, with its foreign headquarters at Antwerp, became, in this narrowed sphere, the monopolistic legatee of the wider trade of the earlier companies: a state of affairs which in the sixteenth century left trading conditions even more precarious and even more dangerously subject to political upheavals than they had been in the fifteenth. The concentration of the country's only significant export on this London–Antwerp axis became, owing to the social dislocations which it produced at home, an ever increasing cause of alarm to Tudor statesmen; and so it remained until the sack of Antwerp in the Spanish Fury of 1576 at last forced reluctant English merchants to seek wider markets.[1]

To sum up, in spite of the fact that in its cloth trade England possessed one of Europe's major export industries, it still remained a rigid agrarian economy and the prosperity of the mass of its people still depended upon a crude ratio between the acreage of its cultivated land and the number of mouths which it had to feed. In the fifteenth century its people were abnormally prosperous, not because of any such modern phenomenon as economic growth, but because bubonic plague had left their numbers so comparatively few. Even allowing for regional changes and regional differences all classes could profit (or, at least, few need suffer) from this new, if fortuitous, prosperity.

1. There may also be a connection between this increasing concentration of English trade in the Netherlands and the growing concentration of English production on undyed and unfinished cloth.

Because so fortuitous, depending as it did upon a Malthusian population cycle, such prosperity could not endure. Changes, already slowly
beginning from about 1430, became obvious enough by the end of
the century and thereafter rapidly advanced until by the end of the
sixteenth century population had probably doubled, once again depressing the standards of the masses. From about 1560 those secure
in the possession of land, from aristocrats to yeomen, could afford
to rebuild their houses to higher standards of convenience and comfort to such an extent that the years between 1560 and 1640 have
been called the years of 'the great rebuilding'. At the same time in a
tightening land market, the eviction of the smaller and legally un-
protected tenants continued, growing numbers could find no place
either on the land or in industry and by 1597, the year of *A Mid-
summer Night's Dream*, the wages of the labourer and the artisan
reached their lowest level for three hundred years. England had
become very different from the land where, Sir John Fortescue (d.
1479?) wrote, no one drank water except 'by way of devotion or
penitential zeal' and where he had compared the abundance of the
peasantry in food and clothing with the miserable diet and bare-
legged, bare-footed poverty of the common people he had observed
in exile in France.

Foreigners, who wrote about their experiences in England, also
stressed its prosperity. The Venetian envoy in 1497 sent home his
impressions for the information of his Doge and Senate. 'The riches
of England', he told them, 'are greater than those of any other country
in Europe, as I have been told by the oldest and most experienced
merchants, and also as I myself can vouch, from what I have seen.
This is owing in the first place to the great fertility of the soil, which
is such that, with the exception of wine, they import nothing from
abroad for their subsistence. . . . And everyone who makes a tour in
this island will soon become aware of this great wealth.' And he added
(some historians might say, all unknowingly pointing to the cause)
'the population of this island does not appear to me to bear any proportion to its riches'. The widely diffused prosperity of the fifteenth
century was indeed the result of the fluctuations of nature rather than
of economic progress and, therefore, could not, and did not, endure.

3 The politics of Lancaster

During the Middle Ages men's memories were, in some ways, short. A habit of twenty years or so could be convincingly designated 'immemorial custom'. In conditions by modern standards always turbulent and disorderly, people tended to look back to some golden age – often in the not so very remote past – to be set forth as an example to the rulers of their own time. Very soon the days of Edward III (1327–77) came to fill this almost mythical role. As his epitaph in Westminster Abbey proclaimed, was he not 'the glory of the English, the flower of kings past, the pattern for kings to come, a clement king, the bringer of peace to his people'?

Peace, in this context, did not mean, as it would today, freedom from expensive wars against other states. It meant internal peace. The epitaph was written very much from the point of view of the nobility. After the civil wars of Edward II's reign, with their wanton treason trials, executions and extensive confiscations of estates, Edward III restored a feeling of security to the landed classes by gradually returning forfeited property and by conceding in 1352 an act of parliament which narrowly restricted the definition of treason. His interests were very much those of the great lords of his day, to whom he made considerable financial concessions. In his prime he led them in successful and, for many of them, highly profitable warfare in France. As his sons grew to maturity he was surrounded by a loyal and devoted family, who, successively married to some of the greatest heiresses in the country, greatly strengthened his prestige and authority.

The attraction of his war policy in France in the long run left a poisonous legacy for his descendants. More immediately the success of his middle years degenerated into stalemate and disillusionment. The general increase in prosperity which followed the plague led, as increasing affluence has led in our own day, to growing discontent amongst the newly prosperous. Their resentment against restrictive social conditions, as Jean Froissart noted, reached its bloody climax in the Peasants' Revolt of 1381. The king himself fell into a kind of premature decrepitude from about the age of fifty-three, and corruption and inefficiency overcast the last years of his reign.

In the medieval and the early modern world there was no substitute for a mature and vigorous king, for a king had to rule as well as reign. The well-being of every country lay in the unpredictable genetics of a single family. Edward's grandson and successor, Richard II, was only eleven years old when he came to the throne. For six years the government was carried on by a series of drearily inefficient councils, unsuccessful both at home and in the French wars. When Richard at last threw off their tutelage, he determined to re-establish the authority of the monarchy against what he considered to be the undue encroachment of the magnates during the years of his grandfather's dotage and his own minority. The ruthless practical methods which he employed badly scared the landowning classes, already disturbed and resentful at the social upheavals of these decades to which they were somewhat painfully readjusting themselves.[1] The king's tactlessly reiterated theories on the power of monarchy or 'regality' – as tactless as those which James I was to make two centuries or so later – added to their insecurity. As with the early Stuarts a theoretical, legalistic case could be made out in Richard's favour. In practice extreme theoretical statements, combined with fitful outbursts of tyrannical, often vindictive, energy, aroused general alarm. In an atmosphere already tense with suspicion of his motives, Richard, on the death in 1399 of his uncle, John of Gaunt, duke of Lancaster, debarred his exiled cousin, Gaunt's son, Henry of Derby, from entering upon his immense inheritance, the duchy of Lancaster, the greatest complex of estates ever accumulated by an English noble family. The sanctity of the inheritance was a feeling so strong that it is almost impossible to comprehend its intensity today. To deprive a man of his rightful inheritance was the most heinous crime in the contemporary calendar, and a powerful section of the nobility, fearing that if the greatest of all English landowners could be thus, at a mere royal gesture, deprived of his rights, lesser men would in future possess little hope of resisting the encroachments of the tyrant.

Therefore when Henry of Derby landed at the now vanished little port of Ravenser in Yorkshire, asserting that he had returned to England only to claim his inheritance, many supported him. Even if at this point he was not already guilty of perjury, he quickly decided

---

1. See above, pp. 23 ff.

to claim the crown. Richard, tricked into surrender, was compelled, not without the suspicion of violence against his person, to abdicate. An assembly consisting of most of the nobility and the knights and burgesses already assembled for a parliament under writs of summons which Richard himself had issued, deposed him. Henry seized the crown, shortly afterwards making a distinctly evasive pronouncement of his right to the succession.

There was at this time no definite public law governing the descent of the crown. Now and in later crises it was therefore, *faute de mieux*, deduced by analogy with the law of real property to justify the claims of a possessor who had taken it by armed force. As this in turn failed to provide an unequivocal claim, the crown itself became entangled in the kind of dispute which disturbed the harmony of not a few private families. Should rights descend to the heir general or to the heir male, through a senior female or a junior male line? Some noble families solved the problem, not entirely without subsequent disputes, by creating entails, which allotted the title and some proportion of the land to the heir male while leaving the bulk of the estates to the heir general. This was obviously not a compromise appropriate to the crown and the kingdom: they could not be thus divided. King Henry IV, as Henry of Derby had now become, was undoubtedly the heir male, being the heir of John of Gaunt, the fourth son of Edward III. Yet in the opinion of many people he was nothing but an usurper, for he ignored the claims of the heirs general, the rights of the Mortimer family descending through Philippa, the daughter of Lionel of Clarence, the great Edward's *third* son, claims which after 1425 passed to her great-grandson Richard, duke of York, the father of the future King Edward IV. Though immediately ignored, these claims were not finally extinguished. They lay dormant. Only continued success could stifle them completely. Incompetence and political failure would therefore be more than usually dangerous to the house of Lancaster: disgruntled subjects would be able to justify rebellion, attacking the title as well as its possessor.

The new king seemed in many ways an admirable man. He had won a considerable reputation as a crusader against the infidel in Lithuania. Handsome, brave, devout, and chaste, he was at the same time well educated, and he saw that his sons were well taught – Henry V was always known as a learned king and he acquired a bad reputation for seldom returning borrowed books. Henry IV spoke French fluently and could understand Latin and Spanish. His court was famous for its music. Henry always chose his confessors on account of their high reputation for learning. According to John Capgrave, when leisure allowed, he liked to spend much of the day discussing moral problems, and his judgment in theology was much esteemed. Critics abroad claimed that he was a cool, calculating man and hard towards his enemies, but Englishmen, like the poets Gower and Hoccleve, and Archbishop Arundel, who knew him well, described him as a humane and merciful man.

These qualities seemed to avail him little. Once king, 'his skirts licked trouble and became a weight to make the glory irksome'. For the first six years of his reign he was never free of trouble – revolt in England and Wales, war against Scotland, the constant threat of a French invasion – all expensive and all bringing him into conflict with the house of Commons over money; a conflict exacerbated by what the Commons regarded as the king's own feckless extravagance in financial matters.

Although Henry's supporters represented him almost as the saviour of society, the saviour had been imposed by a process of violence and chicanery. A few years later Philip FitzEustace, the prior of St Botolph's, Colchester, contemptuously referred to the new king as 'elected' by the London rabble, not by the magnates and the state of England. Others, it is true mainly obscure men, openly accused Henry of unjustly seizing an inheritance not his own. If Richard II had been brought before parliament and allowed to speak for himself, he might well have succeeded in retaining the throne. The fact that justice had not been done through parliament may well, to some extent, explain later revolts.

The first conspiracy against Henry came as early as December 1399. It was easily crushed, but it spelt his end for the unfortunate Richard. In February, probably murdered, his body, to stifle all doubts and to remove excuses for future rebellion, was exhibited to the people at St Paul's, then hurriedly and privately buried at King's Langley. Early in September 1401, conspirators attempted to assassinate the king by placing 'an infernal machine called a coltrap, having poisoned spikes' in his bed. The next summer Henry's reputation suffered from an unsuccessful expedition against Scotland, and then and during the two following summers the royal forces tried in vain to subdue the rebellion of the Welsh chieftain, Owen Glyndŵr. It was the powerful northern nobles, the Percys, who finally defeated the Scots at Homildon Hill (September 1402). Then dissatisfied for a number of reasons (some genuine, others spurious) by Henry's attitude towards them, they claimed (most probably untruthfully) that, misled by Henry's original perjured statement at Ravenser, they had never intended to depose Richard and place him on the throne. Now joining forces with Glyndŵr and the partisans of the disregarded Mortimers, they planned, in a fantastic agreement known as the Tripartite Indenture, to depose the king and divide the realm into three independent parts. Their defeat at Shrewsbury in September 1403 crushed the plot. Yet the Welsh still resisted, and the French were raiding and plundering the south coast. In 1405 the Percy earl of Northumberland began to stir up trouble. The king frustrated a plot to kidnap the Mortimers, but the earl of Norfolk who had been implicated in it joined forces with Northumberland and Archbishop Scrope of York. Defeated in this last attempt, Northumberland escaped into Scotland; Norfolk and Scrope were captured and beheaded.

Henry's record called forth outspoken criticism from his friends as well as armed attacks from enemies and former allies. In May 1401, Philip Repyngdon, abbot of St Mary-in-the-Meadows, Leicester, and one of his confessors, wrote him a bitter letter, denouncing his broken promises to protect his subjects from their enemies, and upbraiding him for a government so dangerously incompetent that those who two years before had shouted welcome to him as to a Christ triumphant now stood weeping and wringing their hands.

To these withering comments, the house of Commons soon added criticisms of his financial ways to which the king was forced to listen. Henry's income was considerably less than Richard's had been, possibly as much as one-sixth less. Although he refused to pay Richard's debts, he could not, for political reasons, deprive Richard's former supporters of lucrative grants which they had earlier received, and his own adherents expected rewards. Henry had to buy political loyalty, and he worked in a seller's rather than a buyer's market. Military operations against the Scots and the French also ran away with vast quantities of money. He wisely secured the cooperation of the nobility by frequently consulting them in Great Councils[1] – there were far more meetings of the Great Council than meetings of parliament at this time. The house of Commons proved much more difficult to deal with. A paramount dogma of late medieval politics held that the king should 'live of his own', his own being the royal estates, the

---

1. Roughly speaking a Great Council was a meeting of the house of Lords – without the Commons.

customs, and a few other minor items of revenue. He was entitled to demand direct taxation to cover only abnormal expenditure such as defence and warfare. The Commons refused to believe that Henry's deficits were due in any great degree to expenditures on defence. They took the line that Henry possessed greater estates than any of his predecessors. As no separate and expensive establishments were required for other adult members of the royal family at this time, if the king cut down unthrifty expenditure on his own grossly extravagant household and by an Act of Resumption revoked grants which he and his predecessors had made from the royal estates, he could 'live of his own' and need not demand from his subjects such burdensome taxation as he had demanded since the beginning of his reign. To enforce sound administration, particularly sound financial administration, on a recalcitrant monarch, the Commons insisted on three occasions – in 1402, 1404, and 1406 – that Henry nominate his councillors in parliament.[1] On the last occasion they spent weeks in wearing down the king's resistance, before he at last submitted and granted them both a nominated council and their Act of Resumption.

By 1408 Henry had solved the worst of his problems. The capture of James, the heir to the Scottish crown, for the time prevented further attacks from the north. The troublesome Percy, earl of Northumberland, was crushed at Bramham Moor (February 1408) and a little later the Welsh were at last subdued. Though peace had come, Henry's last years can hardly be described as quiet and free of care. From 1405 he was a chronically sick man, most probably suffering from some kind of cerebral embolism, though some of his subjects called it leprosy and regarded it as a divine judgment upon him.

The Commons, when they met, still complained. In 1410 many old grievances came up again in various petitions – impartial justice was lacking, the king should 'live of his own', a firmer hand was needed in the Marches of Wales and a stronger fleet upon the sea, great officials should be forbidden to accept corrupting gifts. Quarrels with his eldest son, Henry of Monmouth, clouded his last years. At one point it was even suggested that he should abdicate in the prince's favour.

All through the fifteenth century the head that wore the crown wore it very uneasily indeed, and none more uneasily than the

1. Dr A. L. Brown (*English Historical Review*, lxxix, 1964, 1–30) has shown that the Commons were interested only in practical questions and that no revolutionary constitutional claims were made in these crises as historians once thought.

disillusioned Henry of Derby. Looking back, Adam of Usk claimed to remember that the sacred chrism used at the cornoration produced in his hair a crop of lice only with difficulty eradicated – which men took to be an evil omen. Even death seemed to mock the more noble of his dreams, for he expired in the Jerusalem Chamber in Westminster Abbey – a bizarre fulfilment of a prophecy that he, who had always longed to lead a crusade to the Holy Land, would die in Jerusalem. In the end many stories spread, both at home and abroad, about Henry's unease of mind as, after years of ill-health and political strife, his unquiet life ended. The most notorious, that the ungrateful, impatient Prince of Wales stole the crown from his father's bedside believing him already dead was written down only many years later by the Burgundian chronicler, Monstrelet. The most credible, told by John Capgrave, a friar of Lynn, who claimed to have heard it from Henry's confessor, John Tille, relates that, when urged to repent of his usurpation, the king replied that though he did indeed repent, he could give no remedy, 'for my children will not suffer the regalye to go out of our lineage'. The accession of the new king, Henry V, did not banish the spectre of treason. By the autumn of 1413 suspicions of disloyalty had again become so great that sureties for good behaviour were taken from leading men, including the earl of Arundel. Early in the following year, Henry's old friend, the Lollard Sir John Oldcastle, raised widespread and dangerous rebellion. Henry crushed it swiftly and ruthlessly, but Oldcastle himself escaped, went into hiding and took part in various conspiracies over the next three years until he was captured and executed in 1417. Another plot hatched by the king's cousin, the earl of Cambridge, Lord Scrope of Masham and a Northumberland knight, Sir Thomas Grey of Heton, was discovered on the very eve of Henry's departure for France in 1415. It was put about that the plotters had been bribed by the French, possibly to conceal the fact that they were supporters of the Mortimer family, the heirs general of Edward III, and therefore claimants to Henry's throne.

Very soon after his accession, if indeed such plans had not earlier possessed his mind, Henry decided to revive the glories of his great-grandfather's, Edward III's, reign by invading France. Englishmen have praised Henry's famous victories more often than they have probed his motives, which, indeed, at the deeper levels remain a matter for speculation. Richard II, realistic in this, at least, knew that the Hundred Years War had become an intolerable strain on the resources of the monarchy. So indifferent had he become to his so-called 'French inheritance' that (with the exception of Calais) he had been quite ready to abandon it completely to John of Gaunt, for Gaunt to hold directly as a vassal of the king of France. Sixteenth-century writers surmised that Archbishop Arundel and a clique of churchmen wantonly encouraged Henry V's aggressive instincts to divert his attention from the radical proposals of a section of the house of Commons for a thorough-going disendowment of the church. The king's own deep piety makes any suggestion of this kind implausible. Henry may, on the other hand, have realized that, despite the financial strain which they had ultimately caused, Edward III's successful foreign campaigns had united a major part of the nobility in loyalty to the king, and that peace abroad had coincided with political tension and recurrent crises for the monarchy at home. He may therefore have sought to remove domestic danger by leading a potentially critical aristocracy to expend their destructive energies elsewhere. Obviously, such underlying motives remain, at most, conjecture. The reasons for his invasion of France, which Henry continually repeated (and his reasoning may have gone no deeper), were naturally more respectable. They were very much what the conventions of his day recognized as decent and honourable claims to property: 'the desire of justice and of his right, which every man is bounden to his power to demand and seek only moved him to the war' – as his official biographer remarked. His 'right' was his claim in feudal law to possess the kingdom of France as heir general to the Capetian dynasty, descending to him through Isabella, the wife of King Edward II (1307–27): a 'right' which, inconsistently, he denied at home in order to retain his 'English inheritance' at the expense of the Mortimers. Indeed, the arguments which Henry constantly used to press his claims follow exactly justifications for war advanced by such fashionable writers as Honoré de Bonet and Christine de Pisan. It is necessary to stress this apparently simple point; for traditionally Henry V has been a figure thickly encrusted with later ideals of nationalism – encrustations which must be ruthlessly stripped away to reveal the distinctly legalistic concepts, inherited from a feudal world, on which he acted.

The term nationalism[1] has been used to describe a variety of moods

---

1. The word 'nationalism' appears only in the early nineteenth century. 'Nation' is found as early as *c.* 1300, but it had a variety of meanings; e.g. at the Councils of Constance and Basle in the early fifteenth century, the delegates were divided into four nations, French, Italian, German, and English, but the English 'nation' also included the Scots and the Irish.

which succeeded each other in the consciousness of many generations. The mood which prevailed in the fourteenth and fifteenth centuries, to which the term has often been applied, was but a feeble harbinger of an intense public emotion which developed in the middle and later years of Queen Elizabeth I, when the martyrologist, John Foxe, and his friends, propagated the idea of England as the Elect Nation, in whom, though dangerously threatened by foreign powers, the minions of Anti-Christ, Christ's church and his truth would be preserved. In this atmosphere William Shakespeare invented the long popular tradition of a nation in arms behind the king. For once, in his historical plays, Shakespeare's vision was quite original, owing little to Hall and Holinshed upon whom he usually relied. There is nothing of the high-pitched tone of Shakespeare's St Crispin's Day speech in Hall. He reported Henry as saying that no one would ever have to pay a ransom for him as the result of Agincourt; a hard-headed financial statement much more in keeping with early fifteenth-century sentiment.

The strong attachments, which men certainly felt in Henry V's day for their own locality and language, are more accurately described (though not completely so) as regionalism. Although in their propaganda against the French the English kings frequently appealed for the preservation of the English language and English customs, the language was still so far from being a proud bond of unity that even in Caxton's (1422–91) later years people from different parts of the country found some difficulty in understanding one another. It took the English Bible to make English a genuinely common language. People were as divided in sentiment as they were in accent and vocabulary. Even defence, let alone aggression, failed to unite the country. In 1408 the Commons stated that the Lords Marchers, who alone were interested, should bear the cost of military operations against the Welsh, the northern counties often claimed that they should not contribute towards the French wars as they bore the brunt of the defence against the Scots, and in 1497 the Cornishmen revolted rather than pay taxes for the defence of the northern border against these same Scots. Men carried this negative outlook even further. Some, it is true, equated a 'natural' ruler with a monarch of the same race as his subjects. Others, perhaps a majority, were by no means vehement in their objections to a foreign king as long as he was strong enough to establish his claims without prolonged, destructive warfare, and as long as he was sensible enough to leave the majority of local offices in the hands of local men who looked upon them, by a kind of prescriptive right, as their own. Alien blood in a monarch was a disadvantage – a jealous fear always nagged provincial natives that his foreign entourage would profit to their disadvantage – but it was not an insuperable obstacle. As late as the 1520s Henry VIII seriously thought of settling the succession question by marrying his only legitimate child, Mary, to the Emperor Charles V – a monarch who would be strong enough to enforce her rights. Questions of property still counted for more than abstract ideas of nationhood. Even in 1429 some people gravely doubted whether it was morally and legally correct for the English to besiege Orléans while the duke of Orléans, its feudal lord, was a prisoner in English hands. Regional feeling, regard for the local *patria*, only rarely became an aggressive force in politics. It was important in that it could develop into deep resentment, into violent reaction, if invaders inflicted prolonged cruelties and oppressions upon the population.

Henry V was not a modern, nor even an Elizabethan, type of nationalist. He was through and through a man of his own age in whom certain contemporary characteristics had run to extremes: a bigot of near-heroic mould whose intense religiosity equalled only his intense legalism over feudal property rights. He saw church and state almost as two aspects of a militia of moral right, with himself dominant as its leader. Devout in the extreme, he persecuted the Lollards (partly to placate a jealous God, partly to suppress a sect which, with some justification, he regarded as traitors as well as heretics), tried, unsuccessfully, to enforce reform on the English Benedictine monasteries, and at the same time rigidly excluded the pope from the exercise of any practical power in the English church. The list of his religious foundations and benefactions was long and splendid: a relation of his ostentatious acts of piety would fill many pages. Before he embarked on his first campaign in France in 1415 he demanded fastings, prayers, pilgrimages, and other 'alms deeds' from the clergy and people, and he refused to allow an apostate Carthusian monk to join the invading force even though the man held a papal dispensation. At the same time there are more than hints of superstition and pride, even conceit, in Henry's piety. He dreaded the forces of witchcraft, yet like Constantine, even if unconsciously, he seems to have looked upon himself as something more than an ordinary child of God. So convinced of righteousness was he that religious opposition in particular drove him to furious vindictiveness. On the capture of Rouen, he imprisoned for life, in chains, the archbishop's vicar-general who had excommunicated him during the course of the siege. At Caen, St Vincent Ferrer, the greatest of the revivalist preachers of the day, preached before the king with his hood drawn over his face lest fear should prevent his saying 'all that he had fixed his mind upon'. St Vincent boldly demanded what Henry was, and if he thought himself better than all other kings and conquerors before his days that he had a heart so 'indurate' as to oppress Christ's people by war and devastation. Afterwards Henry saw the friar privately and simply told him 'I am the scourge of God sent to punish the people of God for their sins'. It is said that the friar was convinced, but a modern reader of the tale can hardly resist the feeling that the sin for which the people of God were punished was daring to judge upon, and then to resist, what Henry regarded as a valid legal claim to his *inheritance* in the kingdom of France, a claim which he was determined to vindicate before leading a crusade to the Holy Land.

Henry was fortunate in claiming this inheritance at a time when the kingdom of France was in a state of complete chaos. King Charles VI was insane. Between increasingly rare intervals of lucidity he had the strange delusion that he was made of glass and would break if anybody touched him. The Burgundian and Armagnac factions had been furiously competing, even to civil war, to control the king. Effective leadership there was none.

After prolonged negotiations, which Henry conducted with complete insincerity as a propaganda justification and a cover for his warlike preparations,[1] in 1415 he crossed the Channel with an army of not more than 8000 fighting men, and, after a siege of seven weeks, captured the port of Harfleur. By this time the campaigning season was almost over, with the rather unimpressive achievement of one captured town standing to the royal credit. Dysentery was rapidly depleting his forces and it was therefore unsafe to stay in Harfleur. Henry had the choice of taking back the bulk of his army by sea to England or, for the sake of prestige, of marching 160 miles across country to Calais and disembarking there, after making a kind of demonstration or parade of his right to the land. Against the advice of many of his lords he chose the gesture of the famous march to Calais, setting out from Harfleur with an army of between five and six thousand men. Despite the centuries-old glory of the march to

1. The French felt themselves so weak that they offered to give Henry a large part of Aquitaine and the hand of the king's daughter, Catherine, with the unheard-of dowry of 850000 crowns.

Agincourt it was much less impressive to contemporaries than it appears today when other similar marches have been forgotten. The *chevauchée*, or armed parade across enemy country, had been a feature of earlier phases of the Hundred Years War. In August 1373, with little more than 4000 men, John of Gaunt had made a much longer dash across north-eastern and central France from Calais to Bordeaux. Nor was Henry's own march very impressively organized. The failure of his scouts to detect the French spiking of the ford across the River Somme at Blanche-Taques increased his march by a hundred miles, and his small army ended its journey exhausted and face to face with a French army of at least twice its size.

Henry's splendid victory at Agincourt against such overwhelming odds raised England's prestige abroad and gained him a hero's welcome at home. At the same time it was so wasteful and futile from a purely military point of view that it was not until 1417 that he could raise another army and build up sufficient war stores for a second campaign. He then swiftly and successfully set about the conquest of Lower Normandy. Henry did not come as a foreign conqueror in the modern sense. He took very great care to stress his French descent and as far as possible to induce his 'subjects' to submit to him. As his official biography commissioned by his brother, Humphrey of Gloucester, from the humanist, Tito Livio da Forlì, states, if he pursued his conquests and 'subdue[d] the land by arms without appeasing the minds of the gentlemen and commons, at the last he should bring all the land to desolation which he intended not; . . . he minded rather to lose with all his right in the kingdom of France than to be lord of a void and desolate country'. Once the city of Caen (one of his earliest conquests) had surrendered, he proclaimed that any of the inhabitants who would take an oath of allegiance to him should enjoy their possessions undisturbed. In addition he abolished 'certain unjust and dishonest exactions and imposition of money before used in that country'. Partly because of this clement and, in the circumstances, logical and sensible policy, partly because they knew Henry capable of sack and terror should they reject his offers, and partly because the demoralized French monarchy was showing itself incapable of relieving any of the besieged towns, smaller satellite towns hastened to surrender after the fall of Caen and other major towns, such as Argenton, Séez, and Falaise. Some intransigents there were who protested against this abject submission and fled into exile in other parts of France. The majority were apathetic and about three-quarters of the landowners of western Normandy, though, it is true, none of the very greatest, quietly accepted Henry's government. Citizens, peasants and clergy were equally compliant.

Only Rouen, the capital of Normandy, put up a prolonged resistance, but starvation forced it to surrender by January 1419. By August the English lay outside the walls of Paris. The following month, in an interview arranged to patch up the quarrel between the Burgundians and the Armagnacs, one of the Dauphin's escort assassinated Duke John the Fearless of Burgundy at Montereau-sur-Yonne. His heir, Philip, immediately allied himself with the English, thus for the time shattering any hope of French resistance. Nine months later the Treaty of Troyes (June 1420) disinherited the Dauphin, Charles VI's heir, alleging that he was a bastard, married Henry to Charles's daughter, Catherine, and recognized him as the king's successor and regent of France during his life-time. Henry was now at the zenith of success. Covered with military glory, his triumph in France seemed assured, and in Europe he shared with the Emperor Sigismund the credit of bringing the Great Schism to an end with the election of Martin V as pope at the Council of Constance.

His record of success was now broken, however, by the duke of Clarence's defeat at the battle of Baugé in 1421, a defeat due to Clarence's own incompetent generalship. Henry crossed the Channel for the last time with another four thousand men and laid siege to Meaux, but contracted dysentery as a result of the hardships of the long winter blockade and died at Bois de Vincennes on 3 August 1422.

Brilliantly successful as the last five years of his reign had been, opinion about Henry was already divided. Some men worshipped him as the paragon of splendid hero kings, leading his lords to glorious victory to recover his own just rights, a reputation carefully fostered after his death by his devoted brother, Humphrey, duke of Gloucester, and continued in the London chronicles: the hero whose fame captivated Henry VIII when in his young, romantic, and reckless days he too dreamed against all the dictates of political and financial commonsense of recovering his 'French inheritance'.

Even his enemies admired his generally even-handed justice, the unusually rigid discipline which he maintained over his troops, his merciful consideration towards non-combatants and towards the vanquished populations who took the oath of allegiance which he demanded of them. Even so, in the end, it is doubtful how far his popularity survived the cost of his glory. As early as 1417, on the eve of his most expensive campaigns, Henry was deeply troubled that men, resenting his heavy taxation, *tepide causante* were ceasing to pray for the success of the war; and in 1421 Adam of Usk's Chronicle breaks off[1] vehemently denouncing the king for 'rending every man throughout the kingdom' to raise yet more money for his campaigns, men who paid 'with murmurs and with smothered curses . . . from hatred of the burden', so that Adam, somewhat sanctimoniously, prayed that in the end the king should not become 'a partaker together with Julius, with Asshur, with Alexander, with Hector, with Cyrus, with Maccabaeus, of the sword of the wrath of the Lord'. Later in the century other writers, too, chose to ignore the official panegyrics. Fifty years or so after Henry's death an anonymous Croyland Chronicler wrote 'this most able prince . . . departed this life . . . having ably reigned nine years and five months': surely a distinctly cool appraisal of the warrior king!

It was Henry's ultimate misfortune that he could not, after all, wage a war sustained by national enthusiasm. Both Jean Froissart and Thomas Walsingham in the 1390s noted a natural friendliness between French and English. Fishermen on both sides of the Channel at that time had long ceased to take the war seriously and members of the English and French nobility frequently arranged jousts amongst themselves. Nor could Henry afford to whip up anti-French feeling amongst his English subjects. He claimed to rule the French as in the law their rightful king: they too were his people. Any attempt to stimulate in England a war spirit based on hatred could therefore all too easily boomerang in France. In these circumstances warfare demanded a triple cooperation: that of a king who was an outstanding military leader, the active support of the greater part of the baronage, in his campaigns, and subjects who were prepared to pay the initial expenses; for above all, war, after its initial period, was expected to be profitable. The great mass of Englishmen, with comparatively little aggressive spirit, would not over a long period willingly pay for an expensive war in which they had little or no direct interest, a war waged for the benefit of a dynasty to vindicate a family claim to property.

At the beginning the nobility had been by no means unanimous in their support. Many of the younger peers were enthusiastic, but a section of the more cautious older men, led by the duke of Exeter, would have preferred to attack Scotland. The knights of the shire in parliament expressed misgivings. More important was the monarchy's declining ability to tap the country's wealth in order to support its

1. The rest of it is lost.

ambitions. England, normally, could not hope to conquer France with its vastly superior resources in men and money. It had been able to take over part of the country in the fourteenth century when for a time aristocratic discontent in France (some historians see the earlier stages of the Hundred Years War more or less as a French civil war) coincided with a peak period in the export of English wool, and it was raw wool, very heavily taxed, which paid for the war. The yield of the customs, which had reached £90 000 a year about 1350, steadily declined with the growth of the English cloth industry[1] until by Henry V's day they produced less than £50 000. Henry, therefore, followed the example of his great-grandfather, Edward III, without his great-grandfather's income. In the first Exchequer term of his reign, before the war began, he had to borrow £11 000. Hardly an auspicious beginning – but none of the Lancastrians was blest with any financial sense.

Henry's early death (he was only thirty-five) at once laid bare the weakness of his entire policy. His heir, Henry VI, was only eight months old, and a royal minority always produced acute political tensions. At home, the intransigent ambitions of the late king's brother, Humphrey of Gloucester, and abroad the need to maintain and extend a conquest which had already evoked great resentment, now compounded the usual difficulties. Gloucester claimed the regency under his brother's will. The lords distrusted the idea of a regency with the great powers which it would confer upon a single nobleman and they particularly distrusted Gloucester, who, influenced by some little smattering of Roman law, apparently hoped to establish himself in the position of a 'tutor' to the king, that is, a guardian who could not be called to account for his actions until his ward came of age. The justified suspicions of the lords, encouraged most probably for personal reasons by Cardinal Beaufort, against this arrogant proposal, and a certain aristocratic solidarity, led them to adopt the completely opposite view that during the king's minority the exercise of the royal authority should be vested in the lords spiritual and temporal when met together in parliament or Great Council and in the ordinary, or continual, council, between the meetings of these more august assemblies. They therefore rejected Gloucester's claims, softening the bitterness of his defeat with the titles of Protector and Defender of the Realm and Chief Councillor, taking care, at the same time, to hedge in his powers with very close

1. The export tax on wool stood at thirty-three and one-third per cent, on cloth at only two to three per cent.

restrictions. In spite of embittered political brawls between Gloucester and Cardinal Beaufort in the years to come the arrangement worked reasonably well. The record of the minority council was far better than that of Henry VI's later personal rule.

In France Henry V's mantle fell on his other surviving and very able brother, John, duke of Bedford. For a time, circumstances favoured him. France continued faction-ridden and divided, the monarchy incompetent and ineffective, Burgundy on the English side, though, as time went on, a more and more dubious and wavering ally. The Normans recognized Bedford's rule as fair and just. He worked within the conventions of the day in appointing as many local men as he could to lucrative offices and positions of influence.

Possibly it would have been wise at this point to abandon any idea of more extensive conquests during the king's minority, to concentrate on maintaining good, and cheap, government in Normandy. Unfortunately the terms of the Treaty of Troyes assumed an extension of the conquests into the parts of France still held by the Dauphin. The levies, of both men and money, necessary for this continued aggression roused discontent amongst the inhabitants of Normandy who had meekly accepted English rule, and the draining off of garrison troops for the field armies left the country open to attack from the south. As Charles VI had died only a few weeks after Henry V, there was now one king, Henry VI, who could be represented under the Treaty of Troyes as possessing a new and superior title[1] – a great asset in the thought of the legalistically-minded Anglo-French. Once the decision to continue fighting had been made, Bedford, realizing how essential it was to keep up morale in the Norman population, tried to meet the need by an intensive propaganda campaign, stressing in a spate of political literature and symbolic objects the equal status of English and French under a king descended from the blood royal of both countries. The design of a new gold coin, the *salute*, in a bizarre perversion of an annunciation scene (exceptionally daring because the cult of the Virgin was immensely popular at this time) represented England as an angel announcing to France the

1. This seems to have been the meaning of John Capgrave when he wrote that Henry VI held his titles *nam ex antiqua verum sed ex novo*. It seems that Henry V relinquished his claim (a resumption of Edward III's) to the French crown when the Treaty of Troyes nominated him 'heres Franciae', and Henry VI's title was founded on the treaty and on the marriage of Henry V and Catherine of France. For this point and others in this section see J. W. McKenna, 'Henry VI of England and the Dual Monarchy: Aspects of Royal Political Propaganda, 1422–1432', *J. of the Warburg and Courtauld Institutes*, xxviii (1965), 145–62.

coming of a saviour – even though the saviour was no more than the infant Henry VI. Bedford commissioned from a Frenchman, Lawrence Calot, a poem on the king's dual French and English descent, which together with a pictorial genealogy, he posted on the walls of major churches across northern France. Even the pastries and the jellies at the court banquets were made into shapes symbolic of the dual monarchy.

It soon became necessary to extend the propaganda campaign from Normandy to England. Henry V himself had been forced to recognize the objections of his English subjects on the matter of the dual monarchy by denying any intention of appointing a single chancellor for both countries, and he permitted the re-enactment of a statute of Edward III's securing English liberties if the sovereign became king of France. In 1426 the earl of Warwick ordered John Lydgate to translate Lawrence Calot's poem into English. Lydgate's translation survives in an extraordinary number of copies, no less than forty-six, many of which show signs of being posted as bills or school texts to be learned by heart.

All this activity failed to suppress a swiftly growing feeling that the dual monarchy was not worth the cost. Only a very small number of Englishmen profited directly from the fighting: as little as one-half or one-third of one per cent took part in the pitched battles and a great many of these were gentlemen and their servants. War contracts for victuals, arms, and clothing may have given profitable employment to at most forty or fifty thousand people, probably a good deal less, no more than a tenth of the adult male population. The conquest of France has been called the Norman Conquest in reverse, with all its implications of a lavish endowment of the conquerors with estates as a new aristocracy. This confident assumption is based on a very slender stock of facts. If, as stated earlier, three-quarters of the Norman landowners remained in possession, the quantity of land available for distribution to the invaders must have been limited, and the demands which the prosecution of the war made upon them could hardly have left them sufficient time and energy to exploit their new estates in the most profitable way. Certainly a few men made handsome fortunes, but they are more likely to have come from the windfall profits of loot and ransoms than from land grants. To the end there were always diehard enthusiasts for the war, but less than a quarter of the army contingent leaders of Agincourt were still serving after 1422. Lack of enthusiasm meant that even from this early stage the English failed to maintain a sizeable corps of experienced captains in Normandy. The baronage turned out in force for the last time to meet the crisis of a new French attack in 1429 – but they turned out with no more than 2700 men by way of reinforcements for the now depleted armies across the Channel. It may well be significant of declining interest that the meagre English chronicles of the day say very little about the later stages of the war.[1] Moreover, those who profited most from the war were not those who paid, and for a decade and more after Henry V's death even the stay-at-home taxpayer contributed very little. The English fell back on the comforting proposition that the war could now pay for itself. The king's 'French inheritance' should be self-supporting and should now pay for its own 'defence'.

· This unrealistic attitude reduced political tension in England only at the cost of increasing it in Normandy, thus transforming the original passive acceptance of the conquest into a deep resentment which finally helped to ruin the English cause. The extension of the conquest into the part of France still held by the Dauphin was a costly business. As in Normandy the English proceeded by way of sieges and the establishment of permanent garrisons. To pay for all this, between 1419 and 1435, the government coerced the Norman estates into voting £350000 sterling in taxation, though only about two-thirds of this money was ever paid. From this and from other sources the English forces probably obtained about £650000, not to mention considerable sums taken by local commanders which never appeared in the accounts of the central government.

Financial oppression burgeoned into sufferings far more terrible. The English won their last considerable victory at Verneuil in 1424. From about 1429, the French monarchy and its armies, inspired and revived by Joan of Arc, began to gain ground against the inadequate English forces never sufficiently reinforced from home. More and more Englishmen, possibly including even the duke of Bedford himself, now favoured peace. By 1435, with the failure of a peace conference at Arras due to the almost insensate demands of the English delegation, Burgundy's resulting desertion of the English alliance and Bedford's death, English affairs in France reached a crisis. Sir John Fastolf, one of the most experienced of the veteran captains, now advised the government to abandon Henry V's policy of conquest and consolidation by sieges and the maintenance of garrisons as far too expensive. In its place he recommended a cheap, but ferocious

1. Edward Hall (d. 1547) was forced to rely on Burgundian and French authors when he wrote his Chronicle.

and, in the end, politically disastrous, scorched-earth policy intended to terrorize into submission many of the 'king's subjects' who, he reluctantly admitted, now favoured and assisted the enemy. 'Traitors and rebels must needs have another manner of war, and more sharp and more cruel than a natural and anoien [honourable?] enemy.' A few years later, Fastolf's secretary, William Worcester, admitted that the English had become savage and oppressive in the extreme, and the Norman ecclesiastic, Thomas Basin, bishop of Lisieux, claimed that swarms of brigands and men-at-arms on both sides, who were little better disciplined than the freebooters, reduced vast tracts of the border land where English and French fought for control to a wilderness 'deserted, uncultivated, abandoned, empty of inhabitants, covered with scrub and branches'. So ingrained had the reflexes of terror become that even the oxen, draught-horses, pigs, and sheep ran for shelter when the watch-tower bell rang the alarm of approaching troops. As the English hold grew less firm, Normandy itself grew more turbulent and the population turned more and more against a government which failed to protect them against the resurgent French monarchy.

In 1439 peace negotiations again broke down. During the 1440s the royal council frequently discussed plans for peace until a formal truce was made on the king's betrothal to Margaret of Anjou in 1445. In March 1449 François de Surienne, an Aragonese mercenary in English pay, wantonly broke the truce by attacking the Breton town of Fougères. Charles VII of France to aid his cousin, the duke of Brittany, counter-attacked in Normandy. A fatal combination of brilliant stratagems, treachery in the resentful French population, the defection of a small minority of Englishmen perhaps eager to make their own terms with the enemy and so retain possession of their Norman estates, and inadequate forces weakened by the indiscipline of their petty captains, swept the English out of Normandy in less than sixteen months. By mid-August 1450 all was over.

At home Henry VI, whose minority ended in 1436, displayed the Christian but totally unregal virtues of humility and abnegation which inspire the minds of hagiographers, but he could not have been worse equipped for the incessant cares and demands of personal monarchy. Resenting the intrusion of the detailed tasks of administration on the studies and religious practices to which he was devoted, he rarely presided at meetings of the royal council. In an age when the majestic presence of the king counted for a good deal in the success of government he seldom left the five or six royal palaces of the home counties. As early as 1442 many of his humbler subjects were already calling him a fool, and saying that he was more like a child than a man. By fits and starts feeble and wilful, he allowed himself to be plundered by his entourage and yet sporadically and obstinately asserted himself to impose decisions, particularly in matters of foreign policy, against the advice and much to the embarrassment of his ministers. He utterly lacked the systematic application to business and the ruthlessness essential to the kingly office; and a system of government which stretched, often to breaking point, the capacities of a vigorous and effective monarch, drifted to almost inevitable disaster in such erratic hands.

Henry conspicuously failed in the two most important tasks of a king: control of his aristocracy and control of his finances. The English monarchy, now and much later, weak in coercive power at its direct command, had no option but to rely on that of the aristocracy to maintain order in their own districts. The king therefore had to inspire confidence in most of the baronage, to stand sufficiently above them to arbitrate in their frequent quarrels, so that peace between the great would extend a like peace and order to the countryside.

From the beginning of his personal rule, a narrow faction, led by the Beaufort family, exploited the king's weaknesses. From about 1442, an even smaller group, led by William de la Pole, later duke of Suffolk,[1] isolated him from the influence of possible rivals to such an extent that their enemies even accused Lord Say, the chamberlain of the household, of censoring sermons which were to be preached before the king. With all important decisions taken by a narrow court clique, attendance at the royal council degenerated at times into as little as three or four royal clerks. It thus lost one of its most valuable functions, as the institution which provided for cooperation between the king and the nobility. Henry's prestige inevitably declined, and many of the nobility and greater gentry, now rightly distrusting his impartiality, took to settling their differences by armed force, which, in turn, dragged into conflict their local adherents and dependents. In the late forties and the early fifties violent affrays between the Courtenay earls of Devonshire and the Bonvilles, the Ormonds, and the Cobhams in Devonshire, between the Nevilles and the Percys in the north of England, between the Blounts and the Longfords in south Derbyshire, amongst others, none effectively quelled by the

1. Earl of Suffolk by inheritance, erected marquess (1444), duke (1448).

C

king, brought the royal authority even lower. A dangerous development of armed private feuds preceded the Wars of the Roses. Henry
so conspicuously failed in his dealings with the nobility that between
1448 and 1455 at least one-sixth of the peerage were, at some time or
another, imprisoned for violent conduct: a situation humiliating to
both sides, and politically calamitous.

Humphrey of Gloucester, the most intransigent of the warmongers,
bitterly opposed the truce with France concluded at the time of the
king's marriage. By 1447, his reputation, tarnished five years earlier
by his wife's condemnation for plotting the king's death by sorcery,
appeared to be reviving to such an extent that, for their own safety,
Suffolk and his followers decided that he must be silenced. To accuse
and condemn him the court summoned a parliament to meet at Bury
St Edmunds, a centre of the Suffolk influence. As Gloucester rode
into Bury on 18 February he was arrested. Five days later he died. It
is most likely that he died from natural causes, but appearances were
all against his opponents. They had forbidden his own servants to go
near him, and he died in their hands at the moment they were plotting
his ruin. Foreign chroniclers claimed with one voice that he had been
murdered. Popular opinion in England was soon whispering the
same charge, and within a few years rumours of the political murder
of other noblemen were widespread.

If Suffolk's rule aroused the distrust of the nobility, its notorious
corruption roused the active hatred of the Commons. With the long-
term decline in the customs revenues, made worse in these years by
a slump in overseas trade, the king was more and more thrown back
like any other landowner upon the profits of his own estates. Even
without the continual drain of the French war, which was responsible
for the greater part of mounting royal debts, solvency required constant watchfulness over these resources. Towards the end of Henry's
minority the royal demesne had been exceptionally great in extent.
As in Henry IV's day the legitimate charges upon it were abnormally
small, for the king had few adult members of his family to provide
for. As early as 1437 Henry VI's prodigality had already disturbed
the Great Council of peers. Their protests were ineffective, and the
royal finances sank into ever deeper confusion until in 1449 the
treasurer told parliament that the king's debts had risen to £372 000.
Over the previous twelve years his courtiers and officials had in-
veigled Henry, always too generous to refuse an eager request, into
granting away the royal estates to an extent probably unparalleled
up to this time in English history, and a good deal even of the income

which remained was passing into the hands of members of the royal household. It was notorious that those about the court had wantonly pursued their own profit with no regard for the public weal, leaving the deficit created, at least in part, by their own plundering to be made good by taxation. As one contemporary squib bitterly expressed it:

> . . . ye have left the king so poor
> That now he beggeth from door to door.

Parliament met in February 1449. The Lords, almost wilfully blind to the now desperate situation in Normandy, claimed that any attempt to raise troops would only increase disorder at home. The Commons, for their part, would grant little in the way of taxation. They took an obstinate stand on financial matters which hit directly, and hit hard, at the greed of the court group and of the household officials. Refusing compromise of any kind, they insisted on a full-scale cancellation, or resumption as it was called, of all royal grants of lands and offices. Rather than submit to their demands, the king and his advisers dissolved parliament. This was only to postpone the day of reckoning. Faced by mounting disaster in Normandy, they were forced to summon another parliament for November. The fall of Rouen at the end of October made the new house of Commons more determined and intransigent than ever. On 9 January 1450 at Portsmouth a mob of unpaid sailors lynched Adam Moleyns, the keeper of the privy seal, and Moleyns was supposed *in articulo mortis* to have made most damaging accusations against Suffolk. As soon as parliament reassembled after the Christmas recess, Suffolk tried to quell the murmurs now swelling against him everywhere with a long, emotional speech dwelling upon the loyal service which his family had given to all the Lancastrian kings, and formally demanded that this vindication of his actions should be placed on the Parliament Roll.

He wildly misjudged his ability to sway the Commons. Enraged against him, they delivered to the chancellor and the lords a bill accusing him of treason and, shortly afterwards, followed it with another, denouncing him for a wide variety of corrupt and violent practices. To save him from a worse fate, the king ordered him into exile. A small fleet, commanded by men unknown, captured the duke's ship on its way to Calais. His captors gave him twenty-four hours in which to shrive himself and prepare for death; beheaded him over one of the ship's boats, and cast his naked body ashore on Dover sands.

It was the king's undoubted right to choose his ministers as he saw fit. If he obdurately insisted on retaining them only a capital charge could force their removal from power. The treason charges which had been laid against the dead man, that he had, with French help, planned the king's deposition, that his negligence, duplicity and worse, had been responsible for the loss of Normandy, were, therefore, deliberate, brazen perversions of the truth. The deposition charge was fantastic. While not brilliant, he was not incompetent, and in Normandy he had faced an impossible task which would have defeated the greatest of men. On the other hand the secondary accusations of violence and corruption were certainly well founded. In his statement to parliament Suffolk claimed, though he exaggerated, that he had spent thirty-three years of his life in the French wars, seventeen of them without ever coming home or seeing England, and that his capture by the French had cost him a ransom of £20 000. A study of his career makes one wonder if this prolonged absence from home in the brutalizing atmosphere of war had developed in an originally upright character gangster traits execrable by even fifteenth-century standards. The century's twin characteristics of greed and piety were, in Suffolk, carried to schizophrenic extremes. Exceptionally cultivated, a generous patron of literature, a poet himself, his religious devotion matched only his rapacity. His moral utterances were impeccable: the letter which, just before his death, he wrote to his son, was a pattern of high-minded exhortation. Mindful of terrestrial wealth and of riches in the world hereafter, he could rob a poorer neighbour of an estate with one hand while endowing a church with another, and force an unwilling accomplice in a swindling deal to swear a corporal oath on the gospels not to back out of the tesseration of perjury in which they were both involved. Besides profiting enormously from direct royal grants, in every other way he abused his position to bully, cheat, and extort, bilking the customs on a large scale, perverting the course of justice, appointing sheriffs in return for bribes, allowing his men to terrorize the East Anglian countryside. Finally, to protect himself and frustrate retribution, he had isolated the king from a large section of the nobility upon whose cooperation the internal peace and welfare of the realm depended. It was this aspect of Suffolk's rule which had roused such widespread hatred. The loss of Normandy, which people chose to regard as its result, while adding to their resentment, in reality provided only the perfect excuse for the attack upon him.

Suffolk was murdered on 2 May 1450. Cade's rebellion followed close upon his death. Cade was an Irishman who, claiming to be a cousin of the duke of York, assumed the name of Mortimer. He was a man of abilities great enough to organize in an effective way the long-standing unrest of the Kentishmen which had erupted in sporadic riots and conspiracies ever since the late 1430s. One exceptionally violent rising had in fact been suppressed as recently as February. The causes of the rebellion, unlike the Peasants' Revolt of 1381, were more political than economic. Lord Say, one of the Suffolk group, and his son-in-law, William Crowemer, the sheriff of Kent, had conducted themselves as oppressively as Suffolk and his affinity in East Anglia. The rising was not the work of a rabble – amongst the rebels were a knight, eighteen esquires and seventy-four gentlemen, besides merchants and clergy. The skilfully drafted manifesto in which they set forth their grievances was well informed enough to assert, and to assert correctly, that the courtiers and household officials were impeding the execution of the Act of Resumption. The rebels could therefore claim that they were supporting the intentions of parliament. To put matters right they demanded the almost standard remedy for political ills, government by a council in which all the great nobles took part – and, significantly, they demanded the recall of the duke of York from Ireland to take part in such a council.

At this point, for the first time, Richard of York became the dominant figure in English politics, and its dominant figure he remained for a whole decade until his violent death in December 1460. Five times during these ten years he tried to seize power until, in the end, his persistence won a grudging half-recognition from his fellow peers. York's long struggle now began in an attempt to dominate the king and court. In 1450 there was nothing in his past career which would have led men to prophesy the dynastic claims which he ultimately made. York's ancestor, the earl of March, in 1415 was so negligent of his claim as heir general of Edward III, that he himself denounced to Henry V the conspirators who had plotted to depose the king in his own favour. York, as a royal ward, had been brought up by the Nevilles, one of the greatest families of northern England and then amongst the most loyal of Lancastrian supporters. When he became of age his lands had been handed over to him on exceptionally easy terms. Twice the king's lieutenant in France (1436–7 and 1440–5) he had just managed to hold his own without loss of reputation. He left Normandy in time to save his political future, for no commander's name could have survived the inevitable disasters ahead. York, who had little political sense, failed to realize that he was well out of such a mess, and deeply resented Suffolk's action in refusing to re-new his commission as lieutenant of France. Further, Suffolk, as part of his attempt to stifle criticism, in 1447 sent York into a kind of honourable exile as king's lieutenant in Ireland. By 1450 suspicions about the succession to the throne exacerbated the duke's resentment. Since Gloucester's death, if the somewhat perplexing claims of the Beaufort family were ignored, York was both the heir male and the heir general of Edward III. He showed how jealously he regarded the inheritance by adopting the surname 'Plantagenet', now heard again in England for the first time for about three hundred years[1] – though being ten years older than Henry VI, he can hardly have hoped in the normal course of events to succeed to the throne himself. For some time he may have suspected that Suffolk and Edmund Beaufort, duke of Somerset, were plotting to deprive him of his rights, a sus-picion reinforced by a rumour, for once quite accurate, picked up by parliament in 1450, that Suffolk had secretly married his son to Somerset's niece, Lady Margaret Beaufort – afterwards the mother of King Henry VII, through whom Henry derived such hereditary right as he possessed.

Their financial difficulties also set the two dukes, York and Somerset, at loggerheads. York had taken part in the French war too late to profit from it. On the other hand he had never been burdened, like Suffolk, John Beaufort and Lord Hungerford, with the payment of an enormous ransom. During the later part of his second term of office in France (1440–5) the government had defaulted on a consider-able part of the funds promised him as lieutenant. Part of the debt remained unpaid for years, but York suffered no more from the government's inability to keep its promises than other, and some of them much poorer, men, who remained conspicuously loyal to Henry VI.[2] York's political activities certainly added to his growing debts, until as he stated in parliament in 1454 he had by then been forced to sell 'a great substance' of his lands, pledge his plate and

1. The descendants of English princes normally took the titles of their cadet forebears. York's purpose apparently was to emphasize the purity of his own descent from Edward III in contrast with the doubtfully legitimate Beauforts. The Beauforts were descended from the illegitimate children of John of Gaunt. Richard II had legitimized them by act of parliament, but Henry IV had declared by letters patent that this did not enable them to inherit the crown; legally a some-what dubious restriction.

2. A detailed investigation of the financial dealings between the government, York, and other war leaders would be needed to show whether York's grievances were, or were not, abnormal.

great jewels and borrow money on the credit of his friends. Part of his jewels were indeed in pawn – they were still unredeemed at the time of his death in 1460 – and he did sell two manors and thought of selling more, a most unusual, almost shameful, proceeding for a nobleman of his standing. In addition to the money owing him, the duke was entitled to hereditary annuities valued at £1000 from the Exchequer – no inconsiderable proportion of his cash income compared with that which he received from his apparently badly supervised estates. Somerset was even more vulnerable. His family had been mainly endowed with royal annuities. Partly owing to this, partly to an earlier division of family property, Somerset possessed a meagre £300 a year, or slightly more, from land, as against nearly £2000 from crown annuities, pensions and offices. There was never enough ready cash at the Exchequer to meet all demands. Royal favour determined the order of precedence of its creditors, and each of the two rival dukes dreaded that the other's dominance at court would cut off supplies.

York returned from Ireland at the end of August or the beginning of September 1450 after the royal forces had suppressed Cade's rebellion, probably hoping to assert his own authority in a time of general confusion. In any case he was glad enough of an excuse to leave the country where his government had come dangerously near collapse, and he dreaded lest failure there would ruin his reputation, as failure in Normandy had helped to ruin Suffolk's and Somerset's. By November the Commons (in yet a third parliament), well aware that the courtiers and household officials had skilfully evaded the Resumption Act of May 1450, now, with York's support, demanded and obtained a much more effective act which, rigidly enforced, reversed the dissipation of royal lands and revenues which had taken place since 1437.

The key to the events of the next few years lies in the mutual suspicions of York and Somerset. With Suffolk out of the way and the royal circle forced, however reluctantly, into financial reform, choice between the rivals was not a choice between good and bad government. Later events, indeed, were to show that York's interest in financial reform in 1450 had been merely tactical. For a time York continued to influence the king, but in the summer of 1451 retired, frustrated, to his estates in the Welsh Marches. From there he and his followers made extensive plans for an armed rebellion to be supported by riots and demonstrations in numerous towns in the south-west, the Marches of Wales and East Anglia. The rebellion misfired, and York, after negotiations, surrendered to the king at Dartford in March 1452; surrendering, it seems, upon a promise that Somerset would be imprisoned and made to answer charges that he was responsible for the loss of Guienne.[1] This promise, if made, was soon broken. York had gone much too far, and opinion now turned in favour of the court. York was forced to take a solemn oath to the king in the presence of the assembled magnates in St Paul's Cathedral: an oath which would have spelt ruin in case of future misconduct had the court ever been powerful enough to enforce its penalties, for it more or less imposed a suspended sentence of attainder upon him. It is impossible to gauge the effect of the Resumption Act in detail, but knowledge that reform of the king's hereditary revenues had begun left the Commons more favourably disposed towards the king than they had been for many years. The parliament of 1453 made a notably generous grant of taxation, and attainted York's chamberlain, Sir William Oldhall. By the summer of 1453 the duke seemed to be hopelessly isolated and discredited.

The events of the second half of the year shattered the prospects of this modest revival in the royal authority. By early August the king was insane.[2] On 12 December the queen gave birth to a son, Prince Edward. The prince's birth made York more jealous of his rights than ever. He probably hoped even now to preserve his inheritance to the crown, for with infant mortality at its fifteenth-century level the birth of one child did not make his deprivation certain. More menacing for the present, the king's madness left power completely in the hands of his opponents, and he may have feared that they would use the occasion to inflict the retribution which he had so far escaped.

For seven months the court contrived to avoid any public discussion of Henry's condition. By mid-February 1454 evasion was no longer possible, and the royal council, unable to ignore York's claims of blood as the king's nearest adult relation, granted him a limited commission authorizing him to open parliament as the king's lieutenant. When parliament met, a dismayed delegation from the house of Lords found the king in a state of such extreme prostration, both physical and mental, that a decision on the conduct of government could be postponed no longer. The Lords rejected the queen's plan for her own appointment as regent. Nor, on the other hand,

---

1. Guienne had fallen to the French in January 1451.
2. Dr R. L. Storey (*The End of the House of Lancaster*, London, 1966, p. 136) described his breakdown as bearing 'a fair resemblance to a period of stupor in a case of katatonic schizophrenia'.

would they give York such extensive powers. They would give him no more than the Lords thirty years before had given Humphrey of Gloucester – the title of 'Protector and Defender of the Realm': a title which implied a personal duty for the defence of the land and no more. They made their distrust of York's ambitions crystal clear (as they would have done in the case of any other magnate) by explicitly denying him the titles of tutor, lieutenant, governor, regent, or any other title that would 'import authority of governance of the land'. Even this restricted authority was to continue only until the prince became of age, and the Lords, to make matters absolutely certain, firmly stated that York's authority should in no way prejudice the prince's rights.

This first protectorate lasted only a short time. By the end of the year Henry recovered his sanity and in February 1455 York's period of office came to an end. A tactless attempt by Somerset to exclude him from the Great Council, amongst other things, once more aroused his deep suspicions, and by early May, together with his Neville relations, the earl of Salisbury and Salisbury's son, the earl of Warwick, generally known from his activities over the next sixteen years as Warwick the Kingmaker, he was marching south, attempting once more to impose his will upon the king by armed force. The king and Somerset countered the move (the danger of which they badly underestimated) by summoning another Great Council to meet at Leicester. It was no part of their plan to use armed force, for Somerset was taken completely by surprise when he heard that York had been recruiting in the north. Not until mid-May, when it was already too late, did Somerset begin to mobilize troops for the king. On 22 May the two parties met at St Albans. Prolonged negotiations between them broke down upon Henry's adamant refusal to surrender Somerset to his enemies. Pacific as he was, in the end he chose to fight rather than put himself completely in York's hands. The forces joining battle were small. York led at most 3000 men. The king's 'army', vaguely estimated at about 2000, owing to Somerset's original misjudgment of York's intentions was made up of very little more than the household retinues of the lords who were in attendance at court.

The battle lasted only three hours. Not more than one hundred and twenty men were slain on the field, possibly as few as sixty. The importance of St Albans, however, lay in more than time and numbers. Its political consequences were disastrous. Before 1455 his greater subjects, in spite of his personal weakness, had always treated

Henry VI with the greatest deference. With blood now shed in his presence for the first time, a valuable restraint in public life had broken down. Indeed, for the rest of the decade it never returned to normal.

Somerset had been killed at St Albans. To that extent York and his friends triumphed in their private feud. There is indeed some justification for a contemporary opinion which regarded the battle as an act of private revenge upon some particular lords. It brought them, however, little long-term political advantage. Many bitterly grudged at their proceedings. Somerset may have been much disliked but at this time there is no sign that York was widely popular. York's success had been so negative that he and his friends dreaded the outbreak of quarrels amongst the lords, for they themselves might come none too well out of any new disputes to which recriminations would inevitably lead. They therefore tried to promote an appearance of unity and, at the same time, to provide for their own safety by passing through parliament, which had been summoned after the battle, a pardon for all except Somerset and two other men.

Even then so negative a success could hardly have satisfied the duke. Some of his own friends were uneasy, the attitude of the Lords in the new parliament coldly disapproving. Real power he had yet to gain. While parliament was in recess during the summer and autumn he seems to have planned a peaceful *coup d'état*. When it reassembled in November, possibly making use of a temporary indisposition in the king, he and his friends skilfully organized a deputation from the Commons to stampede the Lords into making him Protector a second time, ostensibly to deal with outrageous disturbances in the west country raised by the earl of Devonshire. His ploy succeeded – but not for long. Just over fifteen weeks later (25 January 1456) the king came to parliament and deprived him of his office.

At this point the court showed no vindictive spirit towards York. The king gave him at least one valuable grant and authorized arrangements to pay off arrears of salary from his first protectorate and the expenses which he had recently incurred. It is indeed possible that Henry, wishing to rule through a widely based council of lords, would have retained him as his principal councillor. If this was true, Queen Margaret, implacable, and perhaps clearer-sighted, would have none of it. At this time John Bocking, in a letter to Sir John Fastolf, described her formidable qualities: 'a great and strong laboured woman, for she spareth no pain to sue her things to an intent and conclusion to her power'. Margaret, only sixteen when she arrived in England, had taken little or no part in politics until the birth of her son, when, her maternal instincts aroused, she was determined to defend his inheritance – and she came of a family in which strong-minded, dominant wives were accustomed to defending the interests of feckless and incompetent husbands. From now on there was political stalemate, disturbed in some parts of the country by the inability of the protagonists to control the more aggressive of their local followers.

So matters drifted; drifted through the failure of a conspicuous attempt at reconciliation in a Great Council assembled at West-minster in January 1458, until the next confrontation in 1459. The earl of Warwick, in spite of government attempts to dislodge him, led an uneasy life in Calais (its possession was one of the few advantages York and his friends retained from his second protectorate) supporting his garrison on the proceeds of piracy in the English Channel. During the winter and spring a new, vicious note, unheard before, ran through murmurings against the court. Its evil reputation acquired in Suffolk's day, left it still a plausible target for the em-bittered scandal which the Yorkists were now spreading against their opponents. The queen and her affinity were alleged to be gathering in riches innumerable. She had taken as her paramour the earl of Wiltshire, the handsomest man in England, too vain of his beauty ever to risk losing it in battle. She had appointed him treasurer and he was using his position to enrich himself by evil and corrupt practices. She had poisoned the earl of Devonshire. The Prince of Wales had been begotten in adultery, and to make certain of his succession Margaret had even planned her husband's abdication – so the venomous stories ran.

By the end of April 1459 Margaret was moving about the Midlands recruiting troops. Late in September, York and his sons at Ludlow, Salisbury at Middleham, and Warwick at Calais, alarmed by news of the queen's preparations, determined to act together. Salisbury, marching to join York, defeated part of the royal forces at Blore Heath in Shropshire. Warwick, landing in Kent with part of the Calais garrison, marched across England to Ludlow unmolested. As events were to prove, time after time, given the advantage of surprise, very small military forces could accomplish a great deal. Both sides during the Wars of the Roses found defence much more difficult to organize than attack. At Ludlow the confederates attempted to nego-tiate with Henry who, in spite of Blore Heath, still commanded con-siderable forces. On the failure of these negotiations, knowing that a large part of their troops would refuse to fight against the king himself, they broke their camp and fled by night in a dash for safety so panic-stricken that they abandoned the duchess of York in Ludlow Castle.

On 20 November 1459 the Parliament of Devils met at Coventry. An Act of Attainder, drafted with an eye to publicity, set out a detailed catalogue of York's offences since 1450 in a way that left no doubt of his guilt. Even allowing that the triumphant loyalists put the most unfavourable interpretation they could on every incident, it was an unanswerable indictment. It convicted of treason York, his two eldest sons, the earl of Warwick, the earl and countess of Salisbury, two of Salisbury's younger sons, and sixteen other men, and condemned them to suffer the most solemn and atrocious penalties known to the common law. Treason was the most heinous of all offences; its penalties ruined the traitor's descendants as well as himself. The law held the offender worthy of death 'inflicted with the last extremity of bodily pain' – castration and disembowelling while still alive. It looked upon his children, their blood corrupted, as unfit to cumber the earth and barred them from both the paternal and maternal inheritances. The traitor died in the flesh; his children died before the law.

York's career sank to its lowest point in the Parliament of Devils. From Ludlow he fled to Ireland, his eldest son (the earl of March), Salisbury, and Warwick to Calais. Within a few months they made a striking *revanche*. On 26 June 1460 Salisbury, Warwick, and March embarked for Sandwich with about fifteen hundred or two thousand men. Their forces grew as they marched towards London where the authorities grudgingly admitted them to the city. A few days later part of their army marched northward to meet the royal forces now advancing upon the capital. They met outside Northampton. Negotiations once more preceded battle and once more failed. Victory fell to the Yorkists owing to the treachery of Lord Grey of Ruthin who came over to them from Henry's side early in the battle. Having taken the king prisoner, the earls returned with him to London, where they installed him in the bishop's palace and treated him with every mark of respect.

All this time York remained in Ireland. It is strange and suspicious to say the least that, in spite of discussions with Warwick, who had sailed from Calais to Dublin and back for that purpose earlier in the year, he made no attempt to coordinate his own landing in the west with that of the earls in Kent – surely the sensible proceeding in so precarious a venture. York began his own preparations for returning to England only after his friends had won the fight for him at Northampton (10 July). It was not until early September that he crossed the Irish Sea to Chester. Even then his progress towards London was slow – so slow that the suspicion arises that he dallied deliberately so as to avoid meeting any of his friends before confronting parliament which had been summoned for early October. York reached Westminster three days after parliament met. He came with five hundred armed men at his back, his trumpets and clarions sounding and his sword borne upright before him – the style appropriate only for a king. Passing through Westminster Hall, he strode into the Parliament Chamber where the Lords were in session and laid his hand on the cushion of the empty throne as if to claim it as his own by right. The expected acclamation never came. In a tense and angry silence he turned and faced the hostile rows of lords. Baffled and angry, impetuous in his disappointment, he strode out of the chamber. Smashing the door bolts, he broke into the king's apartments and 'lodged there for no little time more like a king than a duke'. Only one interpretation could be put on actions such as these – and soon there came 'a noise through the city that King Henry should be deposed and the duke of York should be king'.

Alone in Ireland York had brooded upon his wrongs, and his brooding had led him into political fantasies which had far outstripped the intentions of even the most extreme amongst his friends, the earls of Salisbury and Warwick. If rumour is correct, some of York's entourage, like Sir William Oldhall, had planned to make him king as early as 1450. York himself, whatever his private thoughts may have been, had never *openly* suggested that the king should be deposed until his return from Ireland. When they crossed from Calais, and later, Salisbury and Warwick had strongly protested their loyalty to the king. There is no reason to doubt their sincerity. York had laid his plans alone and the Nevilles felt outraged and deceived.

York never lacked courage. A few days later he formally claimed the throne by right of inheritance. Discussions about his claim went on for over a week. The dismayed house of Lords tried to throw responsibility for a decision first upon the royal justices and then upon the sergeants-at-law. When these refused to give a decision the Lords could evade responsibility no longer. They finally produced a compromise – the Act of Accord – remarkably like the Treaty of Troyes under which Henry V had obtained the French crown. Henry was to retain the crown as long as he lived, York acting as

Protector. After his death, ignoring the existence of Edward, Prince of Wales, York and his sons were to succeed.

We know little or nothing of York's thoughts, but many hypotheses have been advanced to explain the motives and the final, but limited, success of his struggles. Attempts to see him as a frustrated constitutional or administrative reformer may certainly be dismissed. Men in opposition are bound to speak the language of reform, but their words need be taken at face value only if matched by their deeds. The moral sentiments of those denied access to royal patronage were usually loftier than those of the more fortunate men who enjoyed it, for those excluded from the court resented it on hard financial grounds. York in 1450 and 1452, Salisbury and Warwick in 1460, claimed that the laws were disregarded, crime was unpunished and the king's income so plundered by courtiers and officials that he must resort to unlawful means to support his household. Their own hands, and those of their friends, were by no means as lily-white as their propaganda suggested. Salisbury and Warwick between them, as a result of the schemes of Salisbury's mother, Joan Beaufort, held the greater part of the estates which, according to the normal common law rules of inheritance, should have formed the endowment of the earls of Westmorland, the elder branch of the Neville family. The executors of Ralph, Lord Cromwell (d. 1456) thought that Warwick behaved abominably in forcing an unprofitable exchange of lands upon them. After supporting the Commons' demands for financial reform in 1450, ten years later, under the Act of Accord, York took 10 000 marks a year from the royal revenues to support his position as heir to the throne. It is true that the king normally provided for his heir, but the Prince of Wales had no other income, whereas York was a rich man in his own right. The rebels' associates were, if anything, worse. The earl of Devonshire was a notorious ruffian, for years the terror of the south-west. The duke of Norfolk was twice imprisoned for oppressive conduct (1440 or 1441 and 1448) and by 1452 the reputation of some of his followers in East Anglia was as evil as that of Suffolk's men two years before.

Nor can York be considered the leader of embittered war lords and soldiery who, driven out of Normandy in 1450, their occupation and their income vanished, turned on the government at home. There is no obvious connection except for a near-coincidence in time between the end of the Hundred Years War and the beginning of the Wars of the Roses. A few elderly veterans who had made their career and their money in France in the palmy days of Bedford's rule and who had later served under York as lieutenant supported his political ventures in the 1450s. His chamberlain, Sir William Oldhall, was one of them, Sir Edmund Mulsho and Sir Henry Radford others. There could hardly have been many of these embittered survivors of the war period, and they were members of a somewhat *passé* generation, for an unprofitable war career had long ceased to attract young men. Other war veterans, like Viscount Beaumont, Lord Hungerford and Lord Ryvers, never supported York. As for the rank and file, the depleted garrisons which in the end fled from Normandy were far too few in number to have provided the forces which fought against Henry VI at home and, in any case, they arrived in England a demoralized rabble, mentioned, when at all, by contemporaries as the pitiful objects of charity, not the makers of civil war.

Nor is there much to be said for the recently popular theory that a warlike aristocracy took first to political gangsterdom and then to civil war to compensate themselves for declining agrarian revenues. As we have seen, given careful management, aristocratic incomes had not universally declined as a result of social change. On the contrary, owing to marriage alliances and the acquisition of property which they brought with them, the greater lords on both sides were richer than their grandfathers had been. The richest property owners in England had more to lose than other men. Disorder was not in their interest, and they did not rush light-heartedly into civil conflict. They all held estates widely scattered in different parts of the country and prolonged fighting would inevitably lead to the loss of part of their vital agrarian incomes.

There is the other point that, ready enough as they were, at times, to take to violence to settle their own quarrels, treason was another matter, and they became involved in it only reluctantly. Considering how feeble and incompetent he was, it is astonishing how loyal they remained to Henry VI.

More than we know may have sympathized with York's quite genuine grievances, and some younger sons of noble families, who had little to lose, fought for him. Yet the fact remained that, by 1460, after ten years of intrigue and violence York had conspicuously failed to rally the peerage to his side. Twenty-eight secular peers, including York's uncle, Lord Abergavenny, his brothers-in-law, the duke of Buckingham and Viscount Bourchier, and his nephew, the duke of Norfolk, took an oath of loyalty to Henry VI and the Prince of Wales in the parliament of 1459. By that time only six of his fellow peers had taken the considerable risk of joining the duke in arms.

All but one did so to further quarrels of their own, not out of conviction for the justice of his cause. In 1452 the earl of Devonshire and Lord Cobham were with him at Dartmouth gambling on his victory to triumph in their own violent feuds with the earl of Wiltshire and Lord Bonville in the south-western counties. Neither lord supported York's later attempts. In 1454–5 the sudden alliance of Salisbury and Warwick rescued him from almost complete political isolation. They joined him then because a quarrel of several years' standing between Salisbury's younger sons and their cousins, the sons of the Percy earl of Northumberland, had reached a crisis in riots and tumults which threatened their interests in the north, and because Warwick was quarrelling with Somerset over the division of the Despenser inheritance in South Wales. Apart from the Nevilles, Lord Clinton was the only peer who fought with York at the first battle of St Albans, and he too went over most probably as the result of a personal quarrel with Lord Say and Sele. In 1459 only Lord Clinton and Lord Grey of Powys joined the rebels.[1]

The nobility would not support York. Neither would they take a firm stand against him. The leadership of a strong king or the blatant injustices of a tyrant were always essential to formulate or to provoke firm political decisions. The lords may well have remembered the sufferings and losses of their ancestors when they had taken sides in the violent political feuds of Richard II's and Henry IV's day. Fear of like retribution may have checked them now. Certainly the period of the Wars of the Roses, generally held notorious for noble treachery and violence, saw the majority of peers in a remarkably cautious frame of mind. Moreover, the uncertainties produced by Henry VI's long minority, followed by many years of feeble personal rule, already seem to have produced a kind of abdication of the will in great men. The peers, and others, had developed a tendency to dissociate themselves, as far as they could, from responsibility; a tendency shown in the practice of placing on record excuses for themselves, even in advance of action, in the parliament rolls or council minutes. In the crisis of 1454 most people were above all things anxious to avoid committing themselves on the major question of the regency. Attendance in the house of Lords was generally thin during the later Middle Ages. On this occasion an exceptionally large number of lords were so averse from committing themselves that they stayed away from parliament altogether. This tacit exhibition of dis-

1. Grey was a very young man whose status as a peer was dubious. He was also impoverished.

approval had not suited York's plans at all. As the king's nearest adult relation his authority could not be denied, but he wanted more than this: to force the widest possible show of approval from those who were most powerful in the country's affairs. York, in February 1454, decided for the first and only known occasion in English history to fine peers for non-attendance. The fines were stiff, but they produced only the slightest effect. Even those who did put in an appearance were hardly enthusiastic for York. No one wished to accept the final responsibility for making him Protector. York, ruthlessly as he enforced his claims, wished it put on record that the Lords had freely appointed him. The Lords in turn insisted that 'for their discharge' the Commons must agree. During Henry VI's minority, when the king for other reasons had been incapable of government, the Lords had claimed that the authority which he could not exercise lay with them. Now, in more difficult, more dangerous, circumstances, when faced with the choice of supporting or rejecting a fellow magnate, who had so recently come near to treason, they shuffled away, too bewildered to find any other way out. Dr J. H. Roskell is probably right in claiming that in 1454 rather than in the more spectacular crisis which was to follow in 1460, the Lords unwittingly sold the pass to York. By ignoring Queen Margaret's claim to the regency they may well have given the duke the impression that, although he failed to obtain wide approval for his actions, he could, by sheer determination, impose his will upon a reluctant and leaderless group of men.

In the parliament of 1459 the Lords showed no greater anxiety to shield York than they had formerly shown to support him. The royal advisers, like York in 1454, probably wished for the approval of the largest and most influential body of peers they could bring together. In this they were more successful than York had ever been. The Parliament of Devils was in fact (on the evidence available) the most fully attended parliament ever summoned by the three Lancastrian kings. It seems that with York out of the way the peers were prepared to demonstrate their loyalty to the king, feeble though he was. This impression is very much supported even by the parliament of 1460, for the absence from it of many prominent court peers who were with the queen in the north made its hostile attitude to York doubly significant.

In other quarters York received equally little support. He fled from Ludlow at the eleventh hour because the troops which Warwick had brought from Calais under the command of the famous war veteran, Andrew Trollope, the Master Porter of the town, refused to fight against the king. The Yorkists, aware of the danger, attempted to deceive Trollope by bringing men into their camp who swore that Henry was dead. To make the story more plausible, their priests even sang a mass for his soul. Their discreditable subterfuge was a miserable failure. Trollope and many of his troops went over to the king. The London records make it clear that the city fathers admitted the earls from Calais most reluctantly, hoping, by so doing, to avoid damage to property. An enthusiastic Yorkist poet could claim no more than 'The people rejoiced *inwardly* and thanked God of his goodness'. Even the Merchants of the Staple in the late 1450s provided funds because they knew that only a Yorkist victory gave them any immediate prospect of getting back the money which they had lent to pay the Calais garrison during York's second protectorate.

There is no evidence that any *widespread* group of people flocked to York's banners. In some districts he could count on the support of gentry families like the Pastons in East Anglia; families prepared to take his side if, in so doing, they could push their own local interests over those of their rivals. Robert Poynyngs in Kent joined in Cade's rebellion and later sided with York. He had little interest in reform or in the justice of the causes which he espoused. He hoped to use them to gain an advantage in his prolonged quarrel with the countess of Northumberland over the Poynyngs' inheritance.

Apart from a few war veterans, most of the duke's adherents, varying in rank from greater gentry to simple squires, some of them linked by family and marriage ties, were men who had profited from a long-standing connection with his estate and household administration. Some, even of these, held back at the critical moment. Lord Grey of Wilton, to whom he had granted a fee of twenty marks a year, never supported him. Three of his councillors ejected Sir William Skipwith from the stewardship of the duke's manor of Hatfield in Yorkshire and the constableship of Conisbrough Castle for refusing to follow the duke at St Albans, and Sir William Herbert of Raglan, the steward of his lordship of Usk and one of the richest of the Marcher gentry, never lifted a finger to help him between 1457 and 1460.

It was only after the attainders of the Parliament of Devils that a significant part of the nobility at last came over to York. In fifteen months after the flight from Ludlow fourteen peers swung over and fought for the Yorkists, so that by early 1461 their fighting strength was about seventeen: a substantial proportion of a total lay peerage of about sixty. All this is less impressive, however, if the shortage of the higher ranks is taken into account. Warwick apart, it included only two dukes, one earl and one viscount. The earl of Worcester, like the duke of Norfolk in 1457, even went on pilgrimage to the Holy Land to avoid such acute political difficulties. It is impossible to explain why so many peers turned their coats at this time. It was certainly not due to York's attempt to become king: that the peers in parliament had greeted with dismay. Some may have felt that he was treated too harshly in 1459. One of the most deeply rooted emotions of the age was its conviction of the near-sanctity of the inheritance. In the minds of the landed classes, if not in law, the 'life-lode' or landed inheritance was a family trust. They felt with a deep passion that not even treason should permanently extinguish the rights of an heir. York's title to the throne (that of the heir general) was uncertain enough to be disputable, his right to his lands and estates was not. From at least 1452 York had publicly, if somewhat vaguely, accused his opponents of plotting to deprive him of his inheritance. In a skil- fully drafted manifesto issued from Calais in 1460, Salisbury, Warwick, and March accused self-seeking lords about the king, in particular the earls of Wiltshire and Shrewsbury and Viscount Beaumont, of deliberately plotting the attainders of the Coventry Parliament to enrich themselves; no longer content with plundering the king of his lands and goods, they had turned their covetous eyes upon other men's inheritances. This skilfully slanted appeal may well have seemed plausible enough to be effective. Others may have gone over for personal reasons now unknown. York's pertinacity may have worn them down at last. For a whole decade he had shown that he was not prepared to give anyone else the chance to govern. By 1460 some may have felt that, indiscreet and violent as his conduct had been, the results of admitting him to power would at least be an improvement on the growing disorders and political chaos which had resulted from his exclusion. Whatever it was, the duke's limited success in 1460 was the triumph of *force majeure*. Principles, though advanced, were not fundamentally involved. York claimed the throne through the alleged superior right of the heir general over the heir male. This right had lain dormant through, but could not be defeated by, the Lancastrian usurpation. As he said, 'though right for a time rest and be put to silence yet it rotteth not nor shall not perish'. The law of inheritance was so confused that the particular point was disputable. Why the Lords would not fully approve the claim we shall never know. In spite of his hopeless incompetence, their loyalty to

Henry VI remained surprisingly strong. Can it be that York was not a man whose personality inspired much confidence?

Even now, in spite of this pronounced swing to York, Henry still commanded the support of greater numbers. Between the first battle of St Albans (May 1455) and the battle of Towton (March 1461) thirty-seven peers (and possibly five more), the heads of thirty-two noble families, fought for him and only three of these ultimately deserted to the Yorkist side.

So by 1461 the greater part of the peerage – at least forty-nine out of about sixty families – became involved in the fighting. They became involved tardily and reluctantly in a factional struggle for power at court, for until York suddenly and unexpectedly astonished parliament by asserting his title to the throne in October 1460 they obviously did not regard these quarrels as a dynastic issue. Once the dog fight for political control became transformed into a dynastic conflict the interest of the nobility rapidly waned. After 1461 no more than thirty per cent of the peerage at most fought in the political crises of the next three decades.[1] Their long-suffering loyalty to Henry VI had been remarkable but they were not prepared to risk their lives and their estates for the sake of untried politicians like Edward IV and Henry VII whose lack of experience could have inspired little confidence in anybody.

Although the Lords in 1460 at last gave way to Richard of York, compromised and made him Protector and heir to the throne, Margaret of Anjou's continued resistance forced him to fight for his position. Margaret, determined and energetic, with the help of a still impressive number of loyal nobles – the dukes of Somerset and Exeter, the earls of Northumberland and Devonshire, Lords Latimer, Roos, Neville, Greystock, and Dacre – succeeded in concentrating several thousand men in the area between York and Hull with such speed that the Yorkists seem to have been incredulous when the news first reached London. To counter the threat York marched north, hampered by waterlogged, sodden roads and broken bridges caused by the worst rains and floods for many years, to meet defeat and death at the battle of Wakefield (30 December 1460) – a disaster caused by his own impetuosity in leading the few men he had with him in a wild rush from the safe defences of Sandal Castle against the attacking Lancastrian forces, rather than waiting to call in the greater part of his troops which had scattered over the countryside in search of food.

1. See below, pp. 92, 94–5.

After the battle Margaret marched on London, allowing her unpaid troops to plunder the countryside relentlessly on either side of
their line of march. Warwick determined to intercept her at St
Albans, but his scouts served him so ineffectively that he was unaware of her approach and was still changing the disposition of his
troops when her army struck. Even then he might have won the day
had not ill-luck and treachery combined against him. The weapons of
his small mercenary force of Burgundian hand-gunners proved more
lethal to his own men than to the enemy, and, as Lord Grey of Ruthin
had gone over to the Yorkists at Northampton, now a Kentish squire
called Loveless deserted with his contingent to the Lancastrians.

All was now thrown back into confusion. After the battle Margaret
marched on towards London – only to pay the bitter price of past
folly. London might well have admitted her (as it had admitted the
Yorkist earls a year before) but for its terror of the evil reputation
which her troops had gained.[1] They had sacked St Albans Abbey after
the battle and had looted and plundered to the very walls of London.
Margaret had let loose furies which she could no longer control, and
panic-stricken people now regarded the Yorkist cause almost as a
defence of the south against the north. Messengers from the city
authorities told Margaret that they would open the gates if she would
solemnly guarantee that there would be no plundering. Margaret, to
her credit, to avoid sack and rapine, withdrew the main part of her
forces to Dunstable during several days of negotiation with the city.
This delay gave the Yorkists time to recover the initiative.

A fortnight before St Albans, York's eldest son, Edward, earl of
March, had defeated another Lancastrian army at Mortimer's Cross,
near Wigmore in Herefordshire. Marching quickly east he met
Warwick and the remnant of his forces somewhere in the Cotswolds,
and together they marched towards London. They arrived on the 28
February, ten days after the battle of St Albans, and the city gates
were immediately opened to them. Margaret then quitted Dunstable,
and the Lancastrian forces started their long march back to the
north. Still nothing was solved! The small band of noblemen and
clerics who entered London with Edward – Warwick, the duke of
Norfolk, Lord Fitzwater, Lord Ferrers of Chartley, the archbishop of

1. Rumours and tradition seem to have exaggerated these horrors. Mr L.
Tebbut, the borough librarian of Stamford, has informed me that the town
charters, allegedly destroyed in the sack of 1461, are extant and that several
buildings commonly said to have been destroyed at the same time still existed at
the Reformation.

Canterbury, and the bishops of Salisbury and Exeter[1] – knew they were in a desperate situation. Technically they were rebels, and although the queen's army was retreating, it was a tactical retreat. It was still intact, undefeated, and Henry VI himself was once again with the queen. Probably to shield themselves from the retribution due to rebels, this small fragment of a faction did for Edward what they had refused to do for his father: they proclaimed him king. As six weeks later the papal legate wrote to Francesco Sforza 'in the end my lord of Warwick has come off best and has made a new king of the son of the duke of York'. Edward, according to his own propaganda, had taken possession of his inheritance, but the country had yet to be won. Immediate action was imperative, or disaster might overwhelm the Yorkists. They followed the Lancastrians north and on 29 March 1461 at Towton, in the greatest and most desperate battle so far, defeated them utterly.

1. Fitzwater's status was somewhat dubious. He had never been summoned to parliament. The bishop of Exeter was Warwick's brother, and the duke of Norfolk his cousin.

4 York and Tudor

Edward IV was nineteen. Although a few months later the papal legate, Francesco Coppini, a witness prejudiced very much in the new king's favour, wrote that the population of the Kentish towns adored him like a God, he was unknown and untried. We know little of his education. He spoke fluent French and possessed a copy of the pseudo-Aristotelian *Secreta Secretorum*, but there is nothing to show that he received anything like the thorough education given to Louis XI of France and his brother Charles (Charles of France was studying Roman law at the age of twelve) – the type of intensive grounding for kingship which both Philippe de Commynes and Sir John Fortescue thought essential for a future ruler. A quarter of a century later, after his victory at Bosworth, Henry VII, although nine years older than Edward, was even more unknown, untried, and inexperienced.

The problems which faced both kings were fourfold, much the same and all interconnected: to devise a foreign policy which would enable them to govern undisturbed at home, to restore confidence and discipline to the greater part of the nobility, to restore better public order and to put the monarchy on a sound financial basis.

The Wars of the Roses from 1461 onwards were far from being merely a matter of domestic concern. Until the death of Duke Charles the Bold in 1477 the rulers of England, France, and Burgundy looked upon each other with a deep suspicious fear which gave to their intricate diplomacy an unscrupulousness, not to say chicanery, worthy of Machiavelli. With their expulsion from Normandy in 1450 the English had lost the lands on the northern French coast which to some extent had protected them from invasion. When in 1477 Picardy and the Somme towns and in 1492 Brittany passed to the French crown, England was even more exposed to the possibility of French attack, more so because, for technical reasons,[1] naval defences were at this time inadequate.

1. Early sixteenth-century ships could not sail very closely to windward, a serious handicap, as the prevailing winds in the Channel and its western approaches blew from between west and south, and before the 1580s very few ships could carry sufficient supplies to remain at sea continuously for more than a few weeks.

More immediately, in spite of the English defeats between 1450 and 1453, a nightmare vision of an aggressive alliance between England and Burgundy, and to a lesser extent Brittany, haunted the dreams of Louis XI and haunted them to such an extent that he was prepared to meet trouble halfway by stirring up sedition in England. The Lancastrians still held the great Northumbrian castles, Bamborough, Dunstanborough, and Alnwick; surrendered them in 1462; recovered them the following year, only to lose them again, and this time for ever, in 1464. Even these strongholds would have been of little use to them without foreign help. This, in April 1462, when Margaret of Anjou went from Scotland to France, Louis XI, desperately afraid of Burgundian ambition, undertook to provide. Then, as the diplomatic situation changed, he quickly lost interest. By September, when Margaret sailed from Brittany to Northumberland, the force which Louis had allowed her to recruit was disappointingly small, and her expedition ended in disaster when a storm wrecked her tiny fleet off Bamborough. In spite of various treason scares, this fiasco wrecked for several years any prospect of a Lancastrian *revanche*. The so-called battles of Hedgeley Moor and Hexham early in 1464 hardly deserve the name: the first was a mere chance encounter between a Lancastrian raiding party and the Yorkist escort for a Scottish embassy; at the second all but five hundred Lancastrians deserted because their wages were unpaid.

The origins of the major crises of 1470 and 1471 lay more in foreign apprehensions than in domestic seditions. In 1468 Warwick and the king's irresponsible nineteen-year-old brother, the duke of Clarence, had raised rebellion and captured Edward IV, but were forced to release him when passive resistance proved so great that they found it impossible to govern in the name of a captive king. When a second attempt on their part, the Lincolnshire rebellion early in 1470, quickly collapsed, they fled to Calais, which refused to admit them, and then to France. Louis XI, fearing that Edward intended to renew preparations for an invasion of France, which he had made in 1467–8, now took up a scheme which had been suggested to him during this earlier crisis – an alliance between the disgruntled Warwick and the queen, Margaret of Anjou, for whose disasters the earl had been so largely responsible. As a result of this seemingly fantastic alliance, Warwick with French help, returned to England and quickly drove Edward, a penniless refugee, to Burgundy. Edward's brother-in-law, Charles the Bold, in turn fearing an Anglo-French attack on Burgundy, provided him with the means of returning to England, where he defeated and killed Warwick at the battle of Barnet (14 April 1471). Margaret, who had delayed her own departure from France, landed in England just in time to hear of the earl's defeat, and her own forces were crushed, and her son Prince Edward slain, at Tewkesbury (4 May). In foreign affairs the remainder of Edward's life consisted of a diplomatic duel with the king of France. The high point of his success came in the Treaty of Pécquigny (1475) when, after taking over to France one of the largest armies which ever left English shores in the fifteenth century, he returned, after a bloodless 'campaign', the richer by an indemnity of 75 000 crowns, an annual pension of 50 000, a ransom of the same amount for Margaret of Anjou and an agreement that his eldest daughter should marry the Dauphin. Edward died in the middle of one of the adverse turns of his relations with France. Alarmed by a combination of Charles the Bold's successor, the Emperor Maximilian, and France, he was, in fact, making preparations for war; preparations which Richard III continued. The advisers of the new French king, Charles VIII, therefore provided Henry of Richmond with 60 000 francs and 1800 mercenaries for his successful attempt on the English crown.

Henry VII soon realized that England's days as a continental power were over – if indeed he had ever thought otherwise. For the first of his two attempts at military intervention in Europe – his invasion of Brittany in 1489 – parliament reluctantly voted £100 000, but only £27 000 was ever collected, and the people of Yorkshire rose in rebellion rather than pay. The second was an invasion of France in 1492. On this occasion, like Edward IV in 1475, he bargained and Charles VIII bought him off with an indemnity and an agreement to pay off the arrears due under the Treaty of Pécquigny. Expensive commitments abroad led to discontent at home dangerous to a monarch with a feeble title to the throne and one, moreover, whose subjects regarded him with no overwhelming affection. On the other hand, both France and the Hapsburgs (and the Hapsburg power 'bloc' after the marriage, in 1496, of the emperor Maximilian's son, the archduke Philip, and Joanna, the daughter of Ferdinand of Aragon and Isabella of Castile, also meant Spain) valued English diplomatic support against each other. Although England became more vulnerable to attack as France acquired the Picard and Breton coasts, fortunately for Henry from 1494 the storm centre of Franco-Hapsburg hostility moved south of the Alps. Charles VIII abandoned his ambitions on Flanders in an attempt to gain control of the wealth of Italy, which the Hapsburgs also coveted with a lust quite equal to his own. The English position, therefore, became less precarious, though certainly not free of danger, and Henry restricted his aims to protecting English commercial interests in the Hapsburg-dominated Netherlands (now the principal outlet for English woollen cloth) and to protecting his country from foreign invasion by two powers, either of which would be prepared to attempt, by force, if necessary, to prevent what they considered his valuable support from being given to the other. The Hapsburgs could bring pressure to bear on England through its merchants in the Netherlands, the French by encouraging their traditional allies, the Scots, to invade the north of England. These prime considerations of defence account for the extremely complicated twists and turns of Henry's foreign policy, and for what, in its later stages, have been condemned as its rather squalid expedients. In 1506, he was even prepared to marry the recently widowed Joanna the Mad, though to do him justice he seems to have thought reports of her insanity to be yet another political trick of Ferdinand of Aragon's. Over the years he was successful enough, though he was prepared, as in 1493, to damage English trade by placing embargoes upon it to further his political schemes. Henry's reputation for the farsighted encouragement of English trade is, in fact, grossly exaggerated. The thirty or so statutes of his reign passed to protect the interests of ship-owners, merchants, and artisans were no part of a wisely formulated royal programme. Self-interested sections of the trading community pressed them through parliament, and, unless the interested parties acting as common informers saw to their execution, many of them from the beginning must have been more or less dead letters, for Henry himself seems to have been concerned to enforce only those which would add to his customs revenues.

The most malign development in English life under Henry VI's personal rule had been the decline in the always weak restraint of the nobility in settling their quarrels by violence and, consequently, the spread of such violence throughout the countryside. The circumstances in which a small group of rebels had placed Edward IV on the throne, and in which Richard III and Henry VII had snatched it for themselves, were hardly likely to inspire immediate confidence in such kings. Nor, in spite of Edward's propaganda for legitimacy or Henry's combination of a somewhat exiguous claim by birth to the Lancastrian inheritance and to that of York through his marriage with Edward's eldest daughter, Elizabeth, did dynastic feeling inspire many men to loyalty: dynastic sentiment, indeed, seems to have been more of an *ex post facto* justification than a prime cause of civil strife. Both kings, therefore, had to inspire confidence through their actions.

Both began with a mass proscription of those who had fought against them. The parliament of 1461 attainted one hundred and thirteen people of treason including thirteen peers. Yet only a hard core of about seven great families remained irreconcilably anti-Yorkist.[1] The king's brother-in-law, the duke of Exeter, a man of violently unstable character, dangerous because he had apparently put forward a claim to the throne in 1454, Edward kept imprisoned as long as he lived. The king, however, knew quite well that he could not base his rule successfully upon the narrow support of the fragment of the faction which had made him king, or even upon the limited support of that wider, but still limited, section of the peerage which had swung over so tardily and reluctantly to his father. Always inclined to overlook the past in return for present support, he first, in 1463, pardoned Henry, duke of Somerset, and to the extent even of rousing the disgust of his own supporters, flaunted this act of clemency before the world, jousting with the duke, sharing his bed with him, even making him captain of his guard on an expedition to the north. The gamble failed and Somerset fled to his Lancastrian friends. In 1469 Edward released another great peer, the Percy earl of Northumberland, and restored him to his estates. This time he won – for two years later on Edward's return from Burgundy, Northumberland did not join his enemies. Two other peers he later pardoned, and from early days many attainted gentry found it possible to make their peace with the king. As many as thirty-three did so during the parliament of 1472–5.

The king's secret marriage to Elizabeth Wydeville – according to legend the only woman who ever denied him her bed, saying that though she might be too base to be a king's wife she was too good to be his harlot – was hardly so grave a cause of offence to the nobility as slanders put out by Warwick later alleged. Indeed, once he had revealed the marriage, Edward seems to have used her coronation as an occasion for bringing the nobility together and reconciling their differences. The quick marriages of her relations into the families of Arundel, Norfolk, Grey of Ruthin, Herbert, and Buckingham, served to bring these families into closer contact with the throne (a contact

1. Exeter, Oxford, Beaumont, Clifford, Hungerford, Roos and Jasper Tudor, earl of Pembroke. Although Lord Clifford's attainder was not reversed until 1485, he received a pardon in 1472. Somerset and Devon died without direct heirs, but the earldom of Devon was re-created for the earl's nephew in 1485.

which members of the peerage never despised) and avoided the resentment which a continued, ostentatious dependence upon the Nevilles would certainly have caused. The Nevilles' appetite for property and their unscrupulous methods of acquiring it were something of a by-word even in this acquisitive century. Warwick's own 'insatiable covetise' became notorious, and since 1461 Edward had created his uncle William (earlier married to an idiot child to get her property) earl of Kent and his brother John earl of Northumberland.[1] Warwick might well have served as an illustration of Machiavelli's opinion that those who help a new prince to power to slake their own discontent against an existing government are afterwards kept friendly only with great trouble and difficulty. Warwick having supported the house of York to serve his own ends grew sour as he found that he was not to dominate its now enthroned representative, his young cousin who possessed an iron will and maybe enough political sense to realize that to deliver himself to a faction might well be to deliver himself to a nemesis not unlike that of Henry VI. When, however, having failed to dominate court patronage in his own interest, having failed to impose a pro-French foreign policy over Edward's preference for a Burgundian alliance, and after the king had refused to allow his brother, the duke of Clarence, to marry his daughter, Isobel, Warwick rose in revolt in 1469, the only peers to rise with him were his brothers-in-law, the earl of Oxford and Lord Fitzhugh. This domineering malcontent failed to inspire confidence even in his own family, let alone the rest of the peerage. The following year only two others, Lord Willoughby and Welles and Lord Scrope of Bolton, joined him in the Lincolnshire rebellion. When that quickly collapsed, showing how completely he had failed to divide Yorkist England, there was nothing left for him to do but go over to the exiled Lancastrians; who were quite prepared to receive him, for, well aware of his discontents, for two years or so they had already toyed with the idea of so bizarre an alliance.

Early in 1473 the earl of Oxford[2] captured St Michael's Mount and held it for five months and people murmured the duke of Clarence's

---

1. John Neville's elevation and endowment with most of the Percy estates were probably most offensive to aristocratic conventions, as the Percy earl of Northumberland, though attainted, was still alive and most men felt that attainder should not be a permanent bar to the recovery of estates.

2. The Oxford family was amongst the very few which remained permanently hostile to Edward IV. The earl's father and elder brother had been executed for conspiracy in 1462.

name in connection with this and various other obscure conspiracies. Clarence also dangerously threatened Yorkist security by quarrelling with his brother Gloucester over property settlements and by demanding, on the suggestion of their sister Margaret, the dowager duchess of Burgundy, that Edward allow him to marry Mary, the heiress of Charles the Bold and all the vastly rich Burgundian territories – a marriage which would certainly have led to an expensive war abroad. When in 1477 Clarence, by intimidating a jury, procured the judicial murder of Ankarette Twynyho, one of his dead wife's former attendants, on a fantastic charge of poisoning the duchess, the king's patience at last broke. Upon an indictment signed with his own hand parliament attainted Clarence of treason, and this handsome, eloquent, feather-brained, unmitigated family nuisance ended his life, according to a probably accurate rumour, drowned in a butt of malmsey.

Edward lived his last years peaceably enough. According to Sir Thomas More he left 'this realm in quiet and prosperous estate, for the displeasure of those that bore him grudge for king Henry's sake the sixth . . . was well assuaged, and in effect quenched, in that many of them were dead in more than twenty years of his reign, a great part of a long life. And many of them in the mean season grown into his favour of which he was never strange.' Unfortunately he left as his heir a boy only twelve years old. A royal minority, now as ever, became the signal for mutually suspicious factions to compete for power. The late king's brother, Richard of Gloucester, fearing the dominance of the queen's relations, the Wydevilles, determined to forestall any bid for power on their part, and wrested from them, by a stratagem, control of the boy king. This hasty action seems to have been no part of any premeditated plot to seize the crown. It resulted, however, in difficulties with some of his supporters, particularly Lord Hastings, who now began to negotiate with the Wydevilles. At this point it may be that Richard, a nervous, apprehensive and impulsive man, began to fear for his own safety, and fear drove him to the summary execution of Lord Hastings. Violence settled nothing, leading only to more violence and Richard in desperation, proclaiming (according to different stories) that either Edward IV or his sons, or all three, were bastards, seized the crown, claiming to be its rightful heir.

Richard III was an able soldier, a cultivated man, fond of music and architecture, a great builder, a patron of learning and deeply pious. His single parliament saw a useful, if modest, programme of legislation. According to the bishop of St David's, writing probably in September 1483, he was popular amongst the people. Though often stated to have been a good administrator during his rule of the north in the last years of his brother's reign, it seems more likely that his popularity there amongst certain groups, particularly the ruling faction on the Common Council of York, was due to an excessively generous exercise of patronage to curry favour for his own purposes – for other citizens of York voiced far less favourable opinions and in 1482 the council of the duchy of Lancaster had informed him, in a remarkably outspoken letter, of their disapproval of his laxity as chief steward of the duchy north of the Trent. Be that as it may, unfortunately for Richard's reputation, neither Edward V nor his younger brother were ever seen again after the end of August 1483 and soon rumours widely spread that he had made away with them in the Tower of London. Whatever excuses his modern admirers advance in his defence they overlook the fact that by the early part of 1485 many of his subjects believed him evil enough to have murdered his queen as well as his nephews: his reign presents the uniquely shameful spectacle of a king of England forced to deny publicly before the mayor and aldermen of London rumours that he had poisoned his wife. Whether or not this indicates that his popularity amongst the people had now vanished, he certainly retained only narrow support amongst the nobility and gentry. When, a fortnight after landing in Milford Haven, Henry of Richmond, with at most 8000 men, confronted him at Market Bosworth, only nine peers[1] rode into battle with him and the earl of Northumberland, upon whom he had relied, stood idly by and watched the conflict.

Before Bosworth Henry gained as little support as Richard, perhaps even less. Amongst the peers only the diehard Lancastrian earl of Oxford and his own half-uncle, John, Lord Welles, fought for him. There is a strong presumption that another uncle, Jasper Tudor, earl of Pembroke, was there, but no contemporary source states his presence as a fact. Although troops raised by the Stanleys played a major part in the battle, Thomas, Lord Stanley, Henry's stepfather, remained aloof because his son, Lord Strange, was a hostage in Richard's camp. As far as the aristocracy was concerned only a little

1. The duke of Norfolk and the earl of Surrey (father and son), the earl of Nottingham, Viscount Lovell, Lords Ferrers, Zouche, Scrope of Bolton, Dacre of Gillesland, and Greystoke. Richard had allowed the first three claims to vast properties which Edward IV had denied them. Lovell, Scrope of Bolton, and Dacre of Gillesland had also profited financially from royal grants.

family group gave armed support to Henry of Richmond. Even the Welsh came to his banners in disappointingly small numbers. What one could achieve so might another, and the fact that he had won the kingdom with so minute a band of men seems to have haunted Henry all his days, making him withdrawn and suspicious. Constant sedition indeed threatened his security. Eight insurrections and rebellions and three changes of dynasty in thirty years had debased the vision of kingship, making men more inclined to treason than they had been in the middle years of the century. Sedition eternally menaced the king: from the insurrection of Viscount Lovell and the Staffords in 1486 to the crazy 'mawmet' of 1499 who 'confessed that being at Cambridge at school he was sundry times stirred in his sleep that he should name himself to be the duke of Clarence's son and he should in process obtain such power that he should be king'. More men (51) were attainted in Henry's last parliament, that of 1504, than in any other parliament of his reign.[1]

Moreover, Henry had no heir of mature age[2] and this may well have encouraged conspiracy. Two decades after Bosworth Henry's only surviving son was still a child and, if a spy's report can be credited, in private discussions prominent men could still ignore his claims to the succession. The conspiracies of the Yorkist pretenders, Lambert Simnel (1487) and Perkin Warbeck (1491–7), especially the latter, were dangerous enough. Certain Irish lords, the better to secure their own independent position, were always prepared to rise in support of Yorkist pretenders – 'My lords of Ireland, you will crown apes at last', Henry once sardonically told them. In spite of her niece's marriage to the king, Edward IV's sister, the dowager duchess of Burgundy, remained implacable and always eager to foment and sustain conspiracies; and members of the de la Pole family, the descendants of one of Richard of York's daughters, were ready enough to put forward their claims to the throne. The independently-minded Irish, one sister and the somewhat feckless descendants of an aunt did not, however, make a Yorkist party. Amongst the English nobility at least, though again a number of men of lower rank were less cautious, there was no more of a Yorkist party now than there had been in the 1450s. Apart from the de la Pole earl of Lincoln, who probably hoped to snatch the throne himself, Viscount

1. This is exactly the reverse of Edward IV's reign when after the mass attainders of 1461–3 only twenty-seven new names were added to the list.

2. Prince Arthur died in 1502, aged fifteen. Henry VIII was only eighteen when he came to the throne.

Lovell was the only recruit of first importance to Lambert Simnel's cause, and Lord FitzWalter was the only peer who supported Perkin Warbeck. Lord Audley, who supported the Cornish rebels in 1497, had no Yorkist connections.

With little overt dynastic attachment, the nobility appear to have become guarded, uncertain and wary, prepared to compromise themselves with a pretender, if at all, only when he looked like winning. Even Sir William Stanley's notorious treason in 1494 may have been little more than taking out an insurance policy with the other side in case it should win. Nevertheless Sir Francis Bacon, writing a century later, judged that Henry 'was possessed with many secret fears touching his own people' and added 'for his nobles, though they were loyal and obedient, yet did not cooperate with him, but let every man go his own way'. This may have been the reason why in military matters he relied to so great an extent upon his household. His suspicious watchfulness may well have stimulated much of the nobility's already existing caution. Long before the end of his reign he controlled most of the peers, many other great men and many officials by means of suspended fines and ruinously great recognizances for good behaviour (see below, p. 174). These became so numerous that one historian[1] has claimed 'the point had almost been reached where Henry VII governed by recognizance'. Whatever the cause may have been, if many of the nobility thought treason in their minds, only a very small number of them allowed it to erupt into action. They had little cause to love Henry, but they at least respected the care and vigilance which enabled him to survive a reign which, as Bacon again remarked, 'proved for many years together full of broken seas, tides and tempests'.

Recognizing strenuous attempts by both Edward and Henry to improve public order, historians in the same breath have pilloried their methods of justice as arbitrary and tyrannical – condemning Edward for intimidating juries and dismissing at least one judge for refusing a condemnation which he desired,[2] seeing Henry terrorizing his subjects through the harsh methods of the court of Star Chamber. These legends, like so many others about the fifteenth century, are fit for the rubbish heap. If Edward 'laboured' juries and employed civil law in the court of the constable to condemn suspected rebels in periods of crisis he did no more than earlier kings. Indeed, in late

---

1. The late K. B. McFarlane, *E.H.R.*, lxxxi (1966), 153–5.
2. The case of Sir Thomas Cook and Chief Justice Markham. The charge is extremely dubious.

medieval England, if the king 'recorded' a man's guilt from his own knowledge, that, in theory, was enough to obtain a conviction. Edward, in these matters, was firm and determined, but his judicial methods were neither new nor particularly ruthless: considering the disturbances of his reign he acted with comparative restraint. The tradition that Henry VII repressed disorder, and in particular retaining, livery and maintenance, through the Star Chamber is without foundation. The Star Chamber became a court for imposing royal discipline upon the gentry only later in the sixteenth century. In Henry's day private suitors initiated nine-tenths of the cases heard there. There is no extant evidence to show that in Henry's time the court tried a single offender for offences against the law of retaining.

Both kings made various judicial innovations. Edward in 1467, and again in 1483, appointed a special officer to 'promote', that is to investigate and prosecute, crimes of *lèse-majesté*, though nothing is known of any action which these men took under their commissions. Henry VII and his advisers were particularly given to creating new judicial machinery. Searching for effective instruments, he established at least four special courts to supersede or supplement the common law tribunals for various purposes. As far as we can judge from the rather thin surviving evidence, nothing much seems to have come of at least three of them:[1] they were almost certainly experiments that failed. Although methods of investigation used in the royal council and in these so-called prerogative courts were a great improvement upon those of the common law courts, they worked under disadvantages which neutralized their greater efficiency. Apart from large fines the penalties which they could inflict were comparatively trivial: they had no jurisdiction over life and limb. Public opinion also played a part, though probably a minor one, in diminishing their utility, for, as Edmund Dudley remarked, offenders resented punishment through their 'extraordinary justice' more than that of the common law tribunals even if the penalties happened to be lighter.

Recent investigations show that, despite Henry VII's experiments, the judicial policy of the 'New Monarchy' was as improvised, as personal and as conservative as most of its other activities. Edward IV took so keen a personal interest in justice that for the first fifteen

1. One set up under the misnamed 'Pro Camera Stellata' Act of 1487; a court to try servants of the king's household accused of trying to destroy the king, a peer or a royal councillor (1487); a court for trying corrupt juries (1495). The 'Council learned in the Law' active from *c.* 1499–1500 mainly as a court for collecting the royal debts was successful – and harsh.

D

years of his reign he well-nigh reverted, perhaps unconsciously, to the itinerant practices of early Angevin monarchy, becoming a peripatetic king visiting and doing justice upon every part of his realm. In 1464 between January and May he rode from Coventry to Worcester, from Worcester to Gloucester, across country to Cambridge and then to Maidstone in Kent, sitting in justice in all these places. In December 1467, when travelling to the north Midlands to settle violent disputes, including a murder, between Lord Grey of Codnor and the Vernons, he personally interviewed their retainers as well as members of the families involved in the quarrel and wrote to the chancellor for the hasty dispatch of commissions of oyer and terminer to cover six whole counties.

The commission of oyer and terminer[1] seems to have been the institution upon which Edward most confidently relied, for the Chancery issued no less than seventy-seven such commissions in the course of his reign. A familiar instrument, it was the most flexible part of the traditional common law system. As many as twenty or thirty men might be appointed to it and it could investigate and give judgment upon anything from a single felony to all those committed in half a dozen designated shires – or even occasionally over the whole country. An important nobleman headed the commission to give it power and prestige, several might be appointed if difficult cases were involved, and one or two of the royal judges provided expert professional assistance. As few as two members of such a commission could hold its pleas and a large commission could therefore split up, and different groups could carry on its work simultaneously in different places. Henry used the oyer and terminer somewhat less than Edward – only forty-one commissions issued from the Chancery between 1485 and 1509. He may possibly have relied rather more upon the justices of the peace and quarter sessions. The royal council, under both kings, heard a number of cases every year, many of them concerning disputes of nobles and great men, not only from the fear that the course of justice in lower courts might be perverted, but because the nobility expected their quarrels to be ironed out at this high level. Chancery too dealt with riot cases. All in all, however, the traditional common law system, not the council, the Star Chamber, and new prerogative courts, sustained the attack against violence and disorder and brought about whatever improvement there was in the life of the countryside.

1. i.e. to hear and determine.

Continuous progress is not one of the more conspicuous features of English history, and financially the fifteenth century was a period of regression for the monarchy. The fossilization of the system of direct taxation on personal property from 1334 onwards[1] and the gradual but, by the mid-fifteenth century, colossal decline in the customs revenue due to the growth of the lightly taxed cloth industry at the expense of heavily taxed wool exports left the kings of England much poorer than they had been in the middle of the fourteenth century. Both Edward IV and Henry VII knew that, as Sir Thomas More remarked, 'The gathering of money is the only thing that withdraweth the hearts of Englishmen from their Prince'. Direct taxation, being sporadic, roused more resentment than it does today when it is regular and continuous. When Edward IV came to the throne his advisers recognized that he must above all be circumspect in his demands for money. The very narrow basis of support which was all he enjoyed in 1461 would never be widened if he made heavy direct demands upon the purses of his subjects. In his earlier years when he was often in the most desperate need for money, living precariously from hand to mouth and forced to raise cash by all kinds of shifts and contrivances, he delayed asking parliament for a grant for two years, and there were only two direct grants in his first decade.[2] Even in his later years, when he was more firmly established, his attitude towards the taxation of the lay population[3] in general was only slightly less wary than in the days of his insecurity. During his reign Edward took, through parliamentary grants, no more than an average of £10 700 a year from his lay subjects. They could not justifiably complain, though complain they did, of the extent of direct taxation. Henry VII, on paper, did a little better with something between £12 000 and £13 000 a year, but by no means all of it was collected. Both kings, following Lancastrian precedents, used the excuse of foreign war in an attempt to tap new sources of wealth in the country by levying an income tax. The results were so discouraging that neither tried again. In 1472 inefficiency and peculation frustrated the scheme, and that of 1489 resulted in dangerous riots in the

1. Parliament cut the proceeds of personal taxation by 10·4 per cent in 1433 and 15 per cent in 1446, a cut which then remained permanent. The excuse was relief for towns and districts which had decayed since 1334 but in fact each county received an exact percentage remission.

2. In 1463 and 1467–8, Henry VII, likewise, did not ask for a grant for two years – until 1487.

3. The clergy were separately and (at this time) rather more heavily taxed.

north and produced only £27 000 instead of an expected £75 000. Both kings, having failed to obtain money from parliament, reverted (as Edward did in his judicial itineraries) more or less to the expedients of thirteenth-century kings in the days before money grants had been centralized in parliament, travelling about the country, demanding, with enormous personal trouble, in face to face interviews, 'benevolences', or more or less compulsory gifts, from their richer subjects. Though immensely troublesome, such levies were less politically dangerous than parliamentary taxation. As the *Great Chronicle of London* remarks of the benevolence of 1491, 'Then the king visited many counties, and the commissioners the residue, in calling the people before them, and in such wise exhorted them, that the king's grace was well contented with the loving demeanour of his subjects. And so he had good cause for by this way he levied more money than he should have done with four fifteenths, and also with less grudge of his commons, for to this charge paid none but men of good substance, where at every fifteen are charged poor people which make more grudging for the paying of sixpence, than at this time many did for the paying of six nobles.'

No attempt was ever made during this period to increase the customs duties which, except for wool (a rapidly declining export) were absurdly low, for the conventional valuation of merchandise for some articles was as little as one-seventh of their true commercial value. Both Edward and Henry, on the other hand, made determined attempts to tighten up the customs administration. Circumstantial evidence casts some doubt upon the common opinion that the rate of duty upon all goods except wool were too low for smuggling to appeal to respectable merchants. In 1479 the Merchant Adventurers noted in their minutes that the king had been 'strangely informed' that London merchants were 'embezzling his subsidy', and with the utmost duplicity expressed their great surprise that the king could possibly suspect any of their fellowship, when all the time they knew quite well that the king's attorney was prosecuting sixteen Adventurers and Mercers in the Exchequer Court for smuggling – one of them, John Marshall, having fourteen separate cases brought against him. In spite of their protestations of innocence they were soon lobbying Lord Hastings, Earl Ryvers, the marquess of Dorset, and even the queen, to intercede for them with the king and in the end they were glad enough to compound their offences collectively for £1000 rather than let the cases against them continue.

From the beginning of his reign Edward IV may have felt that the customs administration had deteriorated during Henry VI's last years. In the 1460s he dealt with the problem in a rather tentative way through several acts of parliament. More vigorous executive action followed in the 1470s. In 1475 the king's own secretary, William Hatteclyff, arranged for an investigation into 'great deceits' in Dartmouth and Topsham: an investigation which returned a detailed report of sixty-nine sailings out of the two harbours. Between 1473 and 1481 Edward reintroduced officials called surveyors into eleven of the principal ports,[1] giving them almost absolute powers over the existing staff. Their high rate of pay attests to the importance of these new officials, for Edward IV was a hard-headed businessman, not given to paying out good money without cause. John Taylour, who covered the south-western ports, received £50 a year and half the goods seized as a result of successful prosecutions. William Weston, one of two such surveyors in London who looked to tonnage and poundage in the port, received 100 marks a year and £10 for his clerk. This equalled the income of one of the richer gentry, and even the king's proctor in the papal court at Rome was paid only £130.

There is no doubt that some of these surveyors, like other royal administrators, were, by modern standards, decidedly shady characters. John Taylour was particularly violent and unsavoury and the principle of set a thief to catch a thief was sometimes all too evident. At the same time the new supervisors were stringent enough to inspire resentment and dread. The Croyland Chronicler remarked 'throughout all the ports of the kingdom he [Edward] appointed inspectors of the customs, men of remarkable shrewdness, but too hard upon the merchants according to general report'. By 1480 the Merchant Adventurers were also complaining about their 'straitness', and cowed by their recent brush with the king decided to discipline any of their own members who in future tried to bilk the customs. Offenders were to be fined 100 marks[2] for a first offence, £100 for a second, and expelled from the fellowship if they offended a third time. Henry VII carried on in the same strict way. In 1486-8 he prosecuted no less than twenty customs officials for absence from their posts, illegal trading on their own account or embezzlement.

The proceeds of the customs reached £34 000 in 1478-9 and an average of £40 000 a year during Henry VII's last decade – no

1. Such officials had been sporadically appointed under Henry VI but appointments had ceased after 1447.
2. A mark was 68 n.p.

spectacular increase, and how far it was due to improved trade, how far to tighter administration it is impossible to say, but in spite of low rates of duty the most constant vigilance was required to check smuggling and maintain the yield of one of the two main sources of royal revenue.

During the fifteenth century the royal lands were an equally significant, if not potentially a more valuable, part of the royal endowment. They consisted of a core of hereditary royal estates, lands which the king himself purchased, others which came to him through forfeiture for treason, and estates which escheated (or returned to him as head of the feudal system of landholding) on the death without heirs of his tenants-in-chief. Sir John Fortescue's well-known proposals, in the *Governance of England*, for dealing with the royal lands and the much-sought-after offices which they provided were, by and large, a summary of reforming opinions which he had heard very strongly expressed by disgruntled members of the house of Commons in the 1450s. The royal lands were part of the crown's possessions which even the king himself could not properly alienate. Those which the king had thus improperly granted away he should 'resume' or take back. In future he should avoid making grants in perpetuity, giving only leases to those who had served him well, and he should reserve offices to his own servants on the principle, one man, one place. These restrictions once established, the Exchequer could then extract a maximum cash yield from the royal estates. Though the principle of one man, one place, and reservation to the king's own servants was impractically rigid and doctrinaire,[1] Fortescue's views did recognize that the crown lands had to fulfil two almost contradictory functions: to produce a large cash income and to provide the patronage which helped to keep the 'political nation' loyal to the king.[2]

These problems were not peculiar to England. All over Europe kings found it difficult to maintain the extent of their crown lands in the face of the demands of their powerful subjects. The contrary demands of the taxpayers, however, assisted their attempts to hold their territorial assets together. Their favourite method was the resumption of all previous grants. In the late fifteenth century kings and estates-general carried through such resumptions in Scotland, France, the Netherlands and Spain – and in Sweden as late as 1680. As we have seen earlier, between 1450 and 1453 the Commons had

1. Elsewhere in his writings Fortescue was less rigid.
2. See below, pp. 174 ff.

forced such resumptions upon Henry VI's corrupted court. The York-ist court, fully alive to the popularity which Henry had gained from these concessions, immediately adopted as official policy what had begun in the demands of a disgruntled house of Commons. Edward IV introduced four Acts of Resumption (in 1461, 1465, 1467, and 1473) and Henry VII another three (in 1485, 1487, and 1495). Numerous exemptions, both general and individual, accompanied all these acts. This does not, however, mean that such grants shattered their effect. Office holders and grantees had to apply for exemption individually, and Edward IV, and most probably Henry VII, care-fully scrutinized the hundreds of petitions handed in to the clerk of parliament after each act. During the whole of his reign Edward personally signed every exemption granted. The acts not only in-creased the extent of the crown lands; they enabled the king to review his patronage.

To the considerable estates regained in this way must be added those which fell in as the result of forfeiture for treason, and those which escheated through the operation of the feudal system. Exclud-ing members of the blood royal, between 1453 and 1504 parliament attainted for treason 397 people; 256 of these attainders were, how-ever, in the end, reversed. The higher the rank of the attainted, and the more valuable the estates forfeited, the greater was the chance of reversal. Only five peers out of thirty-four were ultimately left un-pardoned, so that major acquisitions of land through forfeiture augmented the revenues of the crown estate only for more or less short periods.

It has often been alleged that in the long run the most significant increase in the royal lands came from the king's exploitation of his position as lord paramount of the feudal tenures. In theory on the death without heirs of any tenant-in-chief the tenant's lands escheated or passed permanently to the crown, and, if he held by knight service and left a son (or daughter) who was a minor, the child remained a royal ward until he became of age. His estates could be granted out and the right to marry him profitably sold. Practice, however, con-siderably diverged from theory. No one has yet proved that the process of escheat significantly increased the royal lands. Very, very few families were without common law heirs of some kind, however distant. 'Natural' escheats would, therefore, be few. So-called escheats would, in most cases, be somewhat dubious seizures, rather than escheats in the exact technical sense of the term and if the families thus deprived considered such inheritances as their right and were sufficiently powerful, royal seizures of this kind could generate dangerous political tensions – as indeed happened in the later years of Edward IV[1] and alienated political support from his sons.

Nor was the royal exploitation of such feudal rights of wardship and marriage conspicuously successful. Since the middle of the fourteenth century the development of trusts and uses[2] had badly eroded the king's rights in the holdings of his tenants and the concealment of feudal tenures from the royal officials had become notorious. Governments had been well aware of these evasions and deceits. More or less continuous enquiries into feudal tenures under Henry VI were probably ineffective as no protests against them are known. Edward IV's activity in such matters was effective enough to be strongly resented. The beginnings of the strict investigations so notoriously associated with the names of Henry VII's detested ministers, Empson and Dudley, were already under way by 1474. Edward, according to a contemporary writer, 'examined the registers and rolls of Chancery and exacted heavy fines from those whom he found to have intruded and taken possession of their estates without prosecuting their rights in the form required by law and in return for the rents they had in the meantime received'.

It is doubtful how successful all this bustle and activity was. Cases are known where Edward did not enforce his rights of wardship. The problem of trusts and uses was difficult and politically explosive. Somewhat timid legislation against them under both Edward and Henry was hardly successful. Inefficient and unequal application of the law probably caused great resentment. Those caught in the meshes of the law felt outraged that other men were evading them. Even the supposedly powerful Henry VIII, in 1540, after a long struggle with the landed classes both in parliament and in the law courts, finally conceded defeat and compromised with them in an agreement which secured him his feudal rights over one-third of the lands of his tenants-in-chief, giving them the free disposition, exempt from feudal incidents, over all the rest.

This increase in the crown lands was only part of the task. The

1. With the families of Howard, Berkeley, Huntingdon (Herbert), Buckingham and Westmorland. See T. P. Pugh, 'The Magnates, Knights and Gentry' in *Fifteenth Century England, 1399–1509*, Ed. S. B. Chrimes, C. D. Ross and R. A. Griffiths (1972), pp. 86–8, C. D. Ross, *Edward IV* (1972), p. 50.

2. Legal settlements under which estates were placed in the hands of feoffees or trustees who administered them on behalf of the owners and their heirs, thus avoiding feudal incidents etc. at death.

other part was to exploit them more effectively: to make certain that while the exercise of vital political influence, both central and local, was adequately maintained, they should bring in more to the treasury than they had in the past. Following the Acts of Resumption in the early 1450s the Exchequer had managed to raise rents on some crown estates. Its effectiveness, however, was limited. The upper Exchequer (or Exchequer of Account) was an extremely tenacious, if abominably slow, instrument for the collection of debts but, handicapped by over-centralization and inadequate local control of the estates in its charge, it had proved incompetent as a land management office.

During the late fourteenth and early fifteenth centuries the techniques of estate management had considerably advanced: so much so that they were hardly improved upon again until the development of scientific methods of surveying in the late sixteenth century. During the later Middle Ages the rise of the 'gentleman bureaucrat' (for whom the secondary, informal curriculum at Oxford[1] was at least one source of training) provided the owner of any great estate with highly skilled, professional officers – generally a surveyor, receivers, and auditors. Particular families specialized in this kind of work generation after generation – the Heton family employed by the Staffords, the Leventhorpes in the duchy of Lancaster, the Luthingtons in the service of the earl of Warwick. Their employers expected them to ride far and wide the length and breadth of their estates (unlike the Exchequer officials who rarely moved out of Westminster), supervising, checking, keeping the manorial officials up to the mark. Many of them must have spent a great part of their working lives on horseback.

The most extensive system of estate management of this kind was the duchy of Lancaster, with lands scattered over most of the counties of England and Wales. After 1399 the Lancastrian kings had kept these estates as a separate entity, and it says a good deal for their financial incompetence that they never attempted to introduce the efficient methods of their hereditary duchy into the administration of the crown lands. The house of York, too, had derived its income from an organization similar to that of the duchy, though probably far less efficient. Edward IV, or his advisers, immediately applied those methods of private estate management to the lands regained under the Resumption Act of 1461. They firmly excluded the

1. See below, pp. 140–2.

Treasurer and Barons of the Exchequer from such estates, arranged them in convenient groups, often together with existing crown lands, and gave them in charge to selected officers like John Milewater who booamo tho rccciver of a new unit covering ten countles in Wales and the Marches. A bureaucrat of the same stamp, John Luthington, with many years' experience on the Warwick estates behind him, audited Milewater's accounts on the spot in Hereford, not in distant Westminster. Not all royal lands were placed under this kind of control. Some for convenience, and some, undoubtedly, for political reasons, were leased to private people for large annual rents. The new system, however, covered most of the larger estates.

A new organization at the centre surmounted this system of land management. The receivers-general of the estates now paid the rents and dues which they collected for the king into the Chamber (a department of the royal household, prominent in the fourteenth century, which had sunk into obscurity after 1399) and possibly into a number of provincial repositories. The Chamber became Edward IV's principal treasury and his principal spending department. He did not, however, abolish the Exchequer. The Exchequer of Receipt (or Treasury) still carried out useful routine tasks, paying accounts, providing for the normal annual expenses of various departments and thus saving the Chamber from becoming overloaded and clogged with petty detail. The Upper Exchequer became a repository for the accounts which had already been audited locally and took action upon them against defaulting officials: a task for which its relentless (if slow) procedures were admirably suited.

This whole organization, most probably evolved[1] by trial and experiment in the two decades after 1461, was mature enough to be outlined in a long memorandum early in Richard III's reign. Valuable as it obviously was, it then came near to collapse. There are ominous signs in the governmental records of Richard's short reign (and Sir Thomas More remarked that with great gifts he won unsteadfast friendships) that to buy badly needed political support the king rapidly alienated part of the endowment which his brother had so painstakingly built up. Henry VII, after his victory at Bosworth in 1485, inexperienced as he was in English methods of administration, or any other methods for that matter, at first failed to grasp the significance of the new organization and let it decay, only to reconstruct it with the advice and services of former Yorkist adminis-

1. The details are obscure because of the complete loss of the Chamber records before 1485.

trators once they had convinced him of its vital contribution to his revenues. By 1483 the royal lands produced a net income of about £22 000 and £25 000 a year plus (possibly) another £4640 from sheriffs' farms, payments by bailiffs of liberties, vacant temporalities of bishoprics, wards, marriages and various feudal incidents. By 1509 it had risen to approximately £42 000. The increase, however, seems to have owed more to acquisitions of land – the result of deaths in the royal family and more forfeitures – than to any increased efficiency beyond that which the Yorkists had achieved.

Even so the system was considerably less efficient than it might have been. Under Edward IV, particularly in the first part of his reign, considerable estates had to be alienated to buy political support. Moreover, the crown lands could never be run exclusively for cash profits. Patronage above all kept the body politic in harmony.[1] Even now, most probably it still remained the most important function of the royal estates – at least seven hundred officials derived their incomes from these lands, fee-farms and sheriffs' farms to the tune of about £7000 a year. Their pay, together with annuities and pensions granted from the same sources absorbed at least two-sevenths of the value of such estates. Politics and finance were in fierce competition and the second Anonymous Croyland Continuator thought it of supreme importance, politically, that Edward IV had planted reliable officials in all parts of the kingdom.

Nor, in spite of improvements, did the level of administration ever reach a uniform standard of efficiency. In a period of almost universal corruption by modern standards, the larger an organization was the more difficult it became to supervise effectively – and the royal estates were gigantic compared with any complex of aristocratic estates in the country. Bisley was no better run as a royal estate than it had been as one of the estates of the duchy of York. On other lands success and failure seem to have been mixed. Between 1476–7 and 1480–1, following a progress of the duchy of Lancaster council through the duchy estates in Lancashire and Cheshire receipts rose from £347 to £855. On the other hand the profits of the duchy honour of Pontefract remained more or less stable throughout Edward's reign. The gap between the aims and the achievements of the new estate management often remained very wide indeed.

No complete balance sheet can be drawn up for Edward or Henry at any particular time: approximations are the most that can be

1. See below pp. 174–6, 179–80.

attempted. In his earlier years Edward IV could not avoid heavy expenditure to combat French encouragement of Lancastrian resistance. The finances of these early years were a web of shreds and tatters. He lived from hand to mouth, borrowing here, there, and everywhere. In 1466–7 the treasurer of the royal household had a small surplus for the first time, and in 1467 Edward, with apparently justifiable confidence, told parliament that for the future he intended to live upon his own resources and to ask his subjects for money only for great and urgent causes. In 1472 he arranged to pay his outstanding debts, and by his later years he had accumulated enough money to wage war on Scotland for two years before calling upon parliament for funds. Beginning his reign deep in debt, he was the first English king since Henry II (1154–89) to die solvent. A quarter of a century later Henry VII had screwed up the royal income to about £113 000 a year: his endowed revenues increased between one-quarter and two-fifths over those of the Yorkists. At his death he left a modest accumulation of money, plate, and jewels to his son amounting in value to no more than about two years' income. The oft-repeated stories of his immense fortune are yet another myth.

At the beginning of the sixteenth century these modest, inflexible revenues did not place England amongst the greater European powers. They were pitifully low compared with the £800 000 which the king of France commanded and the £1 100 000 which the Emperor enjoyed by the 1520s. Circumscribed ambition, rather than financial strength or the ability to tap new sources of wealth in the country, had contributed, even beyond increased efficiency, to produce the English monarchy's new solvency. In the early part of the fifteenth century the politically powerful classes had shown that they would not pay direct taxes to support the dynastic, continental ambitions of their rulers. Reluctance and evasion were equally apparent in the 1470s and the 1480s. The monarchy was solvent for as long as it could, or chose to, keep out of expensive military entanglements on the continent, for as long as it continued to be insular and unadventurous. The apparent financial strength of the English kings was due in no small degree to the fact that between the end of the Hundred Years War in 1453 and the 1540s they took part only in occasional and short campaigns abroad. As the country was naturally protected by the sea, no great amount of taxation could be justified by the cost of defence. Political convention and the self-interest of the subject alike demanded that the king should 'live of his own'. The kings of England, having no reasons which they could plausibly advance to make taxes acceptable, lost by default great revenues from personal taxation which earlier monarchs had enjoyed, and changing economic circumstances left them powerless to tax the country's foreign trade as heavily as in former times.

Thus, compelled to live like private men upon an inflexible income, mostly the proceeds of their estates and the customs, like private men too, they tried to augment their incomes by trade. Henry VI, typically enough, lost money on such ventures, Edward IV and Henry VII made handsome profits. Moreover, in a society where the powerful expected to profit in their relationships with the ruler[1] even the effective exploitation of the king's 'own' bred resentment – a resentment which, already apparent by Edward IV's later years, grew steadily with the passage of time. Henry VII's rapacity has been a subject for the comments and arguments of generations of historians. Though claiming only the king's just dues, the severity of his officers in searching out concealed feudal tenures, in enforcing any penal statutes concerning trade which brought in revenue – and, after 1499, the severity of the 'council learned in the law' in collecting debts – more and more exasperated the landed and the merchant classes.

Aggravating the effects of this rigid legalism, the king himself indulged in practices which, though common enough everywhere at the time, were distinctly unsavoury, and many of his officials made the most of their positions to enrich themselves. Although the official Chancery grants reveal nothing of the practice, Edmund Dudley's notebook (and the information it contains is probably incomplete) shows that in two and a half years Henry sold at least seventy offices at prices ranging from £1000 for the Mastership of the Rolls to between £80 and twenty marks for clerkships of the peace in various counties. He sold his favours for large sums in matters of justice and litigation, and greed, overcoming his deep, if conventional, piety, drove him to the mortal sin of simony in demanding 1000 marks for the deanery of York and £300 for the archdeaconry of Buckingham. Dudley himself, who in 1494 according to the *Great Chronicle of London* was so impecunious that he found it difficult to take up the office of under-sheriff of London (the implication being that he bought it), after nine years in the royal service owned estates in thirteen counties and left goods valued at £5000. He and his like not only pushed their activities beyond the limits of decency to curry favour with the king, they used their position to buy up properties

1. See below, pp. 162 ff.

from men forced, as a result of their own activities, to sell estates to
pay fines or debts owing to the Chamber. Unable to increase his income by taxation, Henry, with the help of self-seeking officials, certainly took to what Sir John Fortescue had condemned as 'exquisite
means' to fill his coffers, and he carried them to the point where they
created a dangerous backlash of resentment and political tension. In
1509 the repentant Dudley, imprisoned and threatened with death,
was probably right when he claimed that the king lost the hearts of
his subjects by an insatiable appetite for money, and in his fit of re-
pentance he compiled a list of no less than eighty-four cases in which
he considered that Henry VII had gone beyond the limits of financial
decency.

To sum up, one can say that the period between 1450 and 1509 saw
the development, the maturity and, in the opinion of some people,
the abuse of a new financial system. It came to pass that the English
governing classes wished to have their cake and eat it. By 1450 they
had become adamantly resistant to any realistic assessment for direct
taxation and resolutely demanded that the king should 'live of his
own'. By 1509, their descendants, while still equally resistant to
taxation, had come to grudge the king 'his own' and were determined
to encroach upon it to their own advantage. Whether or not Henry
VII had abused the system, his exploitation of the crown lands, had,
by 1509, produced so great a backlash of political resentment that
his son immediately relaxed its rigours, with the resultant disastrous
loss by 1515 of three-eighths of his landed income.

The political necessity, which forced Edward and Henry, in their
insecurity, to put themselves into the antiquated straitjacket of endowed monarchy, laid up troubles for their successors. In face of the
rising costs of government, and more particularly of the rising costs
of war, it was imperative for sixteenth-century states to reduce
dependence upon landowning as their financial base and switch to
taxation. The later Tudors, once again dreading the political resentment of the taxpayer, allowed a new progressive system of direct
taxation, devised in Henry VIII's earlier years, to decay. Simultaneously in a period of inflation the real value of the customs revenues
declined. Henry VIII in the 1540s, reviving his crazy youthful dreams
of being another Henry V, dissipated a great part of the confiscated
monastic lands on war with France. Once this temporary financial
euphoria was over, the inadequate, ramshackle financial structure
inherited from the late fifteenth century cracked under the strain.
Elizabeth I, compelled to sell more and more monastic and crown

lands to pay for the country's defences, was also compelled to destroy upon her diminishing estates the nice balance between cash and patronage which her grandfather and great-grandfather had established. Otherwise she would have lost the loyalty of the landed classes. The claims of patronage triumphed even over her desperate need for money. As time went on the monarchy once again found no alternative but a new resort to 'exquisite means', to squeezing the last penny that was legally possible out of existing crown rights. In Elizabeth's last decade, and much more under the early Stuarts, such action once again generated dangerous political tensions. One of the long-term causes of the Great Civil War of the mid-seventeenth century may well go back to the political insecurity which left Edward IV and Henry VII little choice but to take a conservative, and far from courageous, course in their revenue methods. They gave the country the firm, strong, and cheap government which it demanded and for which their subjects admired them. They did so to the financial sorrow of their successors.

5 Religious life

During the fourteenth century the church, like the state, passed, not altogether unscathed, through an explosion of tremendous violence which seems, in retrospect, almost a frustrated harbinger of the greater assault which shattered its unity in the sixteenth century. Revolutionary developments in philosophy and theology, embittered criticism of the papacy, the scandal of the Great Schism of the West (1378–1417), ferocious attacks on the religious orders and upon clerical property – in this age of discontent, turmoil, and recrimination little seemed immune from the acerbic onslaughts of academic and political extremists.

Within the universities, philosophically trained theologians shattered the marriage of faith and reason so skilfully contrived by St Thomas Aquinas and his followers, developing in its place methods of speculation as destructive to traditional thought as Einstein's theories were to long-established concepts of Newtonian physics. The new generation of philosophers and theologians debated, almost beyond the fringe of understanding, disturbing concepts of God's absolute power, of God's unfettered will, of predestination, of man's free will, of dominion and grace; concepts which applied to politics and to the social and ecclesiastical order could produce revolutionary effects, destructive to authority in both church and state. Radicals soon applied academic theories of dominion and grace to practical problems – to give theoretical justification to bitter attacks on clerical property following Pope John XXII's (1316–34) condemnation of the doctrine of the absolute poverty of Christ and his disciples developed by the spiritual Franciscans in their campaign against what they stigmatized as the scandalously relaxed life of most of their order. In defence of the Spirituals against the Conventuals (as their opponents were called), William of Ockham (d. *c*. 1349), one of the most revolutionary thinkers of his day, extended the attack to impugn the powers and integrity of a papacy which denied their aspirations: a papacy already under attack from Marsiglio of Padua (d. 1342), a propagandist even more radical, who wished to destroy the dual relationship of church and state, hallowed by long tradition in the Latin West, to degrade the church to a mere spiritual department of the state and the clergy, deprived of their endowments, to a class of salaried public officials.

Debate in the European universities was extraordinarily free. At the same time a universally accepted convention safeguarded the faith of Christendom from the more bizarre excitements of speculation. His intellectual peers expected a scholar to withdraw propositions which after due discussion they found to be unsound or heretical. At Oxford, John Wycliffe (*c.* 1320–84), whose brilliance in debate dazzled a somewhat mediocre generation of academics, after years of philosophical study, went on, with all the vehemence of an irascible temperament, unrestrained by any deep religious experience, to apply his conclusions to problems of church government, church property, and the papacy, and ultimately, and far more dangerously, to speculations upon the nature of the Eucharist. Employed like other clerics of the day in negotiations with the Curia, arguing against papal taxation and against papal appointments to benefices, he mistook the opportunist tactics of his employers for rigid principles which to their embarrassment he maintained long after his employment as diplomat and propagandist ended. Possibly also embittered by disappointed hopes of preferment in the church, he began to launch, in language sour and scurrilous in the extreme even for his far from mealy-mouthed generation, attacks upon the papacy and upon the whole system of clerical property. He proposed, with a starry-eyed naïveté in view of the appallingly bad record of laymen in disposing of clerical revenues whenever they had the opportunity, that the church's property would be better taken over and administered by the state.

Wycliffe was a menace, financially and theologically, to the church as then established. Institutionally he became more dangerous than earlier critics, because unlike them he was prepared to leap the academic fence and appeal to highly placed laymen to enforce what his fellow clerics would not yield. Beyond these narrow limits he can hardly be considered the founder of a popular religious movement. Although he may have been prepared to place the Bible in the hands of the laity, he was not anxious that they should listen to theological debate, which in their ignorance they might misinterpret and so fall into heresy. Wycliffe had tried to work through his connections with the powerful in the land, in particular through John of Gaunt, duke of Lancaster. In the end he went further than his influential friends, and his other earlier allies, the friars, were prepared to go. They had found Wycliffe, the anti-clerical, useful for their own purposes; they were not prepared to follow Wycliffe the heresiarch. Wycliffe wrote for his fellow scholars highly technical treatises in a complicated, tortuous Latin. No known work written in English can safely be attributed to him. Sixteenth-century reformers propagated, on very dubious evidence, the Protestant tradition which made him the evangelizing leader of the Lollard movement. In this they seem to have confused the Master's activities with the work of some of his admiring disciples at Oxford who, by preaching in different parts of the country, did what he refused to do, or was perhaps incapable of doing. So that by the time he died in his parish of Lutterworth in 1384 there already existed a powerful, if somewhat disparate, Lollard[1] movement, and its inspiration remained respectable enough as late as 1410 for parliament at least to entertain proposals for a vast dis-endowment of the church. Groups of merchants in various cities and towns, and unknown but numerous cohorts from lower social groups, particularly artisans, completed the sect.

Wycliffe was less 'the morning star of the Reformation' than the last of the fourteenth-century generation of turbulent, adventurous dons. In the end it was Wycliffe's opponents who won. The battered hierarchy not only survived his attacks: it firmly re-established orthodoxy and even managed, gradually and unobtrusively, against the vested interests of many of its own members and of the powerful laymen to whom Wycliffe had so unrealistically appealed, to make some improvement in the church's condition. At the same time it survived at the cost of the spirit and of intellectual vigour. Those in authority had drunk from the bitter cup of extremism and they would drink of it no more. Repressing speculation, they held up as an example to their world a spirit of timid conservatism which, encouraging a conventional and unspeculative, though at its best a deep, devotion, stifled whatever possibility there may have been of any Catholic reform of more than piecemeal scope.

Archbishop Arundel (d. 1414), unfortunately more the rigid administrator than the subtle philosopher or theologian, vigorously imposed a harsher discipline. His predecessor at Canterbury, Arch-

---

1. The word 'lollard', a pejorative term (probably Dutch in origin) meant a mumbler of prayers. It had earlier been applied to various religious movements. It was deliberately confused with the Middle English 'loller', meaning a loafer, and with the Latin 'lolia' (tares).

bishop Courtenay (d. 1396), a man of more discriminating cast of mind, had prohibited discussion of those theological propositions of Wycliffe's which had been specifically condemned, while leaving uncensored the general and academically stimulating corpus of his writings. Arundel resolutely suppressed them all. His *Constitutions*, imposed upon the university of Oxford in 1407, went even further, attempting to impose a rigid censorship on the traditional freedom of philosophical discussion in the schools as well as condemning Wycliffe's works lock, stock, and barrel.

Arundel added to his distrust of academic speculation in the schools a fear of heretical tendencies in the unlearned, stimulated by the slanted translation and glosses of the Lollard Bible, a fear so great that he became excessively wary of any translation at all. His Oxford decrees of 1407 permitted the laity to use vernacular translations under certain restrictions. No decree positively forbade translations: translations authorized by the bishops were permissible reading. Such authorized versions, however, never appeared, and the Oxford decrees came to be commonly, though incorrectly, understood as a complete prohibition. The country which later became famed for its devotion to the Scriptures knew in the fifteenth century notably less of the vernacular Bible than most other European countries. In Germany twenty complete translations, and numerous incomplete editions, were published between 1466 and 1522. England knew not one. Even a man as comparatively liberal as Sir Thomas More could not break away from this repressive tradition. His admired friend Erasmus would have had every yokel singing a text of scripture as he drove the plough. More timidly suggested that each bishop give an English Bible, or part of one, to those of the faithful in his diocese fit to profit by it,[1] which in practice would probably have meant well-born men and women and prosperous burgesses.

It is well to make some comparison between Lollardy and the type of devotion encouraged by the hierarchy. Until Wycliffe's day England had always been singularly free of widespread, popular heresy, so much so that the habit and techniques of religious repression were remarkably undeveloped as compared with those of some continental countries. There was no special legislation against heresy until the statute *de heretico comburendo* of 1401. During the second half of the

1. Admittedly in 1528 when he was disturbed by the spread of heresy and the dissemination of Tyndale's translation of the New Testament. In his later years, Erasmus, also disturbed by fierce religious controversy, became less liberal in his views.

fourteenth century, with the wider spread of lay literacy, there had developed a form of devotion, contemplative, occasionally anti-clerical, somewhat puritanical, which easily shaded into Lollardy, which appealed, amongst others, to some of the veteran captains of the Hundred Years War. A small number of them, in fact, are known to have embraced Lollard doctrines. This type of devotion, orthodox in itself, formed a kind of seed-bed in which more extreme, and definitely heretical, opinions could easily take root and flourish and explains the ease and rapidity with which Lollardy spread. Such laymen (and women like Margery Kempe) could easily be mistaken for, and attacked as, Lollards, and some of the more prominent amongst them may even have been inclined to protect heretics; and the diocesan authorities, closely enmeshed as they were with the higher ranks of lay society and unhabituated to any established tradition of repression, bewildered by a novel situation were slow to react, so that for many years the persecution of Lollards laxly varied from diocese to diocese according to the disposition of particular bishops. The alarm and the failure of Sir John Oldcastle's rebellion in 1414 proved to be the supreme disaster for the Lollard movement. By the accession of Henry V it had already lost the Oxford academic group which had provided intellectual coherence, even distinction and with few exceptions, the few open Lollards of the knightly class, with horrified memories of the Peasant's Revolt of 1381, alarmed by attacks on clerical property, which might easily be extended to lay holdings, had reverted to doctrinal orthodoxy. The terrifying revelation in 1414 that one man could call out such con-siderable rebellious forces from areas as widely separated as Bristol and Derby drove an insecure government to identify heresy with treason and to turn the hitherto sporadic persecution by the bishops into a vigorously directed government campaign. The systematic repression which followed smashed what elementary unity and central organization the movement had until that time possessed. From then onwards Lollardy survived only in small communities. Lollards in different areas were by no means isolated or completely out of touch with each other, but their heroic period and their central organization vanished together. Lollardy became an underground, surreptitious, pertinacious faith, surviving by tradition in a particular family or group of families. The early loss of its learned men deprived it of any intellectual and doctrinal coherence it had earlier possessed, and for the Lollards of this diaspora it was impossible to maintain any consistent body of doctrine. Later Lollardy became a 'series of attitudes from which beliefs evolved rather than . . . a set of doctrines';[1] attitudes vehemently anti-sacerdotal, anti-authoritarian and on occasion anti-sacramental. More positively, though not entirely logically, Lollards combined a scriptural fundamentalism with an equally crude kind of common-sense rationalism. The scriptural basis of the beliefs of many Lollards has been unduly exaggerated. A good deal of their thought often attributed to the Bible was due more probably to hostility to priests, which also combined with a strong anti-papalism and more than a tinge of puritanism.

With controversial discussion at a low level, if not actively discouraged, in the universities and elsewhere for a century and more after Archbishop Arundel's constitutions, the life of the English church lay in its devotional tradition, that new manifestation of lay piety which had formed the background of Lollard extremism. Of the strength of this devotional tradition, an English insular variety of the *devotio moderna*,[2] one might almost call it, there can be no doubt, graced as it was by the intense religious life of such exceptional women as Margery Kempe of Lynn at the beginning of the century and Cecily, duchess of York, and Lady Margaret Beaufort towards its end – and Lady Margaret's religious exercises show that the *devotio moderna* was not (as is so often assumed) incompatible with traditional practices. The demand for traditional religious books, which the new printers very profitably satisfied, also demonstrates its strength. Two-fifths of the works which William Caxton printed between 1474 and 1490 were long-established manuals of piety and devotion, and those of his successor, Wynkin de Worde, contained an even higher proportion of works of the same kind.

This devotional tradition was probably the most powerful strand in English religious life. Amongst the majority at all social levels, from royalty to the comparatively humble, it served, however, to stress, perhaps even to increase, an emphatic and gross materialism. A good deal of traditional religious literature obscured Christ's life and teaching under numerous and often somewhat apocryphal legends of the Virgin and the saints, legends which often stressed miraculous intervention in men's lives. Caxton himself, when printing the thirteenth-century *Golden Legend* of Jacob of Voragine, added to it no less than seventy new saints' lives. King Henry VI 'made a rule that a certain dish, which represented the five wounds

1. J. A. F. Thomson, *The Later Lollards, 1414–1520* (Oxford, 1965), p. 244.
2. A movement, originating in the Netherlands, which stressed personal devotion and good conduct rather than external religious observances.

of Christ as it were red with blood, should be set on his table by his almoner before any other course, when he was to take refreshment; and contemplating these images with great fervour he thanked God marvellous devoutly'.

Many people blatantly practised a horse-trading legalism in their devotions, demanding for a mundane expenditure of austerities or cash, a *quid pro quo* of celestial bliss or at least exemption from purgatorial torments. Even after all due allowance is made for common forms of speech in a society where legal jargon was almost the 'vulgar parlance' of the semi-educated, this mercenary impression remains. John Calvin's vision of God as the stern implacable judge was nothing new or sinister in religious experience. The pious in the Middle Ages worshipped an equally vengeful deity, but more conveniently believed that they could placate his wrath by good works. By this time their belief had flowered into an obsession, as luxuriantly morbid as the ecstasy of the Victorians in the details of grief, with procuring the swiftest possible progress of the soul after death from purgatory to bliss by means of the good works and intercessory prayers of the faithful remaining in this world. Austerities, charities, above all the mass, possessed a market value to be assigned to particular purposes. Every mass, every good work speeded relief from the purgatorial fires. Margery Kempe in one of her numerous visions told Christ 'I make thee mine executor of all the good works that thou makest in me', allotted half of them for the well-being of a certain Master R., and left Christ himself the disposal of the rest. On another occasion, again after a vision, Margery informed a widow that her husband would spend thirty years in purgatory 'unless he had better friends on earth', and advised the widow to pay out three or four pounds on almsgiving and masses as soon as she could. In this, as in his attitude to the Bible, even the humanist Sir Thomas More could not rise above the stultifying atmosphere in which he had been nurtured. His *Supplication of Souls*, though far less crudely expressed, conveys much the same message as Margery Kempe.

Few people would care – or dare – to leave their souls unransomed. Their provision varied with their wealth and social status. The poor shifted for themselves with the few masses which they or their friends could afford at threepence a time. A *nouveau riche* magnate like Ralph, Lord Cromwell in 1436 left money enough for three thousand. That very curious document, Henry VII's last will and testament, one of the last great extravaganzas of pre-Reformation piety, shows the king determined to insure his soul's progress from purgatory on a scale which even the richest of his subjects could only envy. He left funds for the foundation of hospitals and for the celebration of ten thousand masses at sixpence each, double the usual rate, within three months of his death and, shrewdly combining devotion with propaganda for his dynasty, left to every parish and friary church equipped with only a wooden pyx, a pyx of silver-gilt emblazoned with the royal arms. Even during his life, determined to get his religious money's worth, when commanding the prayers of the clergy in the monastic, cathedral, and collegiate churches of England, he had made certain of the services which he required by enforcing their prayers under legal indentures in much the same way as he commanded the recruitment of troops.

It is true that there were attempts to provide an intellectual justification for faith, but at most their effects on popular religion were small. The most distinguished representative of orthodoxy, the Carmelite friar, Thomas Netter of Walden (d. 1430), set out a reasoned traditional answer to the Lollards in works thoughtful and distinguished enough to be reprinted in Venice as late as 1771. It has been suggested, although in the nature of things it would be difficult to prove, that Netter's works were even more effective than the current severe repression in demolishing what remained of the intellectual side of the Lollard movement. If this is so, the efforts of the century's most notorious prelate, Bishop Reynold Pecock (d. 1460–1), to refute Lollardy 'by doom of reason', to use his own phrase, were useless, for his methods of reasoning and the tortuous, complicated prose in which he wrote were hopelessly abstruse for the conversion of the simple artisans who by his day made up the greater number of the sect.

After Pecock's condemnation for heresy in 1457, religious expression remained wholly traditional until Dean Colet began to lecture on the literal meaning of the Scriptures and Erasmus attracted a modest following at Oxford and Cambridge. Even so, until the 1520s their influence was hardly widespread. Pecock had outraged the best and most conscientious amongst the orthodox not only by what he said and wrote but by his perversity (to their minds) in thrusting discussion of complicated, highly technical, not to say highly explosive, theological problems, to a far greater extent than Wycliffe had done, outside the narrow professional circles to which they had been with great difficulty restricted only thirty years earlier, on to laymen ill-equipped to receive them in an English language still insufficiently developed to convey them accurately.

In justice to Pecock's orthodox opponents, they were far from being mere defenders of obscurantism and corruption. Devout churchmen like Thomas Gascoigne (1403–58) were not in the least complacent. Holding that the controversial discussion of matters of faith was best left to professionals, they genuinely doubted the utility of Pecock's methods. They were by no means blind to the philosophical defences of the faith for the educated like themselves; the more ignorant clergy and laity they considered better served by stimulating a luxuriant devotional life through sermons and devotional books. The prolonged reaction of the church's rulers to Wycliffe and the Lollards resulted in a century of stagnation, and ultimately left its traditional faith bereft of any strong intellectual defences.

At the same time the church was both more and less than 'the congregation of the faithful in the unity of the sacraments' as Conrad of Gelnhausen expressed it. Far from being a monolithic community dominated by the popes, as it is all too often regarded, it was made up of churches. Individual churches, from the greatest cathedral or abbey to the smallest parish, had developed over the centuries as legally independent units of property. A church was a benefice (or a great church a collection of benefices) which its holder regarded as a freehold to be financially exploited as well as spiritually served – a legal independence and an attitude of mind which made it extremely difficult for ecclesiastical superiors to maintain a salutary discipline. Moreover, to maintain their rights and their incomes in the tangled legal jungle of the day, ecclesiastical corporations and individual clergy were as perpetually involved as laymen in prosecuting or defending their rights in the courts, an avocation which distinctly tarnished their reputation. A petition presented in parliament in 1414 complained of the scandalous use on legal cases of money originally intended for the service of God.

Money originally intended for the service of God was also lavishly diverted to the service of the state and of powerful laymen. Both the numbers of the clergy and the wealth of the churches were excessive by modern standards. Partly because of this, partly because for at least eight hundred years the superior education of the higher clergy had made them indispensable to the state, the church and the world interlocked at far more points than they interlock today. At the beginning of the fifteenth century the clergy, religious and secular together, made up about two per cent of the population. There may well have been 30 000 or more secular priests in England compared with about 8600 parishes. This is not to say that from the point of

view of its own need the church was grossly over-staffed. Entry to
the priesthood did not, as in the modern world, imply entry upon a
vocation. It meant rather the assumption of a status, within which the
nature of a clerk's employment could be decidedly secular. A benefice
could be held without priest's orders, and many incumbents were
more concerned with service to the state than to the church.

The accumulated benefactions of many centuries had heaped endowments sporadically and unevenly upon the different churches and
corporations which made up the church. Of the forty richest sees in
all Christendom twelve were in England: an amazing number considering the size of the country. The church had uninterruptedly and
inevitably accumulated an undue share of the country's riches, a
share greatly in excess of its own real needs, while the state generally
existed on the razor-edge of insolvency. Some redistribution of
wealth would, therefore, have been reasonable. With the suppression
of Lollardy after Sir John Oldcastle's rebellion, and with a social
atmosphere which placed property amongst the most sacrosanct of
all things, disendowment became unmentionable. From the second
decade of the fifteenth century to the second decade of the sixteenth
century no one was radical enough to suggest confiscating the super-
fluities of the one to relieve the inadequacies of the other. It was,
therefore, by no means unjustifiable, considering the numbers of the
clerics and the haphazard distribution of wealth amongst the
churches, to employ both for the needs of the state.

The system by which the state, and the papacy too when and where
it could, diverted benefices to servants whom it could not afford to
pay in cash added to the mediocrity of religious life. The state had
always employed bishops and other clerics as civil servants. Such men
had been selected by the king. In the mid-fifteenth century a new
abuse crept in. The deplorably weak Henry VI failed to keep these
appointments, like many others, out of the political spoils system of
the magnates. Edward IV and Henry VII once again revived firm
royal control in the traditional way, that is, they ignored the canoni-
cal right of the cathedral chapter to elect its bishop; the king nominated his candidate to the pope, who then (as the technical phrase ran)
provided him to the see. Henry VII appointed only one member of
an aristocratic family – his step-brother, James Stanley to the
bishopric of Ely in 1506.

The minutes of the royal council for 14 January 1426 show the
system working at full blast. Four lay peers and six bishops on that
occasion arranged for the appointment or translation of clerics

prominent in the royal service to seven rich bishoprics, and kindly allowed an obscure friar called Wells (the council did not even know his Christian name) to accept, after being kept waiting for two years, tho papal nomination to the wretchedly poor and undesirable see of Llandaff.

Little or nothing in their education or early careers imbued such bishops with the pastoral vision. Most of them were even less clerical than Jane Austen's or Trollope's parsons, secure and comfortable in rectory and prebend bestowed by a friendly patron after a university course in classics or mathematics, or both, with a little theology incidentally picked up along the way. Although theology is held to have reigned as the queen of the sciences throughout the Middle Ages, ever since the rise of higher learning in the twelfth century the graduate in law had successfully jostled aside the graduate in theology in the queue for lucrative ecclesiastical jobs. Very few universities boasted a faculty of theology. In most countries they multiplied only during the fifteenth century, a fact which may have more than a little to do with the timing of the Reformation. England was unusual in that both its universities taught theology. It did not, however, save English episcopal appointments from going the same way as those of continental countries.

At Oxford the study of theology attracted mainly members of the religious orders. It was not on the whole popular with secular priests, and those seculars who did proceed from arts to theology tended to make their careers within the university walls. Training in law, generally canon or civil law or both, was the golden road to the rich cathedral. In diocesan as well as in royal administration (the one was often the path to the other), the essential qualification was a legal degree. Once the cleric had obtained his degree in law, service in diocesan administration, if possible that of Canterbury, was the most obvious road to profit, and, for the more able or the more fortunate few, to bishoprics.

Under such a system the direction of the churches was as unequal as their endowments. No comprehensive description of the bench of bishops is possible for the century as a whole. Prominent civil servants, sometimes of humble origin, like Thomas Bekynton, said to have been a weaver's son, sat beside well-educated aristocrats like George Neville, Warwick the Kingmaker's brother and some theologians often from the religious orders. Between 1396 and the Reformation ninety per cent of the bishops had university degrees and no non-graduates were appointed after 1450. Of these men (predominantly from Oxford) fifty had studied law (canon or civil or both), three law and theology, and forty theology. After 1485 the decline in the number of theologians became very marked – from then until 1523 there were only eight appointed as against fifteen lawyers.

Only the sees too poorly endowed to attract the magnate's younger son or the great royal servant went to theologians. Paradoxically enough, poor endowments worked to the church's advantage. Undistracted by the demands of king and court, the poorer bishops could reside in and rule their sees in person. The richer bishops, overwhelmed by the demands of the state, were, by this time, more or less permanent absentees. Unfortunately this class made up the majority of the episcopal bench. At any one time over half England, and that the more prosperous half, would be in their hands. The demands of the state were so exigent that they could hardly do other-wise than devote most of their time to secular affairs. Archbishop Chichele (archbishop 1414–43), genuinely concerned to improve the standards of the church, was yet, in 1433, constrained to admit that he had been absent from meetings of the royal council for only thirty-three days in eleven years.

The great absentees carried out their duties through deputies and officials, men of similar stamp who hoped to profit in the same way in the same world. They performed their duties efficiently enough by the standards of the day and at least without fanaticism – their per-secutions of the Lollards were neither particularly cruel nor blood-thirsty. Certainly no inspiring examples of the Christian virtues, they were more judges and executives than preachers or confessors. The diocesan bureaucrats ran a highly developed judicial system, a system of compulsion exercised through the ecclesiastical courts. A cumbrous legalism replaced religious zeal as the dominant character-istic of diocesan administration. Henry VI, who in spite of his piety did nothing to change the system, wrote to Thomas Spofford in 1442 that there were very few who laboured to draw the people from sin by the example of virtuous living. The system of ecclesiastical appointments which made Henry VIII's juridical break with Rome so easy had long existed; so had the mediocre legalistic system of diocesan administration which made the Marian reaction (too early to be inspired by the new zealous spirit of the Counter-Reformation) so limited and so unsuccessful.

With their eyes directed to very worldly places, distracted by the court, by administrative offices, by embassies abroad, the holders of the more opulent sees made their mark in their dioceses by buildings and benefactions rather than in the way of spiritual guidance. Robert Sherburne, whose exceptionally long life covered over eighty years from the reign of Henry VI to Thomas Cromwell's attacks on the church, perfectly illustrates the type of bureaucrat-bishop. After sixteen years at Oxford, where he studied arts and medicine, he became secretary to Cardinal Morton and held office in the Prerogative Court of Canterbury. He went as ambassador to Rome, negotiated Henry VII's entry into the Holy League and was one of the commissioners appointed in 1500 to sit in judgment on Perkin Warbeck's defeated followers. During fourteen years as a civil servant he collected no less than seventeen benefices, though it is true that he held no more than half a dozen simultaneously and only one which involved a cure of souls. Only towards the end of this period, at the age of forty-five, was he ordained even subdeacon, to become a priest at last fifteen months later. Appointed to the poor diocese of St David's in 1505, he left it for the moderate affluence of Chichester three years later. Already over fifty, a comparatively old man by the standards of the day, he was yet able to give more attention to his see than it had earlier received from younger men – including the notorious Reynold Pecock.

Sherburne was a passionate, almost a compulsive, builder. Although he spent very little time in his various benefices, almost all of them owed him something in the way of new buildings or improvements to old ones – the hospital of St Cross at Winchester, New College, Oxford, and the cloister and the Prior's lodgings at St Frideswide's (now Christchurch). When Dean, he spent £550 on St Paul's Cathedral, and it was even said that he built a chapel during his stay in Rome. As bishop of Chichester he viewed with great distaste what he was pleased to call the 'ancient squalor' of his cathedral. Its somewhat dark, heavy Norman and Early English fabric indeed compared ill with the more recent and fashionable glories which he had known at Salisbury, Winchester, and Canterbury. In twenty-one years he spent the enormous sum of £3717 on the cathedral, the episcopal palace and the episcopal manor houses.

Some high-minded clerics deplored the whole wretched system. Thomas Gascoigne blasted William Booth who rose to be bishop of Lichfield (1447) and afterwards archbishop of York (1452) as neither scholarly nor virtuous 'but a common lawyer who confers benefices culpably on boys and comparative youngsters'. Reynold Pecock seems first to have aroused the wrath of the more conscientious clergy by his views on episcopal duty. Illogically, while setting himself up as the converter of the Lollards, he was rash enough to say with the greatest publicity, in a series of addresses at St Paul's Cross, more or less the broadcasting house of the day, what others only tacitly practised – that bishops had better things to do than reside in their dioceses, and that there were more important ways of serving souls than preaching. Others were deeply troubled that at Oxford, and probably at Cambridge too, the opportunities for legal education were increasing faster than those for theological education. When Robert Woodlark founded St Catherine's College, Cambridge, in 1475, he allowed only the study of philosophy and theology 'in exaltation of the Christian faith and the defence and furtherance of Holy Church'. The study of civil law and canon law he totally forbade.

All in all the struggle for improvement was terribly uneven. Too many of the better educated clerics profited from the system: for too many laymen it was a valuable fountain of patronage and a means of saving money. For what the king did with bishoprics, deaneries, and prebends, lesser men did with lesser benefices. Though laymen were generous benefactors to the church, they indirectly took with the left hand at least part of what they bestowed with the right. The dukes of York endowed a splendid collegiate church at Fotheringay, but they, and other magnates, expected, as part of the natural order of things, to support their domestic chaplains and sometimes even stewards and other estate officials by presenting them to benefices in which they were non-resident. At a lower level parish clergy acted as bailiffs and rent collectors. Few had the will to protest. Even More and Erasmus knew the futility of protest on this point. Meddling with patronage would have alienated a good deal of the lay support on which they depended for other matters in their reforming programme.

The bishops and their officials, rising through administration, had little in common with the clergy over whom they ruled. Never having served a parish, they were ill-fitted to guide and advise the parochial clergy. Nevertheless many were concerned for their improvement. Low though their standards were, parish priests as a class hardly merit the scorn lavished upon them by Protestant historians. They faced a problem which many a group of people since their day has also faced. Too many factors frustrated changes which were necessary to meet the needs of a developing society. As the century wore on, the lower clergy failed to keep pace with developments in the lay world and many of them were probably worse educated than the better class of their parishioners. Conscientious churchmen again regarded this state of affairs as deplorable. To do the prelates justice, it was a condition for which laymen must take their meed of blame. The Christian world had for long enough felt the crying need for a less ignorant clergy. The papal constitution *cum ex eo* of 1298, by encouraging bishops to grant benefice holders leave of absence to study at the universities, had done something to improve matters in the first half of the fourteenth century, but later there was certainly something of a decline in the numbers of even the minority of the parish clergy who had benefited from these arrangements. The second Statute of Provisors (1390), while protecting lay patrons from papal usurpation of their rights, had also put an end to the system of collective supplications to Rome for the appointment of university graduates to benefices. Consequently, in the early fifteenth century, laymen, once again, secure in their right to dispose of their patronage exactly as they wished, ignored the claims of the educated in order to promote their own relations and dependents. Many hard-headed parents therefore began to look upon a long and comparatively expensive university course for their sons as an unprofitable investment. Even the house of Commons, or a section of it, recognized the deplorable facts. Archbishop Arundel, though with little success, tried to organize the patronage of the bishops to promote the learned. So did Archbishop Chichele between 1417 and 1438, though it was uphill work – partly owing to sectional disputes between the secular scholars and the religious in Oxford itself. There is, however, some little evidence that he succeeded after a time in pricking the tough conscience of both lay and ecclesiastical patrons.

At best, however, this could have been but a partial solution to the acute problem of staffing the parishes. Late medieval university studies were long and expensive. Few could afford the eighteen years which it took to complete the courses in arts and theology. They were also highly technical and abstruse. Men who had been through such courses may well have been successful in city rectories, preaching to the more sophisticated urban audiences. The potential success of their ministrations to rustics may well be doubted. The work of the rural parson demanded training of a much more practical type: the practical, vocational training provided by the seminary which the Council of Trent first inaugurated in the Catholic world in the sixteenth century – and a reform unknown in the English church until the establishment of two small theological colleges at Chichester and Wells in 1839 and 1840. Moreover, the resident incumbent, highly educated or otherwise, was constantly distracted by the pressing need to earn his bread in an essential by-occupation, agriculture. Most were poor (more than half the benefices brought in less than £10 a year, some much less) and could hardly have kept body and soul together without cultivating the glebe, not to mention the far from simple business of collecting the tithes. The manse, during the fifteenth century and for long after, was nothing like the modest country house or villa of later centuries. A thatched, wattle cottage of the kind occupied by the more prosperous peasant smallholder housed perhaps two or three clerics and a servant, surrounded by the untidy squalors of the farmyard, distracted from the service of the altar by the demands of the fields. At Theddlethorpe in Lincolnshire in 1397 Revesby Abbey, the patron of the benefice, undertook to build for the vicar a hall twenty-four feet by eighteen, with two chambers over it and two cellars below, a kitchen, a brewhouse and a bakehouse, a stable for three horses and a sty for twelve pigs, all roofed over with reeds or straw. Fundamental economic factors, as well as the corrupted relationship of church and state, prevented any rapid rise in standards for the mass of the clergy.

Yet at least in some dioceses in the eighty or so years before the Reformation standards improved. In the diocese of Lincoln the proportion of graduate clergy in the parishes, educated men fit to argue the theories of the schools, rose from about fourteen per cent at the beginning of the fifteenth century to over thirty per cent in 1500. The attainments of the majority of the run-of-the-mill parish clergy also rose in a modest kind of way with the extension of grammar school education. By the end of the century, throughout the Lincoln diocese, they became, with few exceptions, literate enough to conduct the services decently. As late as 1583 a visitation covering the whole country revealed that as few as one-third of the beneficed clergy held university degrees, and of the rest only one-sixth were considered articulate enough to be granted licences to preach. Either Lincoln had been exceptionally advanced before the Reformation, or the coming of Protestantism with all its attendant troubles, particularly the deprivation of clergy who refused to conform under Mary and Elizabeth, for a time frustrated any improvement upon pre-Reformation levels. Before the Reformation, in Lincoln at least (if not in other dioceses), the days of a parish clergy too ignorant even to purvey the sacraments without scandalous error had passed away[1]

1. Information about the Lincoln clergy is derived from a paper read by Mrs M. Bowker at the Anglo-American Conference of Historians, July 1966.

and it was some considerable time before any further advance occurred. Future Catholic and Protestant countries alike found the provision of an educated rural clergy a prolonged, intractable, heart-breaking problem only to be solved in the seventeenth century.

Such advance towards literacy as there was may well have been more of a hazard than a shield for the church. A little learning is a dangerous thing and many priests, like many of their parishioners, now belonged to the dangerous class of the semi-educated, able to read but perilously lacking information and critical sense and therefore all too open to propaganda. They were educated enough to read the books coming from the new printing presses and by the 1520s it was becoming a question of which would most attract them, the almost incredibly conservative manuals of instruction and devotion, dating from the early fourteenth century or even earlier, to which they were accustomed or the novel, and therefore more exciting, pamphlets published by the reformers. Such men would have been most susceptible to propaganda, and this combined with discontent at their financial position (many curates had little hope of a preferment even to a poor benefice) made Henry VIII's actions at least acceptable to them.

The story of the secular clergy was a story of unobtrusive and very slow development, that of the religious orders moved to catastrophe, swift and complete enough to rouse the passions of generations. Until the comparatively recent decline of sectarian bigotry, polemicists of the various sects could turn and rend each other: Protestants exulting in scandals, Catholics, if not ignoring criticism, defensively adopting the Black Death as a disaster which permanently impaired the finances and the fervour of the religious. A less emotional generation has now reached a more sober consensus of opinion, regarding scandals in their due proportion as exceptional, and relegating the long-term effects of the Black Death to the limbo of historical myths. The plague was in no way a turning point in the prosperity or the fervour of the religious orders. After the first appalling mortality their recovery in numbers was, in fact, remarkable. By 1370, possibly affected by declining recruitment as well as plague, there were no more than about 8000 monks, nuns, and friars left in the country, little more than half their former numbers.[1] From then onwards, however, recruitment steadily rose until the early 1420s, and

1. The numbers of the religious had risen to about 17500 in the early fourteenth century, the period of maximum growth for the population generally.

thereafter continued to rise, albeit more slowly, until by the end of the century they reached 12 000, a rise of fifty per cent over the post-plague total; a rate of increase far greater than the most generous estimate for the general population outside the convent walls.

True, in the later Middle Ages, there were empty cells and echoing halls in the greater and richer Benedictine abbeys, but many of them had already been unoccupied long before the Black Death. Fashions in religious devotion change as they change in more mundane affairs. In the twelfth century the Cistercians and in the thirteenth the busier and more exacting vocation of the friars had already attracted a large share of novices who in earlier days would have had no alternative but to enter Canterbury, St Albans, Durham, or Ely or some other of the great Benedictine foundations. At least one great house, Durham (and possibly others) pursued a conservative recruiting policy which wisely restricted its inmates to the numbers which its diminished revenues could decently sustain. The far more numerous lesser houses, most of them of later foundation and far poorer in their endowments, seem to have found little or no difficulty in attracting the modest number of novices to maintain the community of the dozen or score monks for which they had originally been founded.

Nor did the Black Death mean long-continued impoverishment. While it is true that the main current of benefactions now ran to the more fashionable chantries, a comparative dearth of new endowments was by no means the same thing as poverty. Once the monks, like lay landowners, adjusted to the new economic conditions and completed the transformation of their estates from demesne farming to leases, which most of them managed to do by the end of the fourteenth century, there is no evidence that they suffered any undue economic pinch. The greater houses supported many fewer monks than a century before on the same endowments. In the first half of the century they had to bear comparatively heavy taxation for the French war. Later, with the removal of this burden, taxation lay upon them as lightly as it lay upon the rest of the country. The chronic poverty of some of the smaller houses and the everlasting debts of many nunneries were almost as old as the convents which they burdened. The accumulated riches, not the poverty, of the English religious abbeys impressed foreign visitors. The Venetian envoy in 1497 was amazed at what he called 'those enormously rich Benedictine, Carthusian and Cistercian monasteries . . . more like baronial palaces than religious houses'.

E

Even in houses of the second rank there was money enough and to spare if their income were wisely directed. When Bishop Oliver King in 1500 found Bath Abbey church tumbling into ruin he asserted without hesitation that a succession of priors had inexcusably wasted on extravagant living the ample funds which should have gone to maintain the fabric. The bishop, a strong-minded prelate, roundly told the monks that they could live 'with more latitude than the literal observance of the rule required' upon about half their current income and promptly ear-marked the rest for a building fund.

From the beginning of the century monks were constantly building, reconstructing their domestic quarters to higher standards of comfort, embellishing churches and building libraries: many houses now for the first time erected a separate building for their books. It may indeed have been in their buildings that the monks most impressed the lay world. The great precincts of the monasteries, with their fine domestic ranges, enormous, lavishly decorated churches, splendid abbot's or prior's lodgings and their towered gatehouses, were still the most impressive groups of buildings in the country. Aristocratic houses and royal palaces could not yet compare with them in size and splendour.

Though the number of recruits to the religious orders was surprisingly high, their quality was another matter. The Hundred Years War, the Avignonese Captivity and the Great Schism, while they did not entirely sever their English branches from the great international orders of Christendom, left their relationships too tenuous and finely drawn for their continental brethren to stimulate new developments, or even to check decay in the English communities as they had in the past. English communities now became decidedly insular in character, and individual houses even more decidedly local. Most houses recruited from what might be called a 'local catchment area' and their postulants, young men between the ages of seventeen and twenty-three, were of comparatively modest rural origin, often from the estates of the monastery in which they made their novitiate. By the fifteenth century the sons of aristocratic families rarely entered the religious orders. Many country boys, attracted more by the prospect of a secure livelihood than by a genuine vocation, drifted into local monasteries, completely ignorant of the difference in tone between different houses. Their training and the quality of their future lives would thus be, unknown to them, a matter of chance, varying immensely according to the standards of the house, from the staid, decent observances and ceremonious ritual of a great abbey, so nostalgically described in the *Rites of Durham*, to the uncouth rusticity of some small remote house buried in the depths of the countryside, with a church too dilapidated to keep out the rain and dogs and chickens befouling choir and cloister. In such communities the complement of a dozen or so monks or canons, carelessly muttering their offices and bickering in noisy boredom over their post-compline ale, should hardly be blamed for their low standards for they had never known anything better. Only a very small minority of houses – like Ramsey and Dorchester-on-Thames – were permanent black spots. Yet even in most houses where life was decent the world was too much with the inmates. A bored monk of Christchurch, Canterbury, echoing the poet Thomas Hoccleve, repentantly admitted 'Excess at board hath laid his knife with me' and confessed that excess had done so for twenty years. At Croyland, a decent enough house of the second rank, the monastic chronicler was not ashamed to note (as perhaps a decent monk ought to have been) that Brother Lawrence Chateres, the kitchener, had left £40 for the refreshment of the brethren with milk of almonds on fish days, and gave considerable space to a description of the way in which the almonds were to be provided. By this time the richer houses had become pioneers of comfort as in earlier days they had been pioneers of sanitation. Abbots built elegant and pleasant houses for their lodgings, senior monks occupied suites of rooms, waited on by their own servants, much like Oxford and Cambridge dons in more opulent days. They went on holiday, drew wages, and some accumulated nice little personal fortunes. It is not without significance that monastic libraries at this period owed little to purchases from the common funds; they were mainly built up through gifts and legacies of books from individual monks: donors who according to a strict interpretation of the rule under which they lived were forbidden to possess even as much as a penny of their own.

There are a few exceptions to this tale of dismal mediocrity – the seven austere Carthusian houses with their justified boast *nunquam reformata quia nunquam deformata*, Henry V's Brigittine foundation at Sheen, and the six houses of Friars Observant encouraged by Henry VII. The fervour of their upright inhabitants never died, and they were prepared to sacrifice their lives rather than submit to what were, in their eyes, Henry VIII's evil and destructive plans. These few communities apart, English monastic life, while free from the grosser scandals which defiled many continental monasteries and nunneries, was also completely untouched by the reforming zeal which inspired new continental orders like the Windesheim Congregation of Johan Busch. Dom David Knowles, the most learned and judicious historian of English monasticism, sadly concludes that monastic life had reached one of those recurrent and disheartening phases when the numbers of the lukewarm had come to equal, perhaps even to surpass, the numbers of the fervent, that monks, nuns and friars 'were settled upon their lees'.[1] Many quite orthodox Catholics in the late fifteenth and early sixteenth centuries, in England and elsewhere, contemplated the religious orders with an equal lack of enthusiasm. Dean Colet was thoroughly impatient with monasticism. Sir Thomas More, deeply conservative in many ways, in the end rejected entry to the Carthusian cloister which had attracted him in youth. Some of the most active minds in Rome at the time would have thought the labours of some modern writers to defend the monasteries as they were before the Reformation grossly misconceived. While Thomas Cromwell was destroying the English monasteries, at the very moment of the Pilgrimage of Grace, Cardinal Pole and his reforming friends, still hopeful and liberal in their views, excoriated the decadence of the religious orders in Italy and, in the *Consilium de emendanda ecclesiae*, recommended the abolition of most of their numerous branches.

Endowment was the outward and visible sign of devotion. In earlier centuries it had led to the proliferation of monasteries. By this time the day was long since passed when a well-to-do landowner regarded a small proprietary monastery or monastic cell as an almost indispensable sign of respectability. The increasing popularity of masses for the dead, which developed from the end of the thirteenth century, diverted religious fashion to the endowment of chantries at altars in parish, monastic, or friary churches or, with the very rich, the building of entirely new collegiate foundations. This form of devotion, with an endowment placed in the hands of trustees, for the first time allowed laymen an active role in controlling religious funds. The foundation of a chantry was not cheap (it cost at least £200 to meet the initial expenses and to provide an endowment for the perpetual support of a single priest), but it cost less than any other institution and brought into being a new and wider class of founders.

Schools and colleges were the most splendid monuments of piety; a few of royal foundation, the greater number paid for through the generosity of lay and ecclesiastical magnates and some collectively

1. D. Knowles, *The Religious Orders in England*, ii, 364.

endowed by town and city gilds. In London alone there were at least one hundred and sixty religious gilds. At Oxford splendid episcopal foundations like All Souls (1438) and Magdalen College (1448) made more generous provision for scholars. A small proportion, about one-tenth, of the chantries established for the singing of masses for the souls of founders, founders' kin and founders' friends added opportunities for education, from such a lavish royal foundation as Eton College to the small chantry endowed by Dame Agnes Wingfield in an already existing college of priests at Rushworth. As for the gilds, a society like the Candlemas Gild at Bury St Edmunds gave the townsfolk considerable power in a community otherwise dominated entirely by the Abbey, and the gild of the Holy Cross at Stratford-upon-Avon prospered so well that it became in effect the town government. The form of devotion which created the chantries made the century an age of generous religious endowment and, based though it was on an almost morbid concern for the progress of the soul after death, also resulted, at least in part, in a very practical social form of piety.

So far little has been said of the influence of the papacy upon the English provinces of the universal church. Little has been said because, although its pretensions remained high, its powers and influence, whether for good or evil, were by this time slight. This was not because of any alleged deterioration from former peaks of rectitude in Rome. Historians, all too prone to fit the fourteenth- and fifteenth-century papacy into that dubious straitjacket, 'the declining Middle Ages', have perhaps too readily drawn a depressing contrast with earlier times. In condemning this as an epoch of papal confusion and decadence, the history of the thirteen anti-popes who broke the unity of the church between 1045 and 1197, and the lives of a series of mainly French popes in the late thirteenth century who played the game of power politics hardly less completely than their Renaissance successors, are all too often ignored. No one would deny the distinction of the great reforming popes who for a century and a half followed Gregory VII (1073–85), but it is well to remember that their ideals rather than the more limited success of their practical endeavours are generally compared with the sordid realities of a later age. Although the Babylonish Captivity (1305–78) was a scandal to many of the faithful, all the Avignonese popes were personally men of good life, who genuinely tried to introduce reforms. Unfortunately, like so many of the English bishops whose appointment they authorized, all but two of them were lawyers, precise and careful administrators presiding over an increasingly efficient and costly bureaucracy paid for in part by levies on the church; a development unfortunate for their reputation in an age which looked upon taxation, though with less and less realism, as abnormal and wicked. Paradoxically it was increased efficiency, not increased corruption, which made the papacy unpopular.

Once the Council of Constance (1414–18) was over, the English provinces of the church became progressively more isolated and more insular in spirit. English influence at Constance owed more to the development of secular politics than to reforming zeal. Although Robert Hallum, a member of the very distinguished chapter of Salisbury cathedral, supported the cause of reform, and an Englishman, Cardinal Beaufort, arranged the compromise which led to the election of Pope Martin V and thus brought the scandal of the Great Schism to an end, the mass of the clergy, judging from the tardiness with which they made their financial contributions to the expenses of the English delegation, showed no great enthusiasm for the council.

In the following decades Pope Martin V (1417–31) and Pope Eugenius IV (1431–47), despite insistent and prolonged pressure, utterly failed to persuade the English government to repeal the fourteenth-century legislation which, except with the king's connivance, had destroyed their power to make appointments to English benefices. By this time there were so few foreigners in English benefices and so few Englishmen at the Curia – in a hard-headed way they no longer made expensive journeys to a place where the patronage was so thin – that the popes themselves complained of a lack of intercourse between head and members. The *Calendars of Papal Registers* show, beyond the shadow of doubt, that during the second half of the century the Pope could hardly appoint a clerk of his own choosing to any English bishopric or even to a lesser benefice. In theory his right to make such appointments remained intact: in practice he was quite unable to exercise it. In the thirteen years of his reign Pope Sixtus IV (1471–84) nominally provided or translated twenty bishops to sees in England and Wales. Of the seventeen clerics involved, sixteen were the king's trusted councillors. Sixtus tacitly admitted defeat. Even when he wished to reward John Doggett, Cardinal Bourchier's nephew and Edward IV's own representative at the Papal Court, knowing that it was impossible to make any appointment in England, he provided Doggett to canonries in Cambrai, St Omer, and Antwerp.

Nor did the papacy deserve hostility on account of the money it took from the clergy. Despite Henry VIII's mendacious propagandist assertion that 'great and inestimable sums of money be daily conveyed out of this realm to the impoverishment of the same', the English clergy in the half-century before the Reformation contributed little more than £4800 a year towards the expenses of the head of the church. The king himself, at the lowest estimate, was taking over two and a half times as much from the clergy. Although Henry spoke with compassion of the 'great damage' done to the prelates as well as to the realm by the outward flow of treasure, he so increased his own demands upon them that between 1535 and 1547 he wrung from a reluctant clergy about £47 000 a year – nearly tenfold what they had formerly rendered to the papacy, and between two and a half and three times what they had paid to both pope and king together. Moreover, the huge monastic properties having been confiscated, the clergy paid these vastly increased sums from much diminished resources. Financially the English clergy had every reason to look back to the last days of alleged papal extortion as their golden age of immunity.

In matters of jurisdiction Henry VIII could break with Rome so easily because for several generations the papacy had been a mere cipher in the affairs of a deeply insular English church, acting at most as a kind of superior licensing authority for the issue of comparatively minor dispensations and exemptions. Even had it possessed the will to stimulate English church life for good, it lacked the power to do so. It could only assist the activity of a royal servant by providing legal cover for Cardinal Wolsey's policies.

Fifteenth-century religion may seem to many people unattractive. Every age develops its own forms, both of spirituality and mechanical piety. The Christian life has taken many ways from the asceticism of St Mary of Egypt to the calculation of the Vicar of Bray. The church has never been free of the world's slow stain; corrupted in that its ever-growing and almost inalienable wealth became necessary to support the impecunious state, and therefore was so often used to support the ambitious, cleric in name, lawyer or civil servant in vocation. Nor, in ages when learning and the powers of reason were limited to the few, had Christian belief ever been free of the gross superstitions of an ignorant clergy and laity. In some ages the stain had been more deeply corrosive than in others. The intensity of religious life has always been a cycle of decline and revival. Comparisons are dangerous, if not impossible, but at least historians should attempt them. In some ways the reputation of the fifteenth-century church has fared unduly ill, on the one hand, with those who have compared its realities with the high, and forcefully expressed, ideals and reforming efforts of earlier times, overlooking both their limited application and equally forceful contemporary attacks on its corruption, and, on the other hand, those who have until recently assumed that the Reformation brought about a rapid improvement in standards. The bitter, even blasphemous, twelfth-century tirade, the *Gospel According to the Silver Mark*, equals Matthew of Cracow's pamphlet *On the Filth of the Roman Curia* (1403–4) in the virulence of its attacks upon the venality and corruption of the papal court. Without ceasing to admire the sanctity of St Francis and St Dominic, it is also well to remember the devastating complaints about the wealth, corruption, and negligence of the secular clergy against which their sanctity shone the brighter, and the immense gap in the church's system of pastoral care which the friars for a time so notably filled and which, despite the loss of their original fervour, they still filled before the Reformation.

In fifteenth-century England if saints were non-existent, there was nothing in English religious life like the squalor which in 1493 faced Cardinal Ximines in Spain, when he set about the reform of his own order, the Franciscans, whereupon four hundred Andalusian friars chose conversion to Islam and flight to a new life in North Africa rather than give up their concubines. Though reformers who tried to improve the standards of the parish clergy and the instruction of the people were only to a limited degree effective, at least the days of pluralism on the grand scale had gone. No 'possessioner' could now equal the thirteenth-century record of Bogo de Clare with his twenty-four parish churches and a dozen other benefices besides. The more modest pluralists of the fifteenth century earned their pay as civil servants. Bogo had merely lounged about Oxford. In spite of a groundswell of Lollardy, perhaps increasing towards the end of the century, England was remarkably orthodox, even *dévote*. But beneath its apparent security the church was growing increasingly vulnerable, though few could have thought so at the time. From the beginning of the century, a hierarchy terrified by the Wycliffite attack upon the church's dogma and upon its possessions had chosen to suppress intellectual speculation in favour of a passive, unthinking devotion, and, as the century wore on, the church became increasingly isolated from any stimuli which it might have received either from the papacy or from European developments in religious life – it knew neither the evangelical fervour of St Vincent Ferrer's preaching tours nor the monastic reforms of Johan Busch. Even the slow improvements which the century witnessed may well, in the end, have worked against the church, for rising standards left an increasing number of clerics and laymen literate enough to read and to be impressed by the propaganda of the Protestant reformers, but few learned enough or clever enough to combat it.

6 Education and the arts

During the later Middle Ages education became more widely spread. The number of students attending German universities, for example, quadrupled during the fifteenth century. In England ladies took their Books of Hours to church to read during mass, pews with book rests appear and the fashion for wider windows and clerestories may have come in, at least partly, to provide more light for reading. Posters and handbills became for the first time a means of conveying information to the public. In the early sixteenth century Sir Thomas More claimed that three out of every five people in the country could read,[1] and a modern estimate suggests that forty per cent of the householders of London could read Latin.

This new literacy was a widespread phenomenon. Universities and schools cannot, however, be exactly compared with those of today for standards throughout the various stages of the educational system were several degrees lower than in their modern counterparts. The great majority of university students were in the arts faculties – many of them, indeed, altogether outside the traditional faculty system.[2] They did not take even a first degree and they learned what their modern descendants would learn in a secondary school. The English universities dropped the basic study of grammar only in 1570.

The number of country grammar schools in the fifteenth century is a matter of debate and, most probably, always will be, although it seems that it was increasing. William Byngham, a London rector, founded Godshouse (later Christ's College), Cambridge in 1439 as the first teacher training college to remedy what he considered to be a serious shortage of schoolmasters. Probably some schools founded in earlier centuries had been forced to close their doors because the masters' stipends were no longer adequate. On the other hand, noblemen and prelates founded collegiate schools; town gilds promoted others, and chantry schools increased in numbers. Possibly one-tenth

1. It has been suggested, however, that his figures apply only to London.
2. See below, p. 140–2.

of the 2300 chantries or thereabouts in the country had schools of some kind attached to them, though owing to the vagaries of private benefaction they were very unevenly distributed. There were about forty-six grammar schools scattered across Yorkshire, and another sixty-eight appeared between 1545 and 1603. In discussing the development of education in the later Middle Ages, however, writers may have paid too much attention to endowed schools, neglecting overmuch the factor that education at this period was often a kind of vocational training, carried out in the household – for the sons of the nobility and gentry in aristocratic households, craftsmen teaching apprentices in their own shops. Probably many boys picked up what bookish learning they had as a by-product of this system rather than by regular schooling. Even in the early fourteenth century, according to Robert Holcot (d. 1349), magnates employed tutors in their households. Under Edward IV Elizabeth Wydeville engaged a private tutor to instruct the young duke of Buckingham who was being brought up in her establishment. At a lower level a good deal of teaching was carried on by scriveners, curates, parish clerks and chantry priests, and in gild and borough schools unmentioned in surviving records because they were not formally endowed.

Oxford acquired six new colleges and Cambridge nine between the middle of the fourteenth century and the Reformation. William Wykeham's (1324–1404) endowment of New College, Oxford, nearly doubled the number of college fellows in the university. It was, moreover, the first college in Oxford which admitted comparatively large numbers of undergraduates and the first to employ the tutorial system which had already developed in some of the existing privately run halls. When William Waynflete founded Magdalen in 1448 he made it to some extent self-sufficient for teaching purposes by providing foundation lectureships in theology, moral philosophy, and natural philosophy. The lectures were to be open to all members of the university and so, in a way, they also began the system of endowed university professors who ultimately succeeded the regent masters[1] as the teaching body.

In spite of attempts at reform at Oxford in the 1430s the curriculum in both universities in the arts and in the higher faculties remained essentially conservative until Erasmus began to teach at Cambridge and John Colet at Oxford. In the early years of the century there was undoubtedly, for financial reasons, a decline in the number of students

1. MAs of not more than five years' standing.

studying to prepare themselves for a career in the church.[1] Other types of students probably made up the total numbers. England was experiencing, if somewhat faintly, the movement towards a more liberal, bookish education for the nobility already developing in many parts of Europe. Neither the extent nor the kind of this education could compare with developments in Italy, nor was it stimulated by any strong official backing as in Burgundy where Duke Philip the Good (1419–67) established the university of Dôle to encourage learning in the aristocratic and knightly classes – those classes whose cooperation the ruler so eminently needed.

In the fifteenth century the academic population of Oxford and Cambridge was far from being exclusively clerical. The statutes of Magdalen College provided for the admission of noblemen's sons as commoners,[2] and the records of New College reveal a substantial number of young laymen who do not appear in the university records themselves. It is possible indeed that as much as sixty per cent of the undergraduate population went unrecorded by the university, for most of them never graduated and never intended to graduate. Some may have read in the Arts courses, others were taught in an almost informal series of schools which existed side by side with the recognized university faculties from the early years of Henry III until some time before the end of the fifteenth century. Such schools, run by grammar masters, provided a vocational education for some of the business classes of the day, teaching the *ars dictandi* and the *ars notaria*, in other words formal letter writing in Latin and French, conveyancing, the drafting of deeds and the holding of courts: training in all the miscellaneous legal work which great landowners required from their estate administrators – and agriculture was, after all, the greatest business of medieval England.

An increasing number of young men seem to have attended the universities for this kind of instruction in what passed for business administration, and perhaps more towards the end of the century took some kind of instruction in the arts before going on to one of the Inns of Court. According to Sir John Fortescue the curricula of the Inns included such subjects as history, scripture, music, and even dancing. Like the universities the Inns attracted young men of social standing who were not necessarily looking to a legal career to earn

1. See above, p. 126.
2. This seems to have been the precedent for admitting fee-paying students to the common life and teaching facilities of the colleges. Before this they had been boarded and taught in privately run halls.

their bread. In times when the land law was complicated, not to say chaotic, an education with a legal bias was highly desirable for any landowner who wished to preserve his properties intact. The Paston family were typical products of this type of education. Three of Judge William Paston's (1378–1444) sons went to Cambridge, though none of them entered the church. The heir, John, spent some time both at Trinity Hall and the Inner Temple, and his father sent a fourth son, Edmund, to Clifford's Inn. Sir John Fortescue approved the development, but in the 1450s William Worcester commented very adversely upon it. 'But now of late days,' he wrote, 'the greater pity is, many one that been descended of noble blood and born to arms, as knights' sons, esquires, and of other gentle blood, set themselves to singular practice . . . as to learn the practice of law or custom of land, or of civil matter, and so wasten greatly their time in such needless business, as to occupy courts' holding, to keep and bear out a proud countenance at sessions and shires' holdings.' Like all old-fashioned conservatives Worcester sourly condemned the degenerate youth of his day, fallen from the virtue of their manly forebears. What could one say to the credit of an effete generation which took to books and administration rather than training in arms to recover the lost English possessions abroad and to defend the realm?

Book collecting was popular enough amongst laymen. Edward IV was the real founder of the royal library which, under Henry VII, a French ambassador mentioned as one of the sights shown to foreign visitors. Earlier John, duke of Bedford, had bought the famous Valois collection at a knock-down price. The library of his brother, Humphrey of Gloucester, contained between five and six hundred volumes. Larger than both university libraries, it was the biggest in England apart from the collections of a few great monasteries. The Pastons, like others of their class, borrowed and lent amongst their friends. In the *Howard Household Books* there is an entry under the year 1480 listing thirteen of Lord Howard's books, all the titles, incidentally, being French. It may be a rough catalogue of his library, but judging from its place in the note-books the entry is more likely to have been a list of the volumes which he took with him on his naval expedition along the eastern coast of Scotland. This is quite plausible, for he had made all his preparations upon the most opulent scale. Whichever is the case, a library, even of this size (at this date most of the books must have been hand-written manuscripts), represented an extravagant capital outlay. In 1461, an Italian merchant, Pietro de

Buschis, owned eighteen volumes. They were valued at 300 florins, that is about two pounds weight in gold. Although de Buschis was a rich man, these eighteen books represented more than a quarter of the total value of his house, furniture, jewels and working capital. To have spent money for books on the scale which Howard's library implies, even allowing for the possibility that he bought his books for prestige purposes, must show an ability to read easily or that he enjoyed being read to – a distinction certainly not as great at that time as it is today, for silent reading appears to have been very little practised before the sixteenth century. Fifteenth-century prose writers and poets assumed that their works would be read aloud, and they sound much more effective if they are. Many laymen proved generous patrons of literature. Lord Strange of Knockyn (d. *c.* 1449) supported the blind poet, John Audelay. John Lydgate (1370?–1450?), the uncrowned poet laureate of the times, counted amongst his patrons, besides royalty, the duke of Suffolk (himself a poet and the friend of the poet duke of Orléans), the earl and countess of Shrewsbury, Richard Beauchamp, earl of Warwick, Anne, countess of Stafford and Isabella, Viscountess Bourchier (Richard of York's sister), as well as less distinguished men and women. Even the tough, hard-headed Sir John Fastolf in his later years became the patron of a quite distinctive, if minor, literary circle in East Anglia. The nobility also patronized Lydgate's friend, John Shirley (1366–1456), a copyist, and collector of manuscripts, who hired out his volumes for fees, running in fact, from the house and four shops which he rented from St Bartholomew's Hospital the first lending library known in England. Moreover, the fact that William Caxton's press could issue over thirty editions of English romances, poems and histories in seventeen years shows that the schools of his day had educated a public wide enough, with a purchasing power great enough, to support a modest publishing business.

It is possible, in a rough kind of way, to indicate the quality of this lay development. To risk stressing the obvious, no social group or groups ever exhibit a level, common standard. The entire aristocracy cannot be condemned, as they have often been condemned, as bucolic, illiterate boors, interested solely in war and the chase. As with their counterparts today, some read books and some bred horses – some did both. Some were amongst the most highly educated laymen of their day. Moreover, as earlier implied, the fifteenth century witnessed an expansion in the provision for education rather than any fundamental change in the kind of education provided. By the standards of the Italian humanists (though in fairness we should remember that even in their own society they formed a highbrow minority), English laymen were old-fashioned and backward. Humanism, and in particular what little study of Greek there was, remained mainly the avocation of churchmen. Interested laymen like Humphrey of Gloucester and John Tiptoft, earl of Worcester (1427?–1470), were few, though it was a sign of the times that a circle of humanist poets flourished at the Yorkist court, and a visiting Italian noted that the thirteen-year-old Edward V was well versed in most of the standard Latin classics. All the same, the English printing presses never produced a classical text. The demand was far too small for such an enterprise to show a profit.

For most people the very idea of a liberal education did not exist. They would have regarded the notion as extravagant nonsense. The evidence suggests that the gentry looked upon a certain level of education as necessary if their sons were to rise in the world, possibly even to maintain their accustomed place in it. By the beginning of the sixteenth century such people were well aware that their sons would lose jobs to lesser men if their education were neglected. For the ambitious gentleman, as for the ambitious churchman, a legal education was highly desirable. Nine-tenths of the lawyers came from the upper and middle ranks of the gentry, and unlike later periods when younger sons went to the bar to make a living, parents at this time put the eldest son to the law to make a family fortune. Others required the more limited education in law and business methods which would add to their efficiency in running their own estates and which would enable them to join the ranks of the 'gentleman bureaucrats' taking employment on royal or aristocratic estates – the type of men that William Worcester so vehemently deplored.

An increasing number of laymen, many of them in quite humble circumstances, could copy, understand, and even draw up documents in Latin, and from about 1460 masters in a few newly endowed schools (as well as at Oxford) taught such techniques. The ability to draft formal documents in Latin and English, or to read a chronicle or a romance, does not, however, imply a capacity for original thought or even for the lucid expression of ideas outside the scope of normal administrative routine. Outside the universities the standard of teaching was inevitably low. Before the invention of printing, books were too expensive for all but the exceptional schoolmaster to buy. All he possessed was a grammar and perhaps a book of extracts. Nearly all teaching was therefore oral teaching, teaching by rote.

Moreover, the drafting of business documents did not call for any great fluency. Latin was still the vehicle of abstract thought, but layman's Latin was too jejune to permit intellectual discussion or the development of ideas.

For different reasons English likewise failed the layman. A coherent prose style takes time to develop – and in English it developed by slow stages. In the late fourteenth century, with the decline of spoken French, the use of the mother tongue spread rapidly amongst the upper classes. Henry V issued the first English proclamation, the London chroniclers began to write in English towards the end of his reign and the use of English steadily advanced in administration. The results, to say the least, were uneven. The most lucid, forceful English, because work-a-day and unpretentious, was that of some of the government clerks and private letter writers, the most tortuous and opaque that of Bishop Reynold Pecock, a determined pioneer who struggled to express abstract, theological ideas in a language which had hardly begun to develop the abstract noun. It took men like Sir Thomas More, trained in the new humanistic Latin, to develop an effective prose style, capable of flowing narrative and the expression of ideas. As Professor Denys Hay has pointed out, although More's style owed a good deal to the English tradition of devotional writing, he 'and others of his generation who wrote English with a fair degree of vigour, economy, and variety were to a man the products of Latin scholarship'.[1]

In the reign of Henry VII intellectual life and speculation were still, because of difficulties of language, essentially clerical. The growing class of literate laymen was still a semi-educated class, fumbling and somewhat incoherent in its clumsy, imperfect command of language. The fifteenth century was a period when the great medieval gulf between the highly educated churchman and the illiterate layman grew less. Even so, it remained great enough. With few exceptions the educated laity had not yet become part of the intelligentsia. A lay generation capable of abstract thought about the state and other problems developed only in the 1520s. The progress then had been from illiterate through 'gentleman bureaucrat' to intellectual. Education and the state of society are closely related. In the mid-twentieth century industrialists who formerly needed no more than a secondary-school education have now moved up to university level. So in the fifteenth century 'gentlemen bureaucrats' could manage with a

1. *From the Renaissance to the Counter-Reformation: Essays in honour o Garrett Mattingly* (London, 1966), p. 107.

fairly simple type of vocational education. Their successors, if wise, and under pressure from the king and court, gave their sons a more intellectual training in the new humanist, Erasmian style. The steady, if unspectacular, advance of the later Middle Ages had laid a solid foundation for the more rapid sixteenth-century development. Educational opportunities indeed had so far advanced that, even before the great expansion of the sixteenth century, reactionaries moaned that boys far too low in the social scale were going to school and entering careers that should have been reserved for their betters.

Standards of literary taste were very much those one would expect at such a level of education. Nobles and gentry were passionately interested in genealogy and topography, for an intimate knowledge of family trees and the descent of manors was the basis of landown-ing as well as the means of gratifying family pride. The early writers to meet this need, William Worcester and John Rous of Warwick, were the direct ancestors of John Leland, William Camden and the great seventeenth-century county historians. At a higher emotional level readers, like those of most societies deeply conscious of disorder and violence, craved for didacticism – and these generations loved it garbed in elaborate eloquence. As William Caxton wrote, in one breathless phrase, of *Le Morte Darthur*, Sir Thomas Malory gave them 'noble chivalry, courtesy, humanity, friendliness, hardiness, love, friendship, cowardice, murder, hate, virtue, and sin'. If they did after the good and left the evil 'it shall bring you to good fame and renown'. Malory, the sport of fifteenth-century writers, possessed a genius which illumined almost stale romances with a new fire. Other, and more consciously literary, writers strained themselves to the limit – and beyond – to impress didactic reflection and the moral tale upon their readers: and impress it with all the virtuosity of technique they could command, a virtuosity of elaborate construction and 'aureate diction'. Abbot Whethamstede of St Albans, striving to imitate the Italian humanists, produced a highly ornate Latin style – *verborum florida venustas* – 'the flowery beauty of words', he proudly called it. It was not a style which his models would have commended. John Lydgate, in long, traditional-style histories and romances, over-laid their gothic content with classical references and allusions, and, attempting in English verse what Whethamstede attempted in Latin, claimed a complicated, highly flown style as a virtue, and laid down the principle, which he relentlessly practised, that writers should not be 'constreyned under wordes few'. Tastes change and their few modern readers find such works unendurable – more akin to the works of Mrs Amanda McKitterick Ross than to those of the world's great stylists. But tastes took a long time to change. The new printers gave the public much the same books as the old scriveners. They constantly reprinted standard medieval works until about 1600, though, it is true, less frequently in the second half of the sixteenth century. Lydgate, in particular, remained immensely popular – indeed people still read his works with pleasure until the end of the eighteenth century. Its Elizabethan authors planned the *Mirror for Magistrates* as a continuation of his *Fall of Princes*, an epic already 36 000 lines in length; and it was after all in the works of Lyly, whom the Elizabethans so intensely admired, that the passion for 'aureate diction' reached its climax. Our standard selections of their literature leave us with a false idea of what the Elizabethans read. The taste of many of them was still that of the fifteenth century.

Popular literature produced matter more digestible, though not completely so, than the courtly tradition. The late fourteenth and the fifteenth centuries were the great age of the town miracle and morality plays. Miracle plays, developing from the liturgy, came to be specially associated with the Feast of Corpus Christi. Though most popular in the north and in the Midlands, these plays are known to have been performed in more than forty places all over the country – from individual villages, groups of villages which combined their resources for the purpose, to the larger towns. The great cycles at York, Beverley, Wakefield and Chester staged episodes ranging from the Creation to the Last Judgment. In some places responsibility for production, lavishly staged and exceedingly expensive, lay with specially created gilds, in others particular craft gilds each took over one of the plays in the cycle. At York (organized by the craft gilds), the actors performed on large wagons, called pageants which followed each other from stations through the town, repeating the scenes at each one.

The moralities, which, in their turn, developed from sermons and homilies, also developed somewhat later than the miracle plays. *Everyman* and *The Castle of Perseverance* (both of which were very popular) were staged in tavern yards or in specially constructed round theatres, enclosures of clay and turf, outside the towns.

The popular lyrics and ballads of the fifteenth century are attractive by any standards. Lyrics to the Virgin like

> There is no rose of swych vertu
> As is the rose that bare Jhesu

and

> I syng of a mayden
> that is makeles
> King of all Kynges
> to here sone che ches[1]

reach the highest level of lyrical beauty.

On the other hand, the series of London and other town chronicles, beginning early in the century, reveal the new vernacular culture in cumbersome, graceless shape. They offer a very poor substitute for the great monastic Latin histories of the twelfth and thirteenth centuries – their comparatively poorly educated authors ill-informed, myopic in vision, limited and fumbling in vocabulary and expression.

The working of the creative spirit is a thing of mystery. High achievement in literature and in the visual arts does not always coincide. The pageant chivalry tradition so tedious in literature resulted in new masterpieces of architecture. For long, historians condemned the perpendicular, or rectilinear, style of architecture as a degeneration from earlier gothic masterpieces as unfortunate as Lydgate's inferiority to Chaucer. If classical influences had invaded English architecture even to the limited extent to which they influenced such authors as Lydgate and the other courtly poets, the result might well have been a discordant bastard style. Pediments and volutes, like 'aureate' terms in literature, would have added incongruous decoration to gothic structures – as they already defaced churches reconstructed in northern France after the last stages of the Hundred Years War. Classical influence was extremely late arriving in English architecture. At the time when Michelozzo added the Portinari Chapel, with its light and airy dome decorated with Renaissance angels, to the Church of St Eustorgio in Milan, and members of the Portinari family were working in the Medici *filiales* in Bruges and London, Edward IV began to build one of the last great gothic churches, the chapel of the Order of the Garter, St George's, Windsor. Nineteenth-century art historians developed a theory that the perpendicular or rectilinear, style, of which the Windsor Chapel is one of the crowning glories, originated in a local south-western style first seen in St Augustine's, Bristol (*c.* 1320), closely followed by reconstruction at Gloucester Cathedral. More recently writers have seen it as a court style, its motifs, though drastically adapted, influenced by French examples. It developed in London, where its earlier

1. i.e. she chose.

buildings no longer survive, spread first to the west country as a result of frequent visits by the court to that area in the second quarter of the fourteenth century and then more slowly to other parts. The style combined two major features, the layman's taste, particularly heraldic taste expressed in romantic chivalry, and a new conception of vast, unified single spaces which the friars had first developed in the great urban churches which they used primarily as preaching halls. The perpendicular is above all a style of spaciousness and light. In contrast to the elaborate spatial divisions of earlier gothic interiors, the architect-mason now desired an effect of great single vessels, and widened arches to lessen the division between nave and aisles so that great aisle windows could illumine the nave itself, or even, as at King's College Chapel, Cambridge, create one enormous, rectangular aisleless lantern, more glass than wall. To gain this new effect gothic columns shed their earlier composite clusters and accentuated capitals, becoming simple octagonal shafts, often with vertical concave mouldings of extreme elegance as at Chipping Camden (*c.* 1401) or rising without a break into the arches they support as at St Mary's, Bury St Edmunds (*c.* 1440). The sinuous curves or ogee tracery were replaced by simpler, geometrical forms; arcading by rectangular stone panelling; sharply pointed arches by the almost flat four-centred arch, often set in rectangular panels. Rich stained glass gave way to plain or to panes of lighter, more varied colours. Deep carving and curves left walls and window tracery to concentrate in church roofs – either in lierne or fan vaulting, or in the most splendid hammer-beams and double hammer-beams giving a quality of immense depth to almost flat roofs. At March (*c.* 1500) in Cambridgeshire where the beams end in gay angels the effect is that of a *repoussoir*, a trick of stage scenery, so that the whole upper space seems filled with spreading angelic wings. Wood carving indeed reached its peak in the fifteenth century – in cathedral choir stalls and in the roofs, roodlofts, screens, pews, and pulpits with which so many newly built or enlarged parish churches were decorated. The later Middle Ages, and in particular the sixty years before the Reformation, were the great period of parish church building, and the woodcarvers produced excellent work for churches all over the country, though the angel roofs of East Anglia, the roodlofts of the north, and elaborate screens in the south-west are particularly notable.

Domestic, like ecclesiastical, designers developed new forms. Standards of comfort rose, with the nobility and the greater ecclesiastics setting the pace. Contrary to a popular tradition, comfort was an aristocratic, not a middle-class, invention. By the beginning of the century the nobility had already withdrawn from the noisy turmoil of their vast households, which in a great establishment could run to two or three hundred people and more, to the seclusion of splendid private apartments. By mid-century even a modest country home like Stonor (Oxfordshire) had, besides other rooms, a hall hung with black say, three chambers hung with red and green, and a separate study. Only a few of the richer London merchants could vie with the nobility in the accommodation which they provided for their families. Crosby Hall, built in the 1460s, is a splendid memorial of the state which a commercial magnate could afford. Crosby Hall, however, was well above the normal run of merchant accommodation. Most merchants, when they could afford it, did little more than ape the nobility in their growing demand for privacy and comfort. Even so, few traders, even in London, were rich enough to live on the high aristocratic scale and most, faced with the problem of contracted urban building sites, were forced, in any case, to content themselves with lower standards.

The remains of castles and great houses reveal such improved standards of planning and comfort, such magnificence in decoration that the late fourteenth and the fifteenth centuries deserve to rank as the first great age of English domestic architecture. Statements if often enough repeated in print seem to destroy any visual perception in historians. Despite the contrary evidence of tons of stone and brickwork in the countryside (building in brick became very popular for the first time since the days of the Roman Empire, especially amongst ecclesiastics), even recent books continue to echo the hallowed cliché that only in Tudor times were houses first built for comfort and not defence. Nothing could be further from the truth. Even in the thirteenth century stone manor houses were built without fortifications. During the later Middle Ages, except in the Scottish Marches, disorder did not exist on a scale great enough to involve sieges. Some people thought it wise, others did not, to build a house with walls strong enough, and water defences wide enough, to protect them against riots and casual attacks. Others, again, liked a martial show. For the rich, pseudo-military architecture was high fashion, a whim to give the impression of chivalric military splendour, to emphasize the owner's rank. The windfall profit of a French ransom enabled the war veteran, Sir John Fastolf, to plan Caister Castle (*c*. 1432 – *c*. 1440). He built it in the height of the latest French and Rhenish fashion which it had seen abroad. Martial enough in appearance, a moated structure three hundred feet square, with a great tower at each corner decorated with machicoulis and immense gargoyles, its design, with both a winter and a summer hall and with one of the towers originally housing five storeys of handsome rooms with arcaded fireplaces, makes no sacrifice of comfort to the demands of military science.

One of Fastolf's friends, another war veteran, Ralph, Lord Cromwell (d. 1455), replanned and enlarged Tattershall Castle in Lincolnshire and built himself another house, South Wingfield, in Derbyshire. Cromwell designed Tattershall with a double curtain wall and double moats. Seen in the distance on the horizon of the paper-flat Lincolnshire plain, its vast central brick keep with four corner turrets, begun in 1434, looks a grim, forbidding fortress of immense strength. Its appearance is deceptive; military engineers had abandoned central keeps of this kind two centuries earlier. The Tattershall keep has often been called an antiquarian revival as deliberate as the sham gothic castles of the nineteenth century: a somewhat improbable theory for the fifteenth century which always wanted to be up to date. Cromwell and his 'architect', Baldwin the Dutchman (i.e. German), are more likely to have modelled it, as Fastolf modelled Caister, upon the great houses of France and the Rhineland, where such high central blocks, miniature palaces, decorated with martial trappings, were the very peak of fashion.[1] The rooms in the keep at Tattershall are enormous living rooms, containing some of the finest carved chimney-pieces of the age. Large traceried windows pierce the walls on all sides, even on three sides of the ground floor.[2] The immense machicolations of the roof line, which look very military indeed, surround what must have been a charming and most unwarlike roof garden; and in the unlikely event of the inhabitants being called upon to defend the building they would have found themselves sadly hampered fighting from the narrow roofs of an arcaded gallery or loggia running all round the inside of the walls. The keep at Tattershall was not 'the last stronghold of a fortress': it was a great multi-storied solar, a suite of magnificent private apartments for the owner's family.

1. See W. D. Simpson, *The Building Accounts of Tattershall Castle, 1434–1472* (Lincs. Record Soc., vol. 55, 1960).
2. The ground floor of the fourth side had three doors opening into a covered space connecting it with a separate great hall (this arrangement too is French in origin) which would have made it even more difficult to defend. Cromwell also improved existing buildings by putting in enormous windows of the kind he built at South Wingfield.

At South Wingfield (*c.* 1441) Cromwell built, this time in stone, a large manor house which, apart from the walls enclosing its two courtyards, was defended by nothing more than a dry moat – and that only on its most exposed side. The hall and state apartments had battlements adorned with quatrefoils and shields of arms and traceried windows elaborate as those of a church. Over a century later Elizabeth I's council thought it comfortable enough to house Mary, Queen of Scots, during part of her captivity. She had fifteen chambers for herself and her servants, and the house was so far from defensible that her custodian, the earl of Shrewsbury, claimed that he would rather keep her at Sheffield with sixty men than at South Wingfield with three hundred. Magnates built houses such as these to show off their wealth and possessions (the conventions demanded ostentation) and to lead a luxurious, cultivated form of life.

Of lesser houses – to name five, all built during the Wars of the Roses – Ockwells in Berkshire is designed to a harmony of simple, but effective, mathematical ratios with a definite aesthetic effect in view. The main façade of the Prior's Lodging at Much Wenlock in Shropshire is rather more glass than wall. Great Chalfont in Wiltshire is protected only by a moat. Gainsborough Old Hall in Lincolnshire and Neville Holt on the borders of Leicestershire and Rutland are completely open, defenceless houses. That Sir Thomas Burgh chose to design Gainsborough Old Hall in this fashion seems particularly significant, because his earlier house had been destroyed in a riot in 1470. Even in these lesser houses interiors were everywhere growing more comfortable and luxurious. Ockwells and Much Wenlock were flooded with sunlight. Monks and canons as well as private men now built chimneys to their rooms, and at Wells when John Gunthorpe reconstructed the Deanery he decorated his state apartments in a way fit for any nobleman.

Many people who admire late medieval architecture judge it by standards completely alien from those of its own day. Few secular buildings have survived as more than shells, and modern enthusiasm for the greater churches, the fifteenth century's most conspicuous monuments, usually takes a form which contemporaries would have regarded as ill-judged – had they been capable of understanding it at all. The cathedrals, collegiate, and parish churches lost long ago the decorative finish which made them glorious in the eyes of their patrons and builders. The vaulting picked out in red and gold, blue and silver, the diapered panelling, shrines and reliquaries jewelled with glass inlays, gesso and precious stones, all combined in a riot of colour, have vanished. The generations which stood before the brightly gilded and painted screens and retables of their new churches would have condemned modern enthusiasm for bare darkened lime-stone and warm brown sandstone walls as singularly poverty-stricken and tasteless. They preferred a bright jewelled effect to a dim religious light. Their more travelled and sophisticated members admired the high polychrome finish of Burgundian effigies and angels. The tomb of Richard Beauchamp, earl of Warwick (d. 1435), is designed with bronze angels and weepers in the high Dijon style of Claus Sluter. Sir John Donne, one of Edward IV's courtiers, commissioned a Madonna and Child from Memling. Edward himself, fascinated by the sumptuous collection of Louis de Grutuyse, which he had seen in Bruges during his brief exile of 1470–1, became a collector in his thirties, and, developing the somewhat undiscriminating taste of a tired businessman, purchased a whole collection of second-rate, though exceedingly sumptuous, illuminated books, mostly Burgun-dian. With few exceptions, only the miniatures in such books as these, and better ones like the lectionary (*c.* 1400) which John, Lord Lovell of Tichmarsh, presented to Salisbury Cathedral, the Warwick and the Bedford Books of Hours, remain as fresh and gay as they were in the age which produced them – but from their inaccessibility (painted on the leaves of books they can never be shown as completely as pictures painted on wood and canvas) remain, except to art historians, the least known and most neglected part of all European art.

Ideas of courtly chivalry dominated aristocratic taste in both liter-ature and architecture. The fifteenth-century pseudo-castles expressed the courtly romance in brick and stone. Nevertheless, in modern eyes, achievement was astonishingly contradictory. If aristocratic taste in literature was, to say the least, stilted, pompous, and not a little dreary, the same atmosphere and taste produced an architecture of great distinction. Moreover, the forms which dominated both proved to be remarkably enduring. From the middle of the fourteenth century to the early seventeenth, chivalric taste continued strong and persistent. In spite of increasing competition from continental humanism, the ostentatious splendour of this pageant chivalry style never died. Edward Hall (1498?–1547) in his famous *Chronicle* set down descriptions of jousts and tilts at immense length. Under Elizabeth I Lords Cumberland, Arundel and Herbert were painted in full armour ready for the lists. James I held Accession Day tilts as late as 1623. Even Inigo Jones designed carpenter's gothic settings for court pageants and interludes. In literature, in spite of the hatred of humanists like Roger Ascham (1515–68), who excoriated *Le Morte Darthur* in one withering remark – 'in which book those be counted the noblest knights that do kill most men without any quarrel and commit foulest adulteries by subtle shifts' – chivalry returned in Sidney's *Arcadia* and Spenser's *Faerie Queene*, though it is true that Sidney and Spenser thought their own romantic dream world a great improvement over earlier works, a refinement which they conceded to the influence of the classical writers.

Building reveals the same attachment to the past. In Hampton Court Palace Queen Elizabeth I had a cabinet called 'Paradise', its walls panelled in gold and silver, its chair of state standing beneath a canopy studded with pearls and other precious stones, amongst which great diamonds, sapphires and rubies shone 'like the sun amongst stars'. Classicism seemed on the verge of triumph in such monuments as Bishop Gardiner's tomb (*c.* 1550) in Winchester Cathedral, and such buildings as Somerset House (1547–52) and Longleat (1572–80). Then in architecture as in literature the native English tradition surfaced again, developing even further the geometrical, rectilinear tendencies so pronounced in fifteenth-century building, to compete with, and predominate over, crude classical elements to produce some of the most archaic buildings in northern Europe. Original as their variations are, the later Elizabethan and some of the early Stuart country houses developed from the late gothic style. Hardwick Hall (1590–7), like King's College Chapel, is a great glass lantern. At Wollaton the four chimney flues of each corner tower run through flying buttresses which curve together at their summit to form a composition essentially that of the late medieval market cross. At Longford Castle (*c.* 1590), in the great chamber classical corinthian columns support a ceiling with rib vaults and a great hanging pendant, and in the 'Little Castle' (1612–21) at Bolsover, corner-towered and battlemented, with hall and parlour pillared and vaulted, Robert Smythson dreamed a pseudo-gothic fantasy worthy of the *Faerie Queene*.

English cultural achievement was virtually unknown in Europe except for three things – music, embroidery, and alabaster sculpture. Henry IV's court was a famous musical centre and the king himself is said to have been, like Henry VIII, a competent composer. English influence became strong in Europe during the earlier part of the century, it may be, partly, because many musicians went to France with Henry V and the great lords after 1417. By 1450, if not earlier, musicians in Flanders, France, and even Italy held England to be the fount of a new musical art. Tinctoris (*c.* 1436–1511), the most celebrated theoretician of his time, placed English above all other music. John Dunstable (1370?–1453), the most renowned of English musicians before the great Elizabethans, made the most notable contribution to this development. Going to France in the retinue of the regent, John, duke of Bedford, he had reached the height of his fame when in 1437, after Bedford's death, he entered the service of the duke of Burgundy. Breaking away from the mathematical isorhythmics of the *ars nova* style of the day, he developed a more fully concordant harmony, freer and less fettered melodies. Indeed, he seems to have been the first composer fully aware of harmonic sequences as such. The development of the six-three chord is said to have been his great contribution to polyphonic music. In England writers had used such chords for a century and more, elsewhere only rarely. Dunstable both developed English practice and extended it abroad, where his work was carried on by Guillaume Dufay. After a period of decline under Henry VI, Edward IV's chapel royal once again became a famous musical centre. A German nobleman, after hearing the choir, wrote that there were no better singers in the world, and the duke of Milan and the friars of Lucca tried to recruit Englishmen for their own establishments. The music which they admired, the elaborate polyphonic music which graced the English chapel royal up to the Reformation, is now seldom heard and little appreciated, for neither the Roman nor the Anglican church has the slightest use for it.

At court and in the great households minstrels were composing secular music, instrumental as well as settings for songs and lyrics. The minstrels of the fifteenth century were far removed from the vagabond entertainers of earlier times. They were skilled composers and executants, some of them with university degrees in music. Noblemen, and even some towns, maintained groups of such minstrels, who went on tours of the country. Sir John Howard, who was a great music lover as well as a book collector, kept 'Thomas the harper' on his household staff at Stoke-by-Nayland in Essex, as well as a man and four or five boys as a choir for his domestic chapel. His accounts show that when he went to London he hired the city waits to sing before him and the trumpeters to play, and at home he made frequent and generous payments to the earl of Kent's minstrels, the duke of Buckingham's and to other aristocratically supported and town groups who arrived at Stoke to entertain the household.

Opus anglicanum, the craft of embroidery, at first carried on by nuns but long before the fifteenth century passing to professionals, both men and women, mainly working in London shops, had been famous all over Europe at least as far back as the reign of Edward I. Pope Clement V had owned at least three English embroidered copes. The work was at the same time sumptuous and delicate, executed on velvet or heavy silks, with a lavish use of gold thread, and in colours of white shading into blue and green into yellow. During the fourteenth century copes were made with scenes embroidered in panels, much resembling in design the miniatures of contemporary psalters. By the fifteenth century *opus anglicanum* was past its best. The figures of saints worked on vestments were by this time stereotyped, and decoration had become somewhat limited to a few conventional motifs such as angels, thistles, bells, and crowns.

During the second quarter of the fourteenth century alabaster and other soft materials began to replace the marble and harder stones in which earlier sculptors had worked. Alabaster became immensely popular for tombs, images of saints, for retables and reredoses. Although alabaster tombs were popular with the greatest in the land – Joan of Navarre, Henry IV's second wife, commissioned one in London and shipped it to France, for the remains of her first husband, the duke of Brittany – the easily worked material made possible cheaper and more commercialized production and the extension of an 'art market' to much wider classes.

Alabaster figures carved round the quarries near Nottingham, Lincoln, and York became immensely popular for churches and private chapels – often being bequeathed in people's wills. In the early sixteenth century the small priory of Sandwell in Staffordshire possessed no less than nine images of saints. The soft texture of the material allowed the development of intricate and detailed carving, and although most of the figures were shop work of no great distinction, occasionally the carvers produced accomplished pieces of sculpture like the figure of the Trinity at Boston. Alabaster is better suited to reliefs than to free-standing figures, and most of the work of these craftsmen seems to have been panels in relief which were then set in wooden frames to form retables and reredoses. Both the wood and stone were freely painted and gilded, thus harmonizing the two materials and happily concealing the somewhat soapy effect of the naked stone. Hundreds of figures and retables were produced before the Reformation. Most of those in England were later mutilated or destroyed. Others still remain scattered all over Europe from the Baltic countries to Italy. Alabaster sculpture and *opus anglicanum* in their day sold more widely than any form of English art before or since. Apart from music, the English were known abroad only for their minor arts.

7 Society and government

Every schoolboy knows that sixteenth-century Englishmen, assisted by the vigorous propaganda of their rulers, welcomed the harsh government of the early Tudors because they dreaded a relapse into the disorders of the fifteenth-century civil wars. The proverbial schoolboy's knowledge is in one respect insular, in another fallacious. All over Europe, below the level of the magnate class, the basis of political action – it might be better to say of political acquiescence – was fear; fear lest the thin dividing line between good government and disorder should suddenly snap. Pope Pius II (d. 1464) trembled for the future of Christendom, threatened by the Turkish peril from without and (so he thought) decadence within. Machiavelli, Guicciardini, Luther and Calvin, no less than Englishmen, dreaded the collapse of society and the coming of chaos. The desire for strong government sprang from a deeper level than memories of the comparatively superficial crises of the Wars of the Roses, useful though they were to point the moral and adorn the tale. Thoughtful men recognized the dreadful weakness of all forms of government even in normal times.

The myth of the horrors of the Wars of the Roses, so nurtured by Tudor writers, sprang to life in 1461, when Edward IV and his somewhat unimpressive group of supporters, declared that God, to avenge the usurpation of Henry IV, had inflicted upon the land 'intolerable persecution, punicion and tribulation, whereof the like hath not been seen or heard in any other Christian realm . . . unrest and inward war and trouble, unrightwiseness, shedding and effusion of innocent blood, abusion of the laws, partiality, riot, extortion, murder, rape and vicious living have been the guiders and leaders of the noble realm of England'.

As an indictment of disorder the statement was exaggerated: its implication that disorder was the unprecedented result of dynastic sins certainly false. Fifteenth-century England was a turbulent, violent place in which to live. Abnormal extension of armed conflict, however, had not significantly increased its chronic violence.

Between the Norman Conquest and the deposition of Richard II there had been only two periods of more than thirty consecutive years without fighting in some part of the country, and the extent of oivil conflict in the fifteenth century was small compared with the dissensions of former and later ages. The total period of active campaigning between the first battle of St Albans (1455) and the battle of Stoke (1487) amounted to no more than twelve or thirteen weeks – twelve or thirteen weeks in thirty-two years! The most reliable contemporary evidence all points to the limited effect of the dynastic quarrel.

In one way the reputation of these squabbles is a perfect example of misconception produced by a conventional, but inappropriate, vocabulary. The stock terms 'wars', 'campaigns' and 'battles' are misleading, for they convey an impression of military operations on far too great a scale. The 'campaign' in which Henry VII marched unopposed from Milford Haven to his victory at Bosworth Field lasted fourteen days! Some of the battles were equally miniature. The first battle at St Albans (1455) has been described as 'a short scuffle in a street' and the continental experts of the day, who wrote in a well-developed military jargon, would have called Hedgeley Moor and Hexham (1464), which, as noted earlier, were more or less chance encounters between at most a few hundred men, 'besognes', 'rencounters' or 'mêlées' rather than battles. Only at Towton (1461) did the numbers engaged possibly approach fifty thousand. Tactics were, to say the least, haphazard, training non-existent. Towton was fought in a snow-storm which blinded the Lancastrian forces, Barnet (1471) in an April fog so dense that each side badly miscalculated the other's positions. Troops, hastily collected, many of them unwillingly impressed, gathered for each particular crisis, then quickly disbanded as soon as it was over. Neither side could afford the cost of anything more professional. The protagonists from time to time hired small numbers of foreign mercenaries, but they were never numerous enough to become a menace either to their employers or to the population at large. England never offered even the prospect of a career to a military entrepreneur like Perrinet Gressart, who maintained himself for thirty years as military governor of La Charité-sur-Loire, often openly defying the wishes and policy of his employer, the duke of Burgundy. The countryside was so far from being the prey of a brutal and licentious soldiery that on occasion soldiers had to be protected from the civilian population. On the morrow of Bosworth Field Henry VII issued a proclamation 'that no manner of man rob or spoil no manner of commons coming from the field; but suffer them to pass home to their countries and dwelling places with horse and harness'. Plundering was comparatively rare, devastation rarer still. The horrors of war were mild compared with the ravages of the Scots in the north of England during the early fourteenth century or the devastations which the English themselves inflicted on northern France in the period of their 'scorched-earth policy' after 1435 or, two hundred years later, upon each other during the seventeenth century. Whatever the casualties of the Wars of the Roses may have been they certainly did not approach the hundred thousand men (not far short of one-tenth of the adult male population) slain in the years after 1642. Nor were great cities sacked, cathedrals and churches desecrated and looted, great sheep flocks wantonly slaughtered as they were in the seventeenth century – and there were, after all, less than four hundred people attainted compared with over seven hundred royalists whose lands were confiscated in the later period.

The immunity of English towns from attack was remarkable, for they were, and they remained, less defensible than any in Europe. Owing to the early unification of the country and the comparative strength of its government, defences had, for a long time, become less necessary than elsewhere. Little fortified market towns, so common in France and Italy, were unknown, and even major towns like Reading, Derby and Oxford remained unwalled. While mid-fifteenth-century architects developed the bastion in central Italy, and possibly independently in Rhodes, English architecture ignored the demands of warfare. The Wars of the Roses produced nothing comparable to the fortifications and earthworks which both Cavaliers and Roundheads threw up in the seventeenth century. A few towns – Lynn and Canterbury amongst them – strengthened their defences during the 1450s but such additions or reconstructions as they made to the old-fashioned layout of their walls were, except in certain ports, too hastily carried out to have been at all elaborate. The ruinous, and probably obsolete, defences of London may well, in part, account for the pusillanimous readiness of the city fathers to negotiate with both Lancastrians and Yorkists. By 1478 the citizens were so heedless of danger that an ambitious mayor's attempt to rebuild the walls foundered on their reluctance to pay for the work. Strategically castles proved as insignificant as cities. The private castles of the nobility might never have existed for all the effect they had upon the wars. Of the royal castles, only Harlech, for reasons now obscure, withstood a long blockade. The rest of the Welsh castles, like Pembroke and Radnor, and the great northern castles, Alnwick, Bamborough and Dunstanborough, which figure so prominently in the meagre narratives of the 1460s, never held out against a besieging force for more than a few weeks – often it was a matter of days. In the north the inhabitants continued to build peel towers to protect themselves against Scottish raids.

In 1415, there were said to be one hundred and fifteen castles and peels in Northumberland alone, but in the south, after the erection in the last quarter of the fourteenth century of a handful of castles like Bodiam as a defence against the French, serious military fortification on a continental scale was never seen again until Henry VIII, between 1538 and 1540, built from the Thames to Portsmouth a chain of coastal artillery forts in a revolutionary, if distinctly eccentric, foreign style.

Dynastic conflict at most merely added to the chronic disorder of fifteenth-century England: the disorder endemic, there and elsewhere, in the limited scope of government which was all that an under-developed society could afford. Edward Hall (d. 1547) more or less defined the ideals of government in an imaginary speech which he attributed to Archbishop Arundel – 'the noble men shall triumph, the rich men shall live without fear, the poor and needy persons shall not be oppressed nor confounded'. Even within these negative limits, confined externally to defence, internally to the administration of justice, standards of government were by no means high. Although medieval philosophers developed sophisticated theories of political obligation, kings and lawyers impressive courts of justice, all too often majestic façades masked squalid interiors. The intellectual achievements of all pre-industrial societies outstripped their capacity in execution. Standards of conduct were as undisciplined as farming techniques were inefficient, and institutions, as defective in practice as they were impressive to the sight, failed to restrain the violent and the corrupt. By modern standards societies all over Europe were turbulent, feckless, inefficient.

Life showed a level of violent convulsive action often combined with a tolerance of situations which, today, we find barely conceivable. Neither men nor women were accustomed to restrain their emotions. Tempestuous, uninhibited passion was never far from the surface, ready to break through at any time. Grief and anger alike erupted into violent expression. Few women, or men for that matter, would ever have found themselves in the unfortunate predicament of Mrs Tulliver who was unable to squeeze out a decent trickle of tears at funerals. The voluble Margery Kempe, who cried on the least excuse until her eyes were nearly blind, was, even in her day, an abnormally luxurious weeper, but a comparatively sober writer on the religious life could subdivide penitential tears into twenty-eight distinct varieties. The law required every free man between the ages of sixteen and sixty to possess, and practise the use of, arms. The possession of arms combined with the passionate emotional tendency of the day left the temptation to violence irresistibly strong. Sir John Fortescue reflected with a perverse tinge of pride on widespread English crime as a reflection of English valour, and considered the English criminals' penchant for burglary showed their immense superiority to the French who went in more for larceny. The respectable classes themselves were as undisciplined as the mob was brutal and the gentleman thug, like the gentleman bureaucrat, was a recognizable social type. Members of the Mercers' Company drew their knives on each other at the company's meetings. The statutes of more than one Oxford college specifically mention homicide as a cause for the expulsion of fellows. Families which accused each other of every crime in the calendar from riot to mayhem remained on astonishingly social, even amicable, terms with each other. Even during their notorious, protracted quarrel over the Fastolf inheritance, in the course of which the duke of Norfolk blockaded Paston supporters in Caister Castle, relations between the two families were by no means entirely hostile. John Paston the Younger remained all the time in the ducal service, although it is true that, at least in one despairing moment, he thought of seeking employment elsewhere. At the height of the quarrel, with legal actions for murder threatened, and while the Pastons were lobbying royal councillors with accusations against the duke, one of the duchess of Norfolk's servants wrote to the bailiff of Malden asking that the elder brother, Sir John, should be elected to parliament for the borough, and Sir John himself, meeting the duchess in Yarmouth, twitted her upon her pregnancy in coarsely jovial terms, which, reflecting upon later, he thought might have been altogether too familiar for the lady's taste.

Faced with such endemic violence the capacities of the English monarchy, like others, were barely adequate to meet its limited functions. The government was not only poor, it so greatly lacked coercive force, honest officials, even information, that the struggle to maintain control over its resources was desperate – and far from uniformly successful. Government today is largely based upon figures, upon reasonably precise information. All this lay in the

F

future. Even in the late seventeenth century it was still something of a novel idea in England that the study of numbers could give a methodical basis to government. Kings and their councils worked in an ignorance which it takes a major effort of the imagination to grasp. Their lack of quite elementary information is staggering. In 1371 the government, for taxation purposes, estimated the number of parishes at 40 000: the wildest of wild guesses, for there were only about 8600. Expecting an invasion from Ireland, Henry VII hurriedly sent a special messenger to ascertain whether or not the Cheshire ports were capable of accommodating large ships. Judges dealt with cases without copies of the statutes before them until Edward IV, realizing the great advantage of better information, began printing the statutes. Their sessional publication followed under Richard III.

Serious corruption hampered society and government at every turn. The Commons demanded and obtained statutes providing legal remedy against servants who ghoulishly made away with property upon a death in the family (1455–6) and against widows who alienated their dower lands (1495). In 1428 the judges advised the royal council to compound with a merchant who had defrauded the customs rather than prosecute, as it was notorious that juries would not bring in convictions against friends and neighbours. In the 1470s the London authorities brazenly under-assessed themselves for a tax, and not long afterwards a group of the richest and most respectable merchants in the city were in serious trouble with the king over their smuggling activities.

Royal and other officials naturally expected to enrich themselves while serving their employers. In an age when fees provided a large slice of their income it is hard to draw a firm line between the legitimate customary gift and extortion and bribery. Many payments to officials which would be condemned today were then reckoned normal profit. Many, however, from the highest to the lowest, exceeded the limits of conventional decency. Ralph, Lord Cromwell, the builder of Tattershall Castle and South Wingfield, who was treasurer from 1433 to 1443, left his executors, for conscience' sake, the task of making restitution of the enormous ill-gotten sum of £3481 1s. 6d. Even the smug Chief Justice Fortescue was not above taking bribes. In the 1450s the Commons attacked extortion by Exchequer officials, sheriffs and escheators, and officials who held their posts for life. A few years later the king dismissed various duchy of Lancaster officers for taking excessive fees. Accusations of corruption in the customs system never ceased, and when, for a short period under Edward IV, the aulnage[1] was directly administered instead of farmed, the records were a discreditable farce, the aulnagers year after year copying lists of names from earlier accounts and setting imaginary figures against them. Even the most trusted royal servants passed beyond this twilight world to brazen, outright theft. Stephen Preston, a squire of Edward IV's household, who handled important financial affairs for the king, sold for his own profit a large part of the standing timber in the royal forest of North Pederton. In 1506 Henry VII was trying to recover £4000 embezzled by Robert Fitzherbert, 'late customer of London'; and the highly favoured Reynold Bray, the under-treasurer of England, one of whose tasks was to check the customs accounts, cheated him by exporting wool without paying the duty upon it.

It is possible (though dogmatic assertion would be unwise) that standards declined, though not as badly as they declined in the later sixteenth and seventeenth centuries. With the spread of literacy, laymen had taken over the law courts from clerics in the fourteenth century – and had taken them over with far from happy results.[2] Shortly after 1400, laymen began to move into Exchequer offices,[3] and the Signet Office, revived in 1437 at the end of Henry VI's minority, became the first department which they exclusively staffed.[4] The rise of the layman and the decline of the cleric in administration were not an unmixed blessing. Quite apart from the spiritual implications, the church had been wise in its generation in preserving its property and endowments by forbidding the clergy to marry. In government departments clerics generally held office at the king's pleasure, sometimes during good behaviour. The king could dismiss them easily, as they could fall back on their benefices for support or they could be granted others at no cost to the king. Laymen proved more recalcitrant. They possessed no benefices to soften the blow of dismissal and they had families dependent upon them. For greater security they soon began to demand life tenure in their offices, and reversionary interests and the appointment of poorly paid deputies

1. i.e. cloth taxation.
2. See below, pp. 165 ff.
3. In the Exchequer, between 1400 and 1509, there were 27 lay treasurers, and only 9 ecclesiastical, and from 1410 the chancellors of the Exchequer were always laymen. Between 1400 and 1529 there were only two lay lord chancellors. The lesser personnel of the Chancery has not, unfortunately, been investigated.
4. There were only two signet clerks in orders after 1437.

to do the work followed closely upon the life interest. All this, though only beginning in the fifteenth century, led before its end to the concept of royal offices as marketable items, as a form of investment. The drift to lay officials began to create new vested interests, producing as time went on a new rigidity in administration, perhaps even declining efficiency – and in the end an increase in costs. Official salaries were low. Therefore, whenever possible, to get the most out of offices, especially if they had bought them, their holders demanded bigger fees and gifts from the public.

Until recently historians described in glowing terms the development of English legal institutions in the twelfth and thirteenth centuries and reprobated with equal zeal the decay and corruption into which they supposed them to have later fallen. This contrast derived at least in part from the use of different, even somewhat incompatible, types of evidence, a too exclusive concentration upon legal treatises and procedure for the earlier period and an obsession with complaints about the later workings of the courts, due mainly to the early, and isolated, publication of the *Paston Letters*[1] with their endless wails about violence and corruption. However, the publication of vociferous complaint, even its existence, is not proof that conditions have become notably worse. Medieval men always saw rosy visions in the past, believing that a period of good order had existed in some erstwhile golden age, and found their own times wanting by this legendary standard. Foreigners thought crime exceptionally widespread in England. Its notoriety is not surprising, for the execution of criminal law had always been, and still remained, weak. The fifteenth-century records of King's Bench show few convictions except of people like notorious highway robbers. During his period of personal rule Henry VI issued hundreds of pardons to suspected and condemned criminals – probably a tacit confession of weakness, for men under sentence of outlawry found it possible to live openly and unmolested for years together. Except for the developed practice of issuing such pardons there seems to have been nothing new in all this. The good fame of any age generally withers before documentation of its practices as distinct from its legislation, and the publication of some of the judicial records of earlier times shows a state of affairs so appalling that any theory of massive deterioration in the fifteenth century is hardly credible. In the early thirteenth century over three hundred crimes of violence were committed in one year in the single county of

1. Partly published in 1787.

Lincoln. Only a tiny proportion of the offenders was ever brought to justice. An analysis of the records of the session of the peace in the same county towards the end of the fourteenth century reveals that in fifteen years (1381–96) juries indicted 485 felons. Only 81 ever came to trial and all but five of these were either acquitted or pardoned. These horrific figures were not the result of an exceptional crime wave, merely an index to the normal state of law and disorder in the countryside. Improvement came only slowly: even at the end of the sixteenth century the Council in the Marches of Wales levied two hundred and seventy fines for riot alone in a single year.

In civil matters most men regarded the law as a means of gaining their own ends rather than the road to even-handed justice. Agrarian societies are always fiercely litigious, and litigation was a normal avocation for landowners who looked upon their 'lifelode', the complex of family estates, as an almost sacred trust to be defended at all costs and by all means, fair or foul.[1] Readers of the *Paston Letters*, the *Stonor Papers* and the *Plumpton Correspondence* can hardly fail to notice that a large proportion of the violent incidents and the not infrequent riots which they describe flared up out of disputes over landed property or legal rights. Under Henry IV the Commons complained that the clergy spent in the law courts too much of the money which the faithful had given them for the service of God. The clergy probably had little choice in the matter, for in 1455 the abbot of Fountains complained that in recent years malevolent people had brought over twenty vexatious lawsuits against the abbey. At Croyland litigation was so normal a feature of life that the chronicler of the house thought it worth special mention that John Wysbech (d. 1476) had kept the convent free of legal actions during the entire seven years of his abbacy.

Justice in civil actions may possibly have deteriorated with the passage of time. Successive generations of lawyers had failed to adapt the law of real property to meet the needs of so acquisitive a society. The early substitution of laymen for clerics in the courts had been even less advantageous than in administration generally. From the end of the thirteenth century a line of lay judges, cut off from the discipline and rational principles of Roman and canon law in which their clerical predecessors had been trained, became more and more engulfed in the accumulating technicalities of their own profession. By the fifteenth century they were already obsessed by the 'artificial

1. This was nothing new. Thomas II, Lord Berkeley (d. 1321), had during his lifetime fought 24 lawsuits over land or franchise rights.

reason' of the common law,[1] later so revered by Chief Justice Coke (1552–1634) and his generation. The intellectual limitations of a profession thus isolated from jurisprudence, which studied and practised only the technical formulae of the law, bred an intense conservatism which hallowed every ancient, if unvenerable, technicality and only to a very limited degree adapted its procedures to changing social needs. Procedure in the courts excessively favoured defendants. What originally began as safeguards had become abuses of the most pernicious kind. Mesne process, the process of securing the presence of defendants in court, was capable of almost endless delay. The simplest case could rarely be settled in less than eighteen months, cases lasting three or four years were quite usual and a case lasting as many as twenty years by no means extraordinary. The common law only grudgingly recognized entails. By this time, moreover, the richer landed families disposed of their estates by means of trusts and uses, new and more flexible forms of property settlement – devices which only the ecclesiastically run Chancery recognized and dealt with in equity jurisdiction. The common law did not recognize them until 1536. Even at common law, cases concerning land were frequently dealt with according to principles and forms of action which could be adapted only in an evasive and perverted way to fit their needs. To make confusion worse confounded, no statutes of limitation had been passed since Edward I's day. In real actions the term of legal memory went back to 1189. Over the two centuries since that date the descent of many manors had become so obscurely complicated that the illegitimate revival of ancient claims to property could bring serious consequences even to owners long in possession of estates, and careless purchasers might find their titles to land disputed by the subsequent revelation of dower interests, confusion between bond and free tenures, or older, deliberately concealed conveyances. Robert Burton's (1576–1640) remark in *The Anatomy of Melancholy* – 'a man who owns a house must needs own a houseful of evidences' – was as true in the fifteenth century as in his own day. Landed families cherished their 'evidences' almost as dearly as they cherished their estates. In this jungle of the law, in the absence of any system of land registration, they formed the essential, if often thoroughly defective, basis of estate ownership.

Various statesmen tinkered with the problem from time to time, but apart from some legislation on trusts in 1536, it was not until the

1. i.e. the highly specialized conventions and logic developed through the traditions of the legal profession.

mid-seventeenth century that effective legislation provided some escape from such hazard. Bad titles remained as frequent, and as disastrous, for landowners as bad debts for merchants. Most of the notorious attacks on the Paston properties were based at least upon the shadows of old legal claims, and James Smyth, the Berkeleys' steward in the days of Charles I, lamented the history of that murderously litigious house, 'rending her possessions into sundry parts, . . . pressed under bloody brawls and law suits of 192 years agitation between the . . . heir male and heir general, two cousin germans and their issues before they came to peace' – all the result of ambiguous and defective settlements made by Lord Thomas IV (1352–1417). The most scandalous episodes in this great feud took place in the fifteenth century, even allowing that Smyth, the victim of a wildly extravagant oral tradition,[1] exaggerated some of its earlier incidents. Nevertheless, violent brawls, riots and forcible disseizins were almost as notable during its course in the sixteenth century, and, as Elizabeth I's favourite, the earl of Leicester, himself one of the contestants in the later stages of the quarrel, perceptively remarked, the settlements which had been agreed at various times (and quickly broken) owed more to political influence than to a strict interpretation of the complicated legal issues involved.

Exasperated by the delays and expense of the court of Common Pleas, almost as inadequate in its own way in civil pleas as the King's Bench in criminal, litigants had two courses left open to them – to take to force or to arbitration. Some violently seized what they regarded as their own. Others called in arbitrators. The Close Rolls of Chancery teem with entries recording their awards. But, as if there were no end to troubles, arbitration too had its limitations: as the Croyland Chronicle pessimistically noted, the Latin in which some awards were written was so vague and imprecise that it led to yet more disputes. One of the main streams of violence ran directly from the obsolescence and antique deformities of the law of real property.

With institutions in practice so defective, with direct power at the government's command so limited, the maintenance of order depended upon the tolerance and cooperation of the well-to-do, through the combination of patronage and discipline which they could exercise upon their dependents and their neighbours. Government was by the rich and to a great extent for the rich. Writers justified this authority upon theoretical grounds, and ordinary folk in practice demanded it

1. See above, p. 14–15.

because they felt the standards of the wealthy to be somewhat higher than those of other people. Dante had written that only a world monarch could be sufficiently free from the vice of cupidity to make a just ruler. Fortescue claimed that a well-endowed king would be less oppressive than a poor one who would necessarily find himself driven into 'exquisite means' to extort money from his wretched subjects. Riches and honesty dwelt together – though often like a married couple upon somewhat uneasy terms. From the beginning to the end of the century, in parliamentary petitions, in the preambles to statutes, in conversations round dinner tables, complaints ring out against the extortions of *parvenus* insufficiently endowed to maintain official positions decently, and recommending the appointment of men 'of great birth and possessions . . . to lead the people to the greater peace'. In 1439–40 a statute forbade the appointment of justices of the peace with incomes of less than £20 a year from land because of excessive numbers recently appointed in many counties, 'some be of small substance by whom the people will not be governed or ruled and some for their great necessity do great extortion and oppression upon the people'. Edward IV expressed the same view with emphatic clarity in 1478[1] – 'oft times it is seen that when any lord is called to high estate and have not lifelode to support the same dignity, it induces great poverty, indigences, and causes oft times great extortion, embracery and maintenance to be had, to the great trouble of all such countries where such estate shall hap to inherit'.

These 'natural rulers', the well-to-do (what later came to be called the political nation), upon whom such responsibility rested in virtue of their social position, formed no more than about two per cent of the male population. Taxation returns made in 1436 list 51 lay peers, 183 greater knights, 750 lesser knights, 1200 esquires, 1600 men with incomes of £10 to £19 a year from land and 3400 with incomes between £5 and £9, that is on the fringe between yeomen and gentlemen.[2] Of these, historians, until recently, have chosen to regard only the

1. In an act depriving George Neville of the dukedom of Bedford because of poverty.
2. Sir John Fortescue stated that £5 a year was a 'fair' income for a yeoman, but in some counties in 1436 men with such an income could describe themselves as gentlemen. The income of the others (mostly probably under-assessed) was – greater knights average £208, lesser knights £40–£100 (average £60), esquires £20–£39 (average £24).

A modern estimate of peers and gentlemen for *c*. 1500 gives a slightly smaller total (somewhat differently divided): 60 lay peers, 500 knights, 800 esquires and 5000 armigerous gentry.

titled, who received a personal summons to parliament, as the English nobility. The rest, the majority of landowners, they describe as a rural middle class whose interests lay with the urban bourgeoisie. They supposed both this urban and rural middle class together to have tacitly supported the early Tudors in completing the suppression of a peerage of turbulent disposition and troglodyte intelligence, whose ranks were already thinned by the slaughter of the Wars of the Roses. Modern researchers have shattered this tidy theory. If technically the dignity of nobility belonged only to the peerage, their neighbours regarded the richer and more influential knights (some of them were richer than the poorer barons) as lords, and even addressed them as such. The richer landowners, and even many whose incomes were comparatively small, had much more in common with the peers than they had with even the richer merchants. Like the peers they drew the major part of their incomes from land. Their interests and their way of life for those who could afford it (and even for some who couldn't) were those of the peerage. If they waxed rich enough and served the king they could hope, especially in periods of political tension, to break into its ranks. If the possession of a title marked off the major from the minor nobility, the possession of a coat of arms marked off both from the merchants who, indeed, once they had made money, bought estates and entered the coveted ranks of the landowners, the minor nobility.

Contrary to popular delusions, ancient origins and Norman blood were not conspicuous amongst the English peerage. There were fifty-one peers at the beginning of the year 1447, fifty-seven early in the reign of Henry VII. Mortality amongst them, however, was so great that there were far more than six new creations during these forty-odd years. The creation of peerages by royal letters patent, though the earliest example dates from 1387, first became an established practice in the mid-fifteenth century. Kings began, quite deliberately, to create new peers to support the throne and its occupant during seasons of political tension. Between 1447 and 1450 there were no less than fifteen new creations, in 1460–1 nine, followed by another four between 1464 and 1470.[1] Henry VII added only five; all but two, significantly enough, during the first three years of his reign. In the period of calm between 1509 and 1529 his son created only seven. In the years of strain between 1529 and 1547 the number of new creations rose to eighteen.

1. J. E. Powell and K. Wallis, *The House of Lords in the Middle Ages* (London, 1968), chs. 25–9.

Without this sporadic process of creation and the practice of allowing men who married the heiresses of peers to assume the title,[1] the peerage would have come near to extinction. Aristocratic mortality had always been extremely high: during the fourteenth and fifteenth centuries so high that about one-quarter of the peerage families died out in the male line about every twenty-five years. The infant death rate, especially for boys, was appalling, and it may well have been increased by the habit of marrying into decadent stocks for the sake of the land and money to be gained with heiresses. The mortality figures for the second half of the fifteenth century in no way deviate from the usual average. Wild exaggerations, endlessly repeated, of the extinction of *old* noble houses during the Wars of the Roses derive from worthless rumours picked up by foreign letter writers and chroniclers, from the lamentations of a terrified Croyland monk who, giving no details, wrote of 'the deaths of nearly all the nobles of the realm', and from the duke of Buckingham's slanderous propaganda, in Richard III's interest, against the memory of Edward IV. The facts are very different. Excluding descendants of Edward III in the male line, thirty-one peers were killed and twenty executed during the civil wars. During the same period twenty-three titled families died out in the male line. It is, however, mistaken to detect cause and effect between the deaths of individual nobles and the extinction of aristocratic families. Apart from the branches of the royal house (Lancaster, Beaufort and York) the wars extinguished only two *ancient* families (Courtenay and Lovell) and another five, all of which had been ennobled since 1437. It is true that four other families ended on the battlefield, but their representatives had no male heirs, and they and their wives were of an age when they were unlikely to produce more children. Sterility and disease accounted for another six. Six others, all but one recent creations, may have died out partly as a result of the wars, but their end cannot entirely be attributed to them.[2]

Historians have always paid great attention to the dramatic figure of the over-mighty subject, whom no king, strong or weak, could be expected to tolerate. Yet it is well to remember that there was only one Warwick the Kingmaker – and that he died a violent death, after a career hardly conspicuous for prolonged success. The over-mighty subject could hope to succeed in his aims only when, as under Henry

1. Between 1439 and 1504, 21 peerages were continued in this way.
2. See K. B. McFarlane, 'The Wars of the Roses', *Procs. of the British Academy* 1 (1965), where details are given.

VI, the king was too feeble a personality to secure the trust and co-operation of all but a few malcontents amongst his nobility. Contemporary comments and practice make it abundantly clear that kings, well aware of the threat of the over-mighty, also knew well enough that both their own peace and the well-being of their people depended upon confidence and cooperation between themselves and their more powerful subjects. As Henry VI, or his council, wrote to Lord Egremont in 1453 (somewhat hopelessly perhaps, for he was the most shameful thug the Percy family ever spawned) the king had promoted him 'to the worship and estate of baron' for 'the trust and trowing that we had of the good service that ye should do to us in time coming in especial in keeping of the rest and peace of our land and in letting[1] all that should be to the contrary'. Again, in 1483, John Russell, bishop of Lincoln, in a draft sermon intended for delivery to parliament, asserted that the aristocracy were like firm land and rocks in perilous seas and added, 'the politic rule of every region well ordained standeth in the nobles'.

Having no feasible alternative, monarchs practised what they and their advisers preached. Edward IV was glad enough to rely on the power of the Bourchiers in Essex, of Lord Dynham in Devonshire, of the Stanleys in south Lancashire and Cheshire, of the duke of Norfolk, Lord Howard and Earl Ryvers in East Anglia. Far from labouring to destroy the titled nobility, he and his successors promoted to its ranks gentlemen rich enough to sustain the higher dignity and, where local problems were particularly acute, even increased their wealth and power. Edward, in 1461, created William Hastings, Lord Hastings, and by endowing him with part of the confiscated estates of the attainted Butler, Beaumont and Roos families, turned him from a middling landowner into a magnate capable of controlling an area of the Midlands formerly dominated by families conspicuously loyal to Henry VI. Henry VIII still acted in the same way in the 1530s when he endowed John Russell with the greater part of the estates of Tavistock Abbey to give him status great enough to control the turbulent south-west. In 1529, indeed, parliament was even prepared to discuss a private bill (until recently thought to have been an official government scheme), which would have transformed the titled nobility from a group of people with few and, except for trial by peers, trifling legal privileges into a highly privileged caste like the continental aristocracies. The plan would have rendered the fortunes

1. i.e. preventing.

and the local ascendancy of the peerage virtually indestructible, for it proposed to make their estates inalienable except by royal licence under the great seal.

The minor nobility, or gentry, were firmly consolidating their position. In some areas they seem to have been growing in wealth and numbers, if only slowly, for land was hard to come by until the upheavals of the mid-sixteenth century. Their political instincts, or, perhaps more accurately, their desire to profit from contact with the court, also grew stronger. More and more of them became anxious to sit in parliament, for just as rotten boroughs were now first developing, the allied change began which transformed the house of Commons from a body representative of diverse types of communities in the realm to one mainly representative of what was later termed the landed interest. In 1445 a statute laid down that notable knights or such notable esquires and gentlemen who could support the rank of knighthood should represent the counties in parliament, and other evidence shows very strong feeling that the shires should be represented by men who possessed estates within their boundaries. Yet, while creating a monopoly by legislation for themselves in the shire elections, ill-content with the three-tenths share, or less, of the country's representation which the tradition of a century and more allowed them, they quietly and relentlessly broke the law to push the burgesses out of parliament. Despite a statute of 1413 that resident burgesses should represent the boroughs, by 1422 one-quarter of the borough representatives were already non-resident. Another quarter were only technically burgesses: they were lawyers, justices of the peace, members of landed families rather than *bona fide* merchants and traders. Though later parliaments have not been investigated in such detail, the proportion of non-residents seems to have increased considerably by the end of the century.

Over the century, however, their increase in influence may not have been commensurate with their increase in numbers. While the status of the Commons advanced, bringing with it developments in parliamentary procedure which worked in their favour, they never, then or for long afterwards, became regular participants in government. It was already firmly established in the fourteenth century that the king could tax his subjects only with parliament's consent and that law could be changed only by the passing or the repeal of statutes in parliament. Apart from an altercation in 1407 over the Commons' right to initiate the offer for a grant of taxation, these rights were never challenged. The Commons were not yet, however, co-equal with the Lords in the conduct of affairs. Scared by the events of 1399, they formally repudiated any obligation to take part in the 'judgments of parliament', that is, they, in effect, denied responsibility in dangerous questions of high politics, leaving them to the peers. Henry IV conceded their role to be that of 'petitioners and demanders'. They regarded themselves more as watch-dogs against corrupt and inefficient administration than as formulators or directors of government policy. Henry IV also pointed out their additional function as advisers and assenters to legislation. Indeed, during his reign and his son's it became normal in time of parliament for petitions to be presented to the Commons for their sponsorship instead of to the king as formerly. Even more significant, it became normal for the Commons to take part in the enactment of all legislation, and by the middle of the century this had become more or less an established rule. They did not, however, participate as equals. The king and the lords could still change the wording of petitions from the Commons upon which statutes were based without sending back their amendments for the Commons' consent, and the statutes themselves were often drafted by the judges after the end of parliament. Statutes could indeed be 'the government's vague reply to vaguely worded complaints', though from the middle of the century greater precision was introduced by 'the bill containing within itself the form of the act', that is, a formal request containing the actual detailed statute desired. Nearly all the earlier examples were official, but, as Dr B. Wilkinson has remarked, this does not alter the fact that such a feature allowed the Commons more control over the final form of legislation. Despite these and other advances, however, all through the century, the Great Council of peers still met more frequently than parliament, and the very success, particularly the financial success, of the Yorkists and Henry VII reduced parliament's importance. By the 1480s men talked of parliament as 'the place of worldly policy' where every man was represented and the acts of which, therefore, bound him as if he himself were present. Increasingly long intervals between its sessions,[1] however, meant, in practice, that less 'worldly policy' was therein discussed than in the days of the Lancastrians. Except when short of money for foreign war or faced with the legal problems of adequately punishing treason and rebellion, the monarchy gladly managed without it. Henry VII even claimed virtue in sparing his subjects the

1. Parliaments were held in 1461–2, 1463–5, 1467–8, 1469 'summoned, but did not meet', 1470–1, 1472–5, 1483 (2), 1484, 1485–6, 1487, 1489–90, 1491–2, 1495, 1497, 1504, 1510, 1512–14, 1515, 1523, 1529.

trouble and expense of attendance – though there is some little evidence that some people at least resented his attitude. The royal council, not parliament, was, as always, the centre of government.

Parliaments being sporadic occasions and all formal institutions so inadequate, clientage, the personal relationship between lord and man, remained the most powerful bond which held society together. All over Europe a combination of 'pork barrel' morality and fear of the great formed the basis of government. Machiavelli and Guicciardini in Italy, Cardinal Ximines' secretary in Spain, all claimed government to be impossible without the distribution of benefits and rewards. In pre-industrial societies, in almost every European country until the end of the eighteenth century, state service was one of the principal ways of acquiring a fortune, service with magnates for acquiring at least a competence. Rewards went according to status: those who possessed most expected to gain most, and the majority in their relations with the state felt it more blessed to receive than to give. The desire for gain on the one side and the volume of patronage at the disposal of the other was one of the key factors in a political system best looked upon as a complicated series of business relationships touching and intersecting at a great many points. The households of the greater lay and ecclesiastical magnates reproduced the royal court in miniature, and according to men's importance they gravitated to the microcosms or the macrocosm, or both.

Judge William Paston served the bishop of Norwich as steward, no doubt, at least, a semi-sinecure. His son, John I, though he held no formal post, made himself useful to the *parvenu* local magnate, Sir John Fastolf. Of the third generation (two of them at least educated at Cambridge or one of the Inns of Court), John entered the service of the last of the Mowbray dukes of Norfolk and his parents thought of getting Edmund into the 'familia' of Thomas Rotheram, bishop of Lincoln and later archbishop of York. The heir, also confusingly called John, they sent to take advantage of the more lucrative opportunities of the royal household. The Howards served the Mowbray dukes of Norfolk, the Brandons, the de la Pole dukes of Suffolk and ultimately stepped into their ducal shoes.

For those who made the grade the rewards of such service could be enormous. In proportion to their fortunes the gains of lesser men could make up as significant a part of their total incomes as the annuities which magnates like the dukes of Somerset and York drew at the Exchequer.[1] According to the taxation returns of 1436, royal

1. See above, p. 71.

annuities and pensions increased the average income of the peers from £768 to £865 a year – though the figures probably under-estimate their personal incomes. In 1461 Edward IV granted Sir John Fogge, the treasurer of his household, the office of keeper of the writs of the court of Common Pleas. Contemporaries estimated that the office would bring its holder at least 100 marks a year in fees over and above its nominal salary of 10 marks. Again, a successful administrative career brought Sir John Popham of South Chalfont (d. 1463) an annuity of 20 marks from the duke of York, 100 from the Exchequer and he received another 6 as constable of Southampton – a total of £84 to add to the £40 which he drew from his own estates.

English historians have called the method of social and political control exercised through networks of clientage 'bastard feudalism'. Until recently, looking upon it as a predominantly fifteenth-century phenomenon, they largely blamed upon it the century's most prominent social and political abuses, arguing that the late medieval substitution of wages and fees in cash for the fief in land degraded the traditional bond between lord and man into a violently unstable, evil relationship. More recent writers have, on the whole, rejected this argument, pointing out that neither bastard feudalism nor social and political violence were exclusively fifteenth-century developments. Bastard feudalism was already dominant in the early fourteenth century, and it continued strong well into the late sixteenth. The payment of annual wages may well, in fact, have given a magnate firmer control over his dependents – his affinity, as they were collectively called – for it was easier to stop the payment of wages to recalcitrant members than it was to deprive them of fiefs, of landed estates. Social subordination and dependence were constant features of English society for many centuries, and it can be plausibly argued that bastard feudalism based on cash payments was a more subtle and sophisticated form of this relationship than classical feudalism based upon the fief.

The king relied upon the loyalty of those to whom he gave offices. As the Croyland Chronicler remarked of Edward IV during his later years – 'as he had taken care to distribute the most trustworthy of his servants throughout all parts of the kingdom, as keepers of castles, manors, forests and parks, no attempt whatever could be made in any part of the kingdom by any person, however shrewd he might be, but what he was immediately charged with the same thing to his face'. This alone was not enough, and the king also relied, perhaps to an even greater extent, upon the loyalty of his aristocratic clients and through them upon the fidelity of their blood relations and retainers. The *Arrivall of King Edward IV* tells that during his reconquest of the country in 1471, three thousand men joined the king's small army at Leicester 'and, in substance, they were such as were towards the Lord Hastings'. Between 1461 and the time of his death in 1483 Hastings' affinity included ninety indentured retainers in addition to his household and estate servants and legal counsel. Including two other peers, nine knights, fifty-nine esquires and twenty gentlemen, they extended his influence through Leicestershire, Derbyshire and Staffordshire, many of them serving as sheriffs and justices of the peace. Such magnates as these regarded their regional interests with a jealous eye and very much resented poaching. Warwick the Kingmaker detested Lord Herbert because, with Edward IV's support, he reduced the Neville interest in South Wales. In an indenture, dated 28 July 1474, the earl of Northumberland technically became the duke of Gloucester's 'man', but this was less a friendly alliance than a treaty defining their respective spheres of interest in the north. Lower down the scale, when a friend of Sir William Plumpton's, whose 'lord' was the earl of Northumberland, approached Lord Hastings to get Sir William made a justice of the peace, Hastings would have none of it, claiming that such action would make 'a jealousy' between him and Northumberland.

By modern standards such a system of government through the rich was, of course, rank with oppression and injustice. Gangs of retainers, wearing a lord's livery, could, and often did, terrorize neighbours and tenants, and lords were capable of carrying maintenance (the support of a client's case in the law courts) to abominable lengths. Lesser men often found it wise to be circumspect to the point of abnegation in dealing with the powerful. As John Paston wrote in 1452 after several of the duke of Norfolk's servants had assaulted him outside Norwich Cathedral, being 'my Lord's man and his homager . . . as soon as knowledge was had of my Lord's coming to Framlingham, I never attempted to proceed against him as justice and law would, but to trust to my said Lord that his Highness would see this punished'. High ideals of conduct often degenerated into sticks with which to beat opponents. Sir John Fastolf oppressed a London neighbour who, he knew, could not afford the cost of taking legal action against him, while, in his turn, self-righteously accusing the duke of Suffolk of abominable oppressions and assessing his claim for damages at five thousand marks. Dependent as it was upon the great, the crown was often forced to turn a blind eye upon their local vagaries – and it continued to do so as late as the reign of Elizabeth I, if not later.

Bastard feudalism, like every other system, easily got out of hand. In both the fourteenth century and the fifteenth it took an evil turn when the king was weak and his capabilities little respected – under Edward II no less than under Henry VI it gave resentful magnates the military power to turn upon the court. Even under more normal conditions its perennial tendency to abuse called for restraint. Just as parliament restricted membership of juries to men of property, so it restricted affinities to the landed aristocracy. Under Richard II complaints were heard that ex-war captains continued to keep retainers after their return to England. So in 1390 a statute forbade any but peers to take retainers, or any men below the rank of esquire to take such service. Moreover, a retainer not paid as legal counsel or directly employed in the household or estate management of a peer was to be engaged only under written indentures and for life. Edward IV, in a statute of 1468, cut off this last concession and forbade retaining, except for counsel, household, and estate management, for peers as well as lesser men, but probably finding so complete a reversal of convention self-destructive, quietly allowed it to continue within its former limits. Henry VII at first followed Edward's example, then in 1504 returned to the policy of 1468, while in practice operating a system of licensing for retaining.[1]

From 1392 the nobility had sworn oaths upon at least four occasions against taking to violence in future and, when aggrieved, to seek remedy by peaceful means alone. In 1461 and again in 1485 they swore neither to receive nor to maintain criminals. While Henry VII left them free to wield their traditional rods upon other men, he, as they must have thought, flayed them with scorpions in his attempts to fulfil one of the main functions of kingship – that of binding the nobility to the crown, keeping the peace between them and so making certain that, rather than turning their resources against each other and against him, they used them to keep their own rather vaguely defined bailiwicks in order. Between 1485 and 1504 he attainted nine peers of treason. He ultimately reversed five of these attainders and his son a sixth. Henry, however, tempered pardon with caution, mercy with greed, rarely making complete restitution of forfeited property. The reversals took place, if one may

1. Even the statute of 1504 (which anyway expired on Henry VII's death) allowed counsel, household and estate officials. There is evidence that some great landowners, at least, evaded it by multiplying household and estate offices.

use the term, piece-meal. Nobles like Lord Zouche and Thomas, earl of Surrey, were pardoned their lives but their estates were, to a greater or lesser degree, withheld from them, and the hope of recovery held out over long years as an incentive to loyalty and good service.

The king ingeniously tangled others in a web of legal chicanery. Upon some he imposed enormous fines for various offences: fines which he then suspended whilst holding the possibility of collection over the offenders' heads, threatening ruin if they fell out of step. Others he forced to enter into bonds and recognizances carrying heavy financial penalties, binding them to maintain their allegiance and to be of good behaviour towards the king and his heirs. Lord Burgavenny, for example, was forced in 1501 to admit a debt of £100000, the suspended penalty for unlawful retaining. Lord Mountjoy had to provide bonds for 20000 marks that he would be true to his allegiance while he was keeper of Hammes Castle. Henry bullied the marquess of Dorset into making over the greater part of his estates to trustees appointed by the king. If he behaved himself for the rest of his life they would be handed over to his heir: if not, they would be forfeit to the crown. During his reign, and especially towards its end, Henry had pressed the greater part of the peerage, as well as scores of other men, under these brutal forms of control. At some time forty-six or forty-seven out of sixty-two peerage families lay, *in terrorem*, at the king's mercy: seven under attainder, thirty-six under bonds and recognizances, of whom five were also heavily fined, another was probably also fined and three more were at some time under subpoenas with heavy monetary sanctions.

The more remote and ungovernable an area, the more the reliance on great estates and the patronage they carried with them. The tendency is illustrated in the various methods through which the government dealt with the special needs of Wales and the north. Though generally lumped together as if they were more or less identical 'special areas', their problems were, in fact, different. After the collapse of Owen Glyndwr's revolt (1400–9) the problems of Wales were far less acute than those of the northern marches against Scotland. Wales, though always disorderly, became more peaceful, while the north remained a turbulent frontier district. In 1465 Edward IV created for William, Lord Herbert (three years later made earl of Pembroke) the lordship of Raglan, giving him the traditional, almost vice-regal, powers of a Lord Marcher. By 1478, however, he seems to have realized that such great powers were no longer essential for a subject in this area. The Yorkists themselves were the greatest landowners in Wales and the Marches. Apart from the Herberts and the Stafford dukes of Buckingham there was no group of resident nobles powerful enough either to impede or take charge of local affairs. Since 1473 Edward had developed a kind of vice-regal government, nominally headed by the infant Prince of Wales, through the prince's council, later known as the Council in the Marches of Wales, situated at Ludlow. Owing to minorities the Stafford estates were in the king's hands between 1460 and 1498, except for the years 1474 to 1483 when the duke was closely allied to the royal family by his marriage to the queen's sister. The Staffords were therefore left with their hereditary power intact,[1] but in 1478 the king, by inducing, or forcing, William Herbert's eighteen-year-old heir to exchange his earldom for that of Huntingdon, gathered even more local estates into royal hands. The king, therefore, as the greatest landowner in the area, could exercise immense patronage and govern the area directly through the court and council at Ludlow, leaving the pettier Lords Marcher in undisturbed, and harmless, possession of their franchises.

The north was far, far more intractable. With Scotland still independent the north was still a frontier. A frontier in those days was not a neat line of barbed wire fence. It was a march, a no man's land of chronic disorder many miles deep: a land which only magnates with warlike retinues could guard and control. Violent, and remote from the centre of government, harried from Scotland, the north found adequate rulers only in the great local families, the Percys, the Nevilles, the Dacres, and the Cliffords. The Percy household was a replica of the royal court, the estate officers attending on the family in rotation just as the knights and esquires of the royal household alternated service at court with residence in the countryside. All

1. This connection with the crown and the ancient rights of the Stafford dukes of Buckingham (as compared with the very recent extension of the estates and powers of the Herberts) would (though this is admittedly hypothesis) have made it impossible for Edward to reduce their power. In any case long minorities (covering 58 years between 1368 and 1498) had seriously weakened both their wealth and influence during the fifteenth century. By *c.* 1520 Duke Edward of Buckingham found that if he tried to increase traditional rents he lost the loyalty of his tenants, and he was so unpopular that he needed an escort of 300 or 400 armed men to make a tour of his estates. See T. B. Pugh, *The Marcher Lordships of South Wales, 1415–1536* (1963), p. iii. His father (d. 1483) seems to have been equally unpopular. So far from the Lords Marcher being a menace to government, as traditionally held, it seems that the creation of the Council in the Marches of Wales filled something of a power vacuum in a way that the creation of the Council in the North did not.

four of the great families lost some of their power in the 1530s, but their sole legatee was not, as long tradition would have it, the Council in the North. As Mr M. E. James has shown, although the council, originally formed in the early 1480s as the council of Richard of Gloucester, had done a great deal for peace and justice in the Marches, its efficiency fluctuated greatly over the decades. When Henry VIII and Thomas Cromwell broke the Percy hegemony in the north, they did not substitute for it a new council of middle-class bureaucrats. They set (amongst others) in the room of Earl Henry the Unthrifty, a hopelessly unstable character, a Percy retainer, Sir Thomas Wharton, suitably ennobled as Lord Wharton and his income increased for the purpose, largely from the Percy estates, from about £100 to about £600 or £700 a year. Henry at the same time took care to attract the local gentry to the monarchy by exercising directly, as the crown had done for a long time past in Wales, the patronage which the Percys themselves had formerly dispensed in the north. Thus the king could now offer the prospect of greater rewards than the Percys or any other of the great northern magnates could hold out to their dependents. Even so, there was something of a reaction under Edward and Mary and it was only after 1570 that the power of the great families finally passed to civil servants from London. Meanwhile the new Lord Wharton belonged to the same landed society as the magnates, and his far from pleasant personality partook of many of their worst characteristics. The late fifteenth- and the early sixteenth-century monarchy could not smash territorial power in an area such as this. It could only contrive something of a reduction and a change of emphasis within the group of landowners. In the north it still took a gentleman-thug to rule gentlemen-(and other) thugs.

The English state at this time was going roughly the same way as most European states in relying for government and order on co-operation between the monarchy and a powerful aristocracy constantly maintained in numbers from the landed class immediately below it. During the later Middle Ages nowhere in Europe, with the paradoxical exception of the commercial republic of Venice, had the nobility become a tightly closed group. The Italian nobilities generally were comparatively easy of access to men of wealth and personal valour until about 1560. In Germany the nobility tacitly accepted families which achieved riches and prestige. In France the great princely magnates, the dukes of Burgundy, Brittany, Anjou, and Guienne, whose ambitions had seriously threatened the country's unity, disappeared between 1460 and 1500. More of their power, however, fell to the provincial aristocracy than to the monarchy: once more an aristocracy whose ranks would have grown bare indeed without enormous numbers of new creations from lower ranks. In some provinces the average duration of a noble lineage was no more than three to six generations, and by the time of the Wars of Religion very few houses could claim that their nobility preceded the Hundred Years War. From their greater members the king appointed the governors who administered the great duchies which had escheated to the crown. Although feudal relationships based on tenure still prevailed to a greater extent than in England (because in France the greater estates were more compact), developments similar to English bastard feudalism were also strong. The patron-client relationship was normal.

Similar as they were in kind, there was, nevertheless, a considerable difference in degree between England and the continental states. Owing to its smaller size and past history England exhibited a milder, less extreme variation upon the general pattern. Smaller than France or Germany, less geographically and racially divided than Scotland, it had been earlier united and was, still, more easily kept under central control. Provincial feeling in England, though sporadically dangerous, was insignificant compared with the deep gulfs of separatist feeling in France. Moreover, as Froissart noted at the end of the fourteenth century, 'the lands and revenues of the English barons are here and there and much scattered'. Although the possession of wide estates gave particular noblemen predominance in certain areas, it never, as elsewhere, gave them an undisputed legal control. In 1408 a Heidelberg professor (possibly Conrad of Gelnhausen) wrote: 'Every nobleman however modest his standing is king in his own territory; every city exercises royal power within its walls.' No English lawyer could ever have made such a statement or put forward the Norman plea 'Le duché n'est pas du royaume'. At the end of the fifteenth century the Venetian envoy wrote that the English nobility possessed no fortresses and no judicial powers, concluding from this, they 'are nothing more than rich gentlemen in possession of great quantities of land'. He did not think this lack of formal legal power entirely to the country's advantage, claiming that England's appalling level of crime was due to an excessive concentration of criminal justice in over-centralized royal courts, and implying that standards would have been higher had judicial powers been dispersed, as elsewhere, in the hands of the aristocracy. He may have been right. On the other hand, greater powers and greater abuses went together. In France, where many provincial nobles enjoyed almost vice-regal powers such as only the Percys and a few Marcher Lords possessed in England, numerous complaints suggest that the perversion of justice by great men was even more prevalent than it was in England.

Everywhere in the fifteenth century government lay with the men of property. At the same time they required control, or they failed through lack of agreement amongst themselves. Even in the Italian city republics, where the rights of the rich in government had been most unfettered, they were failing owing to violent internal quarrels and the lack of any sufficient degree of self-imposed discipline. By the middle of the century it was everywhere apparent that only monarchy could provide stability through a nice balance of reward and fear. This type of monarchical state, the 'New Monarchy' as it has been called in England, was not, however, as some textbooks still imply, the same thing as the modern state. In the first place, it involved submission to a family, to a dynasty, which tended, indeed was expected (as other landowners treated their estates), to regard the country as a form of property, as the monarchical 'lifelode'. Yet because of its international position, it tended to demand excessive contributions from its subjects to vindicate an alien family inheritance by means of war. This secondary claim the English firmly, if unconsciously, repudiated under Henry VI, forcing, as we have seen, the monarchy back into the increasingly archaic role of estate manager, keeping it, by continental standards, poor, circumscribing its ambitions and, for the future, frustrating the development of more extensive powers.

Secondly, the function of the state being disciplinary, still primarily an institution for the suppression of disorder and violence, its positive appeal was comparatively weak. The formulation of policy lay at the king's discretion to a degree unknown today. At the same time, lacking direct control of coercive power, he could hardly govern at all without the trust and the local cooperation of his nobility and the counsel of that section of them interested enough to attend upon him in person at court. And the nobility in spite of its constant change of membership remained as rich and powerful as it had ever been. The main contestants in the Wars of the Roses were all richer than their grandfathers had been, and the late fifteenth and the early sixteenth century was a period of remarkable stability for aristocratic property. Half a century of political conflict, with all its dangerous threats to property, followed by Henry VII's relentless, legalistic pressure, had not undermined their stability as a class. It had made them more nervous, more tractable, more disciplined, more inclined to co-operate. Even so, however strong the king was, he was still forced, like kings elsewhere in Europe, to leave them considerable freedom in their own areas, bind them to him with offices and annuities and, where necessary, impose sanctions upon a disgruntled minority. Until the Reformation for the first time introduced an ideological opposition founded upon opposing religious convictions, politics still centred upon the relationship between the king and the magnates, and lower in the scale between the magnates and the minor nobility or gentry. Even though the magnates had outgrown an earlier and cruder stage of political life in which they had blatantly expected a king to be lavish with outright gifts,[1] they still expected to be the state's chief beneficiaries. They still expected kings to be generous, and most great estates were still ultimately built up through the royal favour.

Within these limitations the quality of government varied according to the character of the reigning king. The king who administered his vast patronage wisely and fairly and kept reasonably above the personal feuds of the magnates could hope for enough cooperation from the aristocracy and their clients to make the system work. If the king was a minor, senile, or weak in resolution, control of patronage fell to a faction and the excluded revolted. We cannot, therefore, regard the factions which sprang up from time to time as political parties in the modern sense. They were merely groups of people drawn together by a common personal interest, often of the most temporary kind, either to exploit the feeble, yet wilful incompetence of a king like Henry VI, or by reaction to express their resentment against the exploitation of such a controlling group. Once those lower in the social scale, however, as in 1450, tried to influence events and policy by armed rebellion, they dropped their differences to join in suppressing the unruly populace. The 'people' could only protest violently and at intervals in riots and rebellions always, at the last, ineffective before equally violent suppression. Beyond a certain point

1. cf. the letter written in 1097 by Stephen, Count of Blois and Chartres, to his wife Adela, a daughter of William the Conqueror: 'Indeed, I tell you that in these days there is not another such as he [Alexius Comnenus, emperor of Byzantium] alive under the sky. He showers riches on all our leaders, relieves all our knights with gifts, and refreshes all our poor with feasts. . . . Your father, my beloved, gave many and great gifts, but he was almost as nothing to this man.' Quoted from R. H. C. Davis, *King Stephen* (1967), p. 2.

the existence of well-defined factions, or parties, was, of itself, a sign of serious political malaise. They were, in fact, generally found in times when the monarch was weak. Normally politics meant the widest possible cooperation, and the ease with which men crossed the line from one group to another, thus reuniting the shattered ranks, once a new king's accession gave them a new focus for loyalty, can be surprising to minds dominated by twentieth-century ideals of stable political parties based upon well-defined principles and ideas and which are either 'in' or 'out' of office. Though, as pointed out earlier, theologians and lawyers had worked out extremely subtle principles of political obligation, some of which, at times of crisis, men surprisingly low in the social scale could echo, very little in the way of constitutional principles determined the course of political events.

Though conflict there was in plenty, men yearned for stability. It may well be that the aristocracy desired it most of all, for we have seen how tardily and reluctantly they took to armed conflict against Henry VI.[1] Very few felt towards the house of York, or later towards the almost unknown Henry VII, so strong an emotional attachment that they would risk their estates for the sake of a dynasty. Contemporary conventions – political thought would, perhaps, be too dignified a word for these almost superstitious instincts – made changes of allegiance decent and generally, though not always, easy. The belief, by no means yet a mere outworn cliché, that the hand of God was supremely active in directing the affairs of princes, as they were too powerful to be checked by moral means alone, reinforced the dictates of self-interest. God having given his verdict in favour of a prince on the field of battle, it was respectable enough, if a man did not do it too often, to change sides and reap the consequent, and normal, rewards of such divinely indicated action. As Bishop John Morton told the duke of Buckingham when justifying his change of allegiance from Henry VI to Edward IV, he would have preferred to see Henry on the throne, but 'if the secret judgment of God have otherwise provided, I purpose not to spurn against a prick, nor labour to set up that God pulleth down'.[2]

The fifteenth century (possibly because its sources are so intractable

1. Both the late K. B. McFarlane and Dr R. L. Storey have shown that men lower in the social scale seem to have taken to arms much more readily than the nobility. (They had less to lose!)

2. Although the speech is an invention of Sir Thomas More, it expresses contemporary views accurately enough.

and confusing) seems, even more than most, an age of contradictions. Due in part to the Black Death, an epoch of diminished population, it was at the same time for most people an era of modest prosperity between two ages when population growth depressed the standards of a large section of the people. Although there may have been some great landowners, particularly in the Midlands, parts of the south, and Wales and the Marches, who suffered economically, evidence of extensive building, both secular and ecclesiastical, tells strongly against any theory of universal or long-continued depression. Turbulent, violent, and corrupt the age certainly was, though probably not more so than earlier times. After all, King John could live down the murder of his nephew, Richard III could not. Edward I's treatment of the greater nobility was even more arbitrary than Henry VII's, and Sir Maurice Powicke once wrote of the late thirteenth century, 'corruption was the curse of social relationship everywhere'. Whether conditions had changed for the better by the end of the fifteenth century it is impossible on the evidence available to say, but at least men were deeply aware of the need to improve their standards. A good part of Edmund Dudley's *Tree of Commonwealth* (1509) is devoted to exhortations to all sorts and conditions of men, from the highest to the lowest, to strive after standards of conduct which decent men today consider normal, but which until as late as the seventeenth century were considerably above the customary practice of even the upper classes.

It has been condemned as an age lacking in saintliness, heroism, and greatness, with few interesting characters above the gangster level. It is true that outside its architecture and its music, fifteenth-century culture has little appeal today, though before its people are condemned *en bloc* as uninteresting boors we should remember that very little in the way of intimate, personal correspondence has survived. We might well take a different view if letters as well as scrappy financial memoranda had come down to us from the pens of such as Sir John Howard – for even his financial notes indirectly reveal him, harsh and unpleasant though some of his personal traits were, as a man of considerable culture, interested in music and literature. Men of his kind lived in more comfortable houses, read more and, in general, probably lived a pleasanter existence than their forebears a century and a half earlier.

The opinions of outsiders, even if prejudiced, are often revealing. The English were not admired abroad. Foreign propaganda depicted them, from time to time, as a violent race of king slayers – though no

Englishman ever ventured, like Duke John the Fearless of Burgundy (1404–19) and his pamphleteer, John Petit, to write treatises justifying political murder. Even discounting the most extreme opinions, foreign writers from Froissart (1377–1410) to Waurin (1394 – c. 1474) wrote sourly of the violence and treachery of the English: their faithlessness became such a byword that it was only ironically foreigners talked about English loyalty. Though we can discount the jaundiced remarks of the papal envoy, Pietro Aliprando, in 1473 (his experiences in England had been exceptionally unfortunate) – 'In the morning they are as devout as angels, after dinner they are like devils', a less prejudiced observer, the Venetian ambassador of 1497, described the English as almost ludicrously insular, licentious but incapable of love, a mean and stingy race, ready to compound almost any injury for a suitable sum of money. He went on to describe England as a country where men have no 'sincere and solid friendship amongst themselves, insomuch that they do not trust each other to discuss either public or private affairs together in the confidential manner we do in Italy'. Whether the Italians were more trusting or not, the ambassador was right in stressing this tense, suspicious, almost neurotic quality as an English characteristic.

Yet at the same time they were neither fanatical nor vindictive. Fifteenth-century religion, though often a somewhat uninspiring nexus of cash and works, as the bishops' attitude towards the Lollards shows, at least lacked the ferocity which is so often the other face of saintliness and which was to be so repellent an aspect of the Reformation. In secular life too, as noted earlier, men remained on guardedly amiable terms with each other in circumstances which would be almost inconceivable today. This tendency was as prominent in political as in private life. Partly because skilled administrative talent was rare, partly because unity was so highly desirable and the monarchy so badly needed whatever support it could get, very few, except at the highest level, suffered from the effects of revolution. Continuity in office over the revolution of 1399 was remarkable; and, later, out of forty of Edward IV's councillors who were still living after 1485 twenty-two were councillors to Henry VII and even twenty of Richard III's councillors served him in the same capacity. The same applied to estate administrators, though it is true that Henry VII later dismissed former Yorkist servants on the slightest suspicion of disloyalty. In this, as in many other ways, English practices run remarkably parallel to Machiavelli's observations in *Il Principe*: he laid down the general maxim that no ruler who came to power by violence could afford to rely exclusively on those who brought him to power. The circle was too narrow and their demands for spoils so excessive that they would alienate more potential support than they provided.

In financial matters, too, Machiavelli's views appear singularly apposite to late fifteenth- and early sixteenth-century England. He thought a wise prince should be careful with his resources even to the point of meanness, for it was safer to be considered mean than to risk the poverty, and consequent political tension, which an over-lavish dissipation of revenues amongst friends and supporters brought with it. A prince should so manage his affairs that 'he is able to engage in enterprises without burdening his people; thus it comes to pass that he exercises liberality towards all from whom he does not take, who are numberless, and meanness towards those to whom he does not give, who are few . . . when neither their property nor their honour is touched the majority of men live content'.[1] Robert Fabyan, the author of the *Great Chronicle of London*, would have understood such sentiments immediately – and this particular section of *The Prince* might well be a pen-portrait of Henry VII.

In some spheres the modest progress of the fifteenth century laid the base for the more spectacular developments of the sixteenth. The emergence, for the first time, of a cultivated lay intelligentsia would hardly have been possible without the wider diffusion of education during the later Middle Ages, narrowly practical, vocational and prosaic though it was. In other respects the century's main characteristic may well turn out to have been its conservatism: a conservatism which, it has perhaps been insufficiently recognized, continued as, at least, a prominent influence in sixteenth-century England. The Reformation, after all, as the Elizabethan Puritans asserted in season and out of season, failed to eradicate the antiquated administrative structure and the financial abuses of the *ecclesia anglicana*. Its haphazard, medieval iniquities flourished until the nineteenth century. In architecture and in literature humanist, classical style conspicuously failed until the seventeenth century to extinguish the older, native gothic taste.

Politically England's small size and its isolation, guarded by the sea, permitted it to thrive in its peculiar conservative way. Philippe de Commynes remarked that, compared with other countries, it suffered little from its domestic upheavals. In spite of various, and

1. *The Prince* (Everyman reprint, 1952), pp. 88–101.

rather overrated, administrative experiments, both Edward IV and Henry VII, being politically insecure, were highly conventional in their approach to government. Their traditional methods in many ways set the tone of Tudor monarchy which, after the taxation reforms of 1513–15 (which were, in the long run, unsuccessful) and the various plans of Thomas Cromwell, was curiously backward-looking. As noted earlier, by continental standards the English nobility were merely rich landowners. Even during the worst troubles of the fifteenth century they never, unlike some of their French counterparts, sought independence from the monarchy. They sought their due share of the rewards which it could bestow, together with the maintenance of their own local influence. The monarchy, safe from attack in its insular position, but thereby lacking the excuse of defence for developing its powers, could do little to challenge this predominance. True, in the course of the sixteenth century bastard feudalism gradually gave way to less crude forms of clientage, but paradoxically only during the later seventeenth century when the aristocracy and the gentry gained the upper hand in their partnership with the monarchy were they prepared to allow taxation to replace landowning as the mainstay of government finance and thus allow the possibility of development to the modern state. Much as they wished to do so, the Tudors could not escape from the conservative methods which circumstances had forced both the Lancastrians and the Yorkists to adopt. In spite of advances and refinements in the art of government under the Tudors, it was the seventeenth, not the fifteenth century that, in England, saw the end of the transition from the medieval to the modern state.

Select bibliography

Abbreviations used

B.I.H.R.	Bulletin of the Institute of Historical Research
B.J.R.L.	Bulletin of the John Rylands Library
E.H.R.	English Historical Review
Ec. H.R.	Economic History Review
P.P.	Past and Present
T.R. Hist. S.	Transactions of the Royal Historical Society

These notes are intended for those who wish to study the fifteenth century more intensively. To anyone well acquainted with this period my immense debt to many of these works will be immediately obvious.

The standard general work is E. F. Jacob, *The Fifteenth Century* (Oxford, 1961), which contains an exhaustive bibliography. Original sources are discussed in C. L. Kingsford, *English Historical Literature in the Fifteenth Century* (Oxford, 1913, repr. New York, 1964). A. R. Myers, *England in the Late Middle Ages* (London, 2nd ed. 1963) and G. A. Holmes, *The Late Middle Ages, 1275-1485* (Edinburgh, 1962) are good introductions. A. R. Myers, *English Historical Documents*, vol. 4, 1327-1485 (London, 1969) and C. H. Williams, *English Historical Documents*, vol. 5, 1485-1558 (London, 1967) are splendid collections of extracts from contemporary documents with valuable introductions; C. L. Kingsford, *Prejudice and Promise in Fifteenth Century England* (Oxford, 1925, repr. London, 1962), remains interesting and useful. *English Government and Society*, Ed. C. M. D. Crowder (Edinburgh and London, 1967), reprints a number of useful essays from *History Today*. K. Fowler, *The Age of Plantagenet and Valois* (London, 1967), gives a comparative account of England and France during the period of the Hundred Years War.

Chapter 2

The only modern work to attempt an over-all interpretation is A. R. Bridbury, *Economic Growth: England in the Later Middle Ages* (London, 1962), which stresses advancing prosperity. It has been criticized by E. Miller, 'The English Economy in the Thirteenth Century', *P.P.,* no. 28 (1964) for pressing too far a conception of economic growth anachronistic in late medieval conditions. W. G. Hoskins, *The Making of the English Landscape* (London, 1971), gives a fascinating descriptive survey of changes in the English countryside. P. Laslett, *The World We Have Lost* (London, 1971), deals mainly with the seventeenth century, but many of its very stimulating general remarks apply equally well to the fifteenth.

The following is a selection from numerous valuable studies on particular topics and regions. **Population and prices**: J. C. Russell, *British Medieval Population* (Albuquerque, 1948), is a valuable pioneer survey, though its statistics have been seriously criticized. Population trends before the Black Death are controversial, see B. F. Harvey, 'The Population Trend in England between 1300 and 1348', *T.R. Hist. S.*, 5 ser., vol. 16 (1966), and the articles there cited; H. S. Lucas, 'The Great European Famine of 1315, 1316 and 1317', *Speculum*, vol. 5 (1930), repr. in *Essays in Economic History*, Ed. E. M. Carus-Wilson (London, 1962); M. M. Postan, 'Some Economic Evidence of Declining Population in the Later Middle Ages', *Ec. H.R.,* 2 ser., vol. 2 (1949–50); J. M. W. Bean, 'Plague, Population and Economic Decline in the Later Middle Ages', ibid., vol. 15 (1962–3); S. L. Thrupp, 'The Problem of Replacement Rates in Late Medieval English Population', ibid., vol. 18 (1965); Y. S. Brenner, 'The Inflation of Prices in Early Sixteenth-Century England', ibid., vol. 14 (1961–2); E. H. Phelps-Brown and S. V. Hopkins, 'Seven Centuries of the Prices of Consumables, Compared with Builders' Wage Rates', *Economica*, new ser., vol. 23 (1956), repr. *Essays*, Ed. Carus-Wilson, vol. 2 (1962). **Taxation**: R. S. Schofield, 'The Geographical Distribution of Wealth in England, 1334–1649', *Ec. H.R.*, 2 ser., vol. 18 (1965); see also Bridbury (above). **Agrarian development**: M. Beresford, *The Lost Villages of England* (London, 1954), deals with wool production and the enclosure movement. This should now be supplemented by M. Beresford and J. G. Hurst, *Deserted Medieval Villages*, Part 1 (London, 1971). In spite of their titles the following contain a good deal of information about the fifteenth century: P. J. Bowden, *The Wool Trade in Tudor and Stuart England* (London,

1962); J. Thirsk (Ed.), *The Agrarian History of England and Wales*, vol. 4, 1500–1640 (Cambridge, 1967). For recent criticism of these last three works and an opposing interpretation see I. Blanchard, 'Population Change, Enclosure and the Early Tudor Economy', *Ec. H.R.*, 2 ser., vol. 23 (1970), and T. H. Lloyd, 'The Movement of Wool Prices in Medieval England', *Ec. H.R.* Supplements, no. 6 (1973).

The following are a selection from many valuable studies of particular **Estates and regions**: J. M. W. Bean, *The Estates of the Percy Family, 1416–1537* (Oxford, 1958); F. R. H. Du Boulay, *The Lordship of Canterbury: An Essay on Medieval Society* (London, 1966); 'A Rentier Economy in the Later Middle Ages: The Archbishopric of Canterbury', and 'Who were farming the English Demesnes at the End of the Middle Ages', *Ec. H.R.*, 2 ser., vol. 16 (1963–4), vol. 17 (1964–5); R. B. Dobson, *Durham Priory, 1400–1456* (1973); C. Dyer, 'A Redistribution of Incomes in Fifteenth-Century England', *P.P.*, no. 39 (1968); E. M. Carus-Wilson, 'Evidences of Industrial Growth on Some Fifteenth-Century Manors', *Ec. H.R.*, ser. 2, vol. 12 (1959–60), repr. Essays, Ed. Carus-Wilson, vol. 2 (1962); R. R. Davies, 'Baronial Accounts, Incomes and Arrears in the later Middle Ages', *Ec. H.R.*, 2 ser., vol. 21 (1968); R. R. Davies and J. Beverley Smith, 'The Social Structure of Medieval Glamorgan', in *Glamorgan County History*, vol. 3, *The Middle Ages*, Ed. T. B. Pugh (Cardiff, 1971); J. Hatcher, *Rural Economy and Society in the Duchy of Cornwall, 1300–1500* (Cambridge, 1970); H. P. R. Finberg, *Tavistock Abbey* (Cambridge, 1951); R. H. Hilton, *The Economic Development of Some Leicestershire Estates in the Fourteenth and Fifteenth Centuries* (Oxford, 1947); I. R. Jack, *The Grey of Ruthin Valor* (Sydney U.P., 1965); A. Jones, 'Land and People at Leighton Buzzard in the Later Fifteenth Century', *Ec. H.R.*, 2 ser., vol. 25 (1972); A. J. Pollard, 'Estate Management in the Later Middle Ages: The Talbots and Whitchurch, 1383–1525', *Ec. H.R.*, 2 ser., vol. 25 (1972); T. B. Pugh, *The Marcher Lordships of South Wales 1415–1536* (Board of Celtic Studies, University of Wales, History and Law Series, no. 20, 1963), Part 3; J. T. Rosenthal, 'Fifteenth-Century Baronial Incomes and Richard, Duke of York', *B.I.H.R.*, vol. 37 (1964) and 'The Estates and Finances of Richard, Duke of York (1411–60)', *Studies in Medieval and Renaissance History* (University of Nebraska), vol. 2 (1965); for criticism of Dr Rosenthal's conclusions see C. D. Ross, 'The Estates and Finances of Richard, Duke of York', *Welsh History Review*, vol. 3 (1966–7); R. A. L. Smith, *Canterbury Cathedral*

Priory (Cambridge, 1943). **Trade and towns**: E. M. Carus-Wilson, *Medieval Merchant Venturers* (London, 1954); E. Power and M. M. Postan, *Studies in English Trade in the Fifteenth Century* (London, 1933); E. Power, *The Wool Trade in Medieval English History* (Oxford, 1941); P. Ramsey, 'Overseas Trade in the Reign of Henry VII: the Evidence of Customs Accounts', *Ec. H.R.*, 2 ser., vol. 6 (1953–4); G. V. Scammell, 'Ship-owning in England, *circa* 1450–1550', *T.R. Hist. S.*, 5 ser., vol. 12 (1962).

J. Cornwall, 'English Country Towns in the Fifteen-Twenties', *Ec. H.R.*, 2 ser., vol. 15 (1962–3); S. Thrupp, *The Merchant Class of Medieval London* (Chicago, 1948); J. N. Bartlett, 'The Expansion and Decline of York in the Later Middle Ages', *Ec. H.R.*, 2 ser., vol. 12 (1959–60); R. B. Dobson, 'Admissions to the Freedom of the City of York in the Later Middle Ages', *Ec. H.R.*, 2 ser., vol. 26 (1973); E. M. Carus-Wilson, *The Expansion of Exeter at the Close of the Middle Ages* (Exeter, 1963).

Chapters 3 and 4

A. Steel, *Richard II* (Cambridge, 1941), and A. Tuck, *Richard II and the English Nobility* (1974) give a good account of the revolution of 1399. For Henry IV the following should be consulted – J. M. W. Bean, 'Henry IV and the Percies', *History*, vol. 44 (1959) and A. L. Brown, 'The Reign of Henry IV: the Establishment of the Lancastrian Regime' in *Fifteenth-Century England 1399–1509: Studies in Politics and Society*, Ed. S. B. Chrimes, C. D. Ross and R. A. Griffiths (Manchester, New York, 1972); K. B. McFarlane, *Lancastrian Kings and Lollard Knights* (Oxford, 1972).

The following books and articles are all most useful for **Henry V** and **The Hundred Years War**: E. Perroy, *The Hundred Years War* (English trans., London, 1961); E. F. Jacob, 'The Collapse of France in 1419–20', *B.J.R.L.*, vol. 26 (1942) and *Henry V and the Invasion of France* (London, 1947); R. A. Newhall, *The English Conquest of Normandy* (New Haven, 1924); *Muster and Review: A Problem of English Military Administration, 1420–1440* (Harvard U.P., 1940); 'Henry V's Policy of Conciliation in Normandy' in *Essays Presented to Charles Homer Haskins* (Boston, 1929); L. J. W. McKenna, 'Henry VI of England and the Dual Monarchy', *Journal of the Warburg and Courtauld Institutes*, vol. 28 (1965); M. R. Powicke, 'Lancastrian Captains' in *Essays in Medieval History Presented to*

Bertie Wilkinson, Ed. T. A. Sandquist and M. R. Powicke (Toronto U.P., 1969).

J. R. Lander, *The Wars of the Roses* (London, 1965, paperback ed. New York, 1967), provides a selection of contemporary documents. S. B. Chrimes, *Lancastrians, Yorkists and Henry VII* (London, 1964), gives an account of the dynastic conflict. K. B. McFarlane, 'The Wars of the Roses', *Procs. of the British Academy,* vol. 50 (1965), and R. L. Storey, *The End of the House of Lancaster* (London, 1966), see them rather as the result of the collapse of government due to the feeble personality of Henry VI. For the most recent re-interpretation of the king's character and its effect on politics see B. P. Wolffe, 'The Personal Rule of Henry VI', in *Fifteenth-Century England, 1399–1509* op. cit. Significant discussion of various crises in the course of the conflict are to be found in H. M. Lyle, *The Rebellion of Jack Cade* (Historical Association Pamphlet, G. 16, 1950); R. Virgoe, 'The Death of William de la Pole, duke of Suffolk', *B.J.R.L.,* vol. 47 (1965); C. A. J. Armstrong, 'Politics and the Battle of St Albans, 1455', *B.I.H.R.,* vol. 33 (1960); R. A. Griffiths, 'Gruffydd ap Nicholas and the Rise of the House of Dinefwr', *The National Library of Wales Journal,* vol. 13 (1964) and 'Local Rivalries and National Politics: The Percies, the Nevilles and the Duke of Exeter, 1452–1455', *Speculum,* vol. 43 (1968); T. B. Pugh, 'The Marcher Lords of Glamorgan 1317–1485', in *Glamorgan County History,* vol. 3. *The Middle Ages,* Ed. T. B. Pugh (Cardiff, 1971), J. R. Lander, 'Henry VI and the Duke of York's Second Protectorate, 1455–6', *B.J.R.L.,* vol. 43 (1960); 'Marriage and Politics in the Fifteenth Century: The Nevilles and the Wydevilles', *B.I.H.R.,* vol. 36 (1963); J. S. Roskell, 'The Problem of the Attendance of the Lords in Medieval Parliaments', *B.I.H.R.,* vol. 29 (1956); G. L. Harriss, 'The Struggle for Calais: an Aspect of the Rivalry between Lancaster and York', *E.H.R.,* vol. 75 (1960); C. Head, 'Pope Pius II and the Wars of the Roses', *Archivum Historiae Pontificiae,* vol. 8 (1970); J. R. Lander, *Crown and Nobility, 1450–1509* (1976); C. A. J. Armstrong, 'The Inauguration Ceremonies of the Yorkist Kings and Their Titles to the Throne', *T.R. Hist. S.,* 4 ser., vol. 30 (1948).

C. L. Scofield, *The Life and Reign of Edward IV* (2 vols., London, 1923), provides an immensely detailed and accurate political narrative but its general interpretation is out of date. See J. R. Lander,[1] 'Edward IV: The Modern Legend and a Revision', *History,* vol. 41

1. All articles by J. R. Lander are now reprinted in *Crown and Nobility 1450–1509* (1976).

G

(1956). C. D. Ross, 'The Reign of Edward IV', in *Fifteenth-Century England, 1399–1509,* op. cit.; the same author's full-scale study, *Edward IV* (1974) is now the best account of both the politics and institutional developments of the reign. J. R. Lander's studies, 'The Hundred Years War and Edward IV's 1475 Campaign in France', in *Tudor Men and Institutions: Studies in English Law and Government,* Ed. A. J. Slavin (Louisiana State University Press, 1972) and 'The Treason and Death of the Duke of Clarence: A Re-interpretation', *Canadian Journal of History,* vol. 2 (1967), provide new interpretations of these episodes. J. Gairdner, *Richard III* (rev. ed., 1898), still provides the best detailed account of the reign though too uncritical of Sir Thomas More's views. It is corrected by Dominic Mancini's narrative, discovered and published by C. A. J. Armstrong, *The Usurpation of Richard III* (Oxford, 2nd ed., 1969). See also A. R. Myers, 'The Character of Richard III', *History Today,* vol. 4 (1954, repr. C. M. D. Crowder, *English Society,* op. cit.); M. Levine, 'Richard III – Usurper or Lawful King?', *Speculum,* vol. 34 (1959); G. R. Elton, *England Under the Tudors* (London, 1955), provides a good short account of Henry VII. For more recent and very readable interpretations see R. L. Storey, *The Reign of Henry VII* (London, 1968) and S. B. Chrimes, 'The Reign of Henry VII', in *Fifteenth-Century England, 1399–1509,* op. cit. and *Henry VII* (London, 1972). For a short interpretation of the 'New Monarchy' see B. P. Wolffe, *Yorkist and Early Tudor Government 1461–1509* (Historical Association, 1966). See also G. L. Harriss and P. Williams, 'A Revolution in Tudor History: Dr Elton's Interpretation of the Age', *P.P.,* no. 25 (1963). Conflicting views on the king's character and the nature of his government are set out in the following articles: G. R. Elton, 'Henry VII: Rapacity and Remorse'; J. P. Cooper, 'Henry VII's Last Years Reconsidered'; and G. R. Elton, 'Henry VII: A Restatement', *Historical Journal,* vol. 1 (1958), vol. 2 (1959), vol. 4 (1961).

For Yorkist and early Tudor **government practice,** particularly financial and legal, the following may be consulted: A. R. Myers, *The Household of Edward IV* (Manchester, 1959); B. P. Wolffe, 'Acts of Resumption in the Lancastrian Parliaments', 'The Management of English Royal Estates under the Yorkist Kings', and 'Henry VII's Land Revenues and Chamber Finance', *E.H.R.,* vol. 73 (1958), vol. 71 (1956), vol. 79 (1964); *The Crown Lands 1461–1536* (London, 1970), an indispensable book for the study of the royal finances at this period. The same author's *The Royal Demesne in English History:*

The Crown Estates in the Governance of the Realm from the Conquest to 1509 (London, 1971) revises the above-mentioned articles in the *E.H.R.*, but at the same time the articles and book contain different information and to some extent supplement each other; J. Hurstfield, 'The Revival of Feudalism in Early Tudor England', *History*, vol. 37 (1952); W. C. Richardson, *Tudor Chamber Administration* (Baton Rouge, 1952); J. G. Bellamy, 'Justice Under the Yorkist Kings', *American Journal of Legal History*, vol. 9 (1965); C. G. Bayne and W. H. Dunham Jr., *Select Cases in the Council of Henry VII* (Selden Soc., 1958).

Foreign policy and its repercussions on domestic affairs are dealt with in J. Calmette et G. Périnelle, *Louis XI et l'Angleterre, 1461–1483* (Paris, 1930) and R. B. Wernham, *Before the Armada* (London, 1966).

Chapter 5

Wycliffe and the Lollards: J. A. Robson, *Wyclif and the Oxford Schools* (Cambridge, 1961), provides a brilliant analysis of philosophical and religious speculation in late fourteenth-century Oxford. K. B. McFarlane, *John Wycliffe and the Beginnings of English Nonconformity* (London, 1952), is the best account of the great heresiarch's life and influence, and M. Aston, 'Lollardy and Sedition, 1381–1431', *P.P.*, no. 17 (1960), 'John Wycliffe's Reformation Reputation', ibid., no. 30 (1965), 'Lollardy and the Reformation Survival or Revival?', *History*, vol. 49 (1964), deal with his later influence. W. K. Pantin, *The English Church in the Fourteenth Century* (1955) and K. B. McFarlane, *Lancastrian Kings and Lollard Knights* (1972) deal with the devotional background of Lollardy and the latter deals with early Lollard influence amongst the minor aristocracy. J. A. F. Thomson, *The Later Lollards 1414–1520* (Oxford, 1965), traces the suppression and survival of Lollardy in immense detail. V. H. H. Green, *Bishop Reginald Pecock* (Cambridge, 1945) and E. F. Jacob, *Reynold Pecock, Bishop of Chichester* (Raleigh Lecture, 1951), show the complex origins of opposition to Pecock.

The problems of the Lollard Bible are dealt with in M. Deansley, *The Lollard Bible* (Cambridge, 1920) and S. L. Fristedt, *The Wycliffe Bible* (Stockholm Studies in English, vol. 4, 1953).

Ecclesiastical organization and the state of the clergy: The most comprehensive account is A. Hamilton Thompson, *The English Clergy and their Organisation in the Later Middle Ages* (Oxford, 1957). R. L. Storey, *Diocesan Administration in the Fifteenth Century* (St Anthony's Hall Publications, no. 16, York, 1959) gives a particularly vivid account of the character of the episcopate. J. T. Rosenthal, 'The Training of an Elite Group: English Bishops in the Fifteenth Century', *Trans. of the American Philosophical Society*, new ser., vol. 60, part 5 (1970) deals with their social origins, education and careers. See also R. J. Knecht, 'The Episcopate and the Wars of the Roses', *Univ. of Birmingham Historical Journal*, vol. 6 (1958); V. H. H. Green, *Bishop Reginald Pecock* (Cambridge, 1945); E. F. Jacob, *Archbishop Henry Chichele* (London, 1967); A. F. Judd, *The Life of Thomas Beckynton* (Chichester, 1971); R. L. Storey, *Thomas Langley and the Bishopric of Durham* (London, 1961).

The following are now the best accounts of the parish clergy: M. Bowker, 'Non-residence in the Diocese of Lincoln in the Early Sixteenth Century', *Journal of Ecclesiastical History*, vol. 15 (1964), *The Secular Clergy in the Diocese of Lincoln, 1495–1520* (Cambridge Studies in Medieval Life and Thought, new ser., no. 13, 1968) and P. Heath, *The English Parish Clergy on the Eve of the Reformation* (London, Toronto, 1969) and J. R. H. Moorman, 'The Medieval Parsonage and its Occupants', *B.J.R.L.*, vol. 28 (1944). For the character of English devotion and piety see A. G. Dickens, *The English Reformation* (London, 1964) and *The Marian Reaction in the Diocese of York* (St Anthony's Hall Publications, nos. 11 and 12, York, 1957). For an example of aristocratic control, patronage and exploitation of the church see J. T. Rosenthal, 'Richard, Duke of York: A Fifteenth-Century Layman and the Church', *Catholic Historical Review*, vol. 50 (1964).

K. L. Wood-Legh, *Perpetual Chantries in Britain* (Cambridge, 1965), E. F. Jacob, 'Founders and Foundations in the Later Middle Ages', *B.I.H.R.*, vol. 35 (1962), and J. T. Rosenthal, *The Purchase of Paradise: Gift Giving and the Aristocracy, 1307–1485* (London, Toronto, 1972) analyse religious benefactions. Dr Rosenthal's book, though containing valuable information, is unhappily marred by fashionable sociological preoccupations which lead him to pose problems in somewhat anachronistically modern terms.

For **Monasticism** writers on the later Middle Ages must rely on Dom David Knowles' monumental *The Religious Orders in England* (Cambridge), vol. 2 (1955) and vol. 3 (1959) which also contains much fascinating information about the church generally. Some of his conclusions are summarized in 'The English Monasteries in the Later Middle Ages', *History*, vol. 39 (1954).

Anglo-Papal relations: The best short accounts are F. R. H. Du Boulay, 'The Fifteenth Century', in *The English Church and the Papacy in the Middle Ages*, Ed. C. H. Lawrence (London, 1965); J. J. Scarisbrick, 'Clerical Taxation in England, 1485–1547', *Journal of Ecclesiastical History*, vol. 11 (1960); E. F. Jacob, *Essays in the Conciliar Epoch* (2nd ed., Manchester, 1953) and D. Hay, 'The Church of England in the Later Middle Ages', *History*, vol. 53 (1968).

The Book of Margery Kempe, selections in modern English, Ed. W. Butler-Bowden (London, 1936, Oxford, 1954) vividly conveys the atmosphere of popular piety. The full text is available in the Early English Text Society's edition (Ed. S. B. Meech and H. E. Allen, 1940).

Chapter 6

The development of education is discussed in N. Orme, *English Schools in the Middle Ages* (1973); K. Charlton, *Education in Renaissance England* (London, 1965); J. Simon, *Education and Society in Tudor England* (Cambridge, 1966); J. N. Miner, 'Schools and Literacy in Later Medieval England', *British Journal of Educational Studies*, vol. 11 (1963) and H. G. Richardson, 'An Oxford Teacher of the Fifteenth Century', *B.J.R.L.*, vol. 23 (1939) and 'Business Training in Medieval Oxford', *American Historical Review*, vol. 46 (1940–1). R. Weiss, *Humanism in England during the Fifteenth Century* (2nd ed., Oxford, 1957) and R. J. Mitchell, *John Free, From Bristol to Rome in the Fifteenth Century* (London, 1955), discuss the introduction and development of humanism.

Literature, art, and music: E. K. Chambers, *English Literature at the Close of the Middle Ages* (Oxford, 1945); A. Renoir, *The Poetry of John Lydgate* (London, 1967); and T. D. Kendrick, *British Antiquity* (London, 1960) and A. B. Ferguson, *The Indian Summer of English Chivalry* (Durham, N.C., 1960), discuss contemporary taste in historical writing and literature. W. J. B. Crotch, *The Prologues and Epilogues of William Caxton* (Early English Text Soc., 1928, repr. 1956) provides a good short account of England's first printer. K. B. McFarlane discusses a literary group in East Anglia in 'William Worcester, a Preliminary Survey' in *Studies Presented to Sir Hilary Jenkinson*, Ed. J. Conway Davis (Oxford, 1957). For drama see G. Wickham, *The Medieval Theatre* (1974).

Of recent works on **Architecture and the arts** the following are stimulating: J. Harvey, *Gothic England* (London, 1947); J. Evans, *English Art, 1307–1461* (Oxford, 1949); G. Webb, *Architecture in Britain: The Middle Ages* (Pelican History of Art, 1956); M. Rickert, *Painting in Britain: The Middle Ages* (Pelican History of Art, 1954); L. Stone, *Sculpture in Britain: The Middle Ages* (Pelican History of Art, 1955); M. Girouard, *Robert Smythson and the Architecture of the Elizabethan Era* (London, 1966); M. W. Barley, *The English Farmhouse and Cottage* (London, 1961); M. Wood, *The Medieval House* (London, 1965); J. A. Wright, *Brick Building in England from the Middle Ages to 1550* (1972); E. G. Millar, *English Illuminated Manuscripts of the Fourteenth and Fifteenth Centuries* (Paris and Brussels, 1928). F. E. Howard and M. Crossley, *English Church Woodwork* (London, 1917), remain standard works. B. Snook, *English Historical Embroidery* (London, 1960), is interesting. **Music** is covered in F. Ll. Harrison, *Music in Medieval Britain* (London, 1947) and E. D. Mackerness, *A Social History of English Music* (London, 1966).

Chapter 7

Select Documents of English Constitutional History, 1307–1485, Ed. S. B. Chrimes and A. L. Brown (London, 1961), provides valuable extracts from original sources. B. Wilkinson in *Constitutional History of England in the Fifteenth Century, 1399–1485* (London, 1964), has translated a splendid collection of documents, but his commentaries have not met with general approval.

The effects of the **Wars of the Roses** and the question of fortifications are dealt with in Bridbury, op. cit.; B. H. St J. O'Neil, *Castles and Cannon* (Oxford, 1960); K. B. McFarlane, 'The Wars of the Roses', *Procs. of the British Academy*, vol. 50 (1965); and J. R. Lander, *Wars of the Roses*, op. cit.

The following books and articles deal with the position of the aristocracy and gentry and their functions in government. K. B. McFarlane, *The Nobility of Later Medieval England* (Oxford, 1973), offers a fundamentally new approach to the formation of the later medieval nobility and their role in war and politics. T. B. Pugh, 'The Magnates, Knights and Gentry' in *Fifteenth-Century England, 1399–1509*, op. cit., is a most significant article on political influences which should also be consulted. J. H. Hexter vigorously attacks the traditional theories on the decline of the nobility and of Yorkist and Tudor reliance on the middle classes in *Reappraisals in History* (London, 1961), chs. 4 and 5. J. M. W. Bean, *The Decline of English Feudalism, 1215–1540* (Manchester, New York, 1968), discusses important changes in property and land-holding relationships between the crown and the feudal classes. The best analyses of bastard feudalism are G. A. Holmes, *The Estates of the Higher Nobility in Fourteenth-Century England* (Cambridge, 1957) and W. H. Dunham Jr., 'Lord Hastings' Indentured Retainers, 1461–1483', *Trans. of the Connecticut Academy of Arts and Sciences*, vol. 55 (New Haven, 1955). J. R. Lander, 'Attainder and Forfeiture, 1453–1509', *Historical Journal*, vol. 4 (1961) and 'Bonds, Coercion and Fear: Henry VII and the Peerage', in *Florilegium Historiale: Essays Presented to Wallace K. Ferguson*, Ed. J. G. Rowe and W. H. Stockdale (Toronto, 1971), provide further suggestions.

The following are also instructive: J. Cornwall, 'The Early Tudor Gentry', *Ec. H. R.*, 2 ser., vol. 17 (1964–5); F. W. Brooks, *The Council of the North* (Historical Association Pamphlet, G25, revised ed., 1966); P. Williams, *The Council in the Marches of Wales under Elizabeth I* (Cardiff, 1958); M. E. James, *Change and Continuity in the Tudor North: The Rise of Thomas First Lord Wharton* (Borthwick Papers, no. 27, 1963); T. B. Pugh, *The Marcher Lordships of South Wales*, op. cit.

M. Keen, 'Brotherhood in Arms', and J. Hurstfield, 'Political Corruption in Modern England', *History*, vol. 47 (1962), vol. 52 (1967), give perceptive comments on contemporary attitudes towards government; Professor Hurstfield's article is now reprinted in *Freedom and Corruption in Elizabethan Government* (London, 1973), part 3, no. 5. W. T. MacCaffery, 'England, the Crown and the New Aristocracy', *P.P.*, no. 30 (1965); J. Russell Major, 'The Crown and the Aristocracy in Renaissance France', *American Historical Review*, vol. 49 (1963–4), and P. S. Lewis, 'Decayed and Non-Feudalism in Later Medieval France', *B.I.H.R.*, vol. 37 (1964), provide respectively interesting material for contrast with later English and contemporary French government.

The following are good studies of **Parliament**: J. S. Roskell, *The Commons in the Parliament of 1422* (Manchester, 1954) and the same author's article on the Lords (see ch. 4); A. R. Myers' 'Parliamentary Petitions in the Fifteenth Century', *E.H.R.*, vol. 52 (1937) and H. M. Cam, 'The Legislators of Medieval England', *Procs. of the British Academy*, vol. 31 (1946), repr. *Lawfinders and Lawmakers* (London, 1962).

Government departments and methods are discussed in S. B. Chrimes, *Introduction to the Administrative History of Medieval England* (2nd ed., Oxford, 1959). The author's earlier work, *English Constitutional Ideas in the Fifteenth Century* (Cambridge, 1936), is a penetrating analysis of contemporary ideas.

Useful specialized studies are J. F. Baldwin, *The King's Council in England during the Middle Ages* (Oxford, 1913); A. L. Brown, 'The Commons and the Council in the Reign of Henry IV', *E.H.R.*, vol. 79 (1964); T. F. T. Plucknett, 'The Place of the Council in the Fifteenth Century', *T.R. Hist. S.*, 4 ser., vol. 1 (1918); J. R. Lander, 'Council, Administration and Councillors', *B.I.H.R.*, vol. 32 (1959); R. Virgoe, 'The Composition of the King's Council, 1437–1461', *B.I.H.R.*, vol. 43 (1970). J. Otway-Ruthven, *The King's Secretary and the Signet Office in the Fifteenth Century* (Cambridge, 1939); J. C. Sainty, 'The Tenure of Office in the Exchequer', *E.H.R.*, vol. 80 (1965); C. Phythian-Adams, 'Ceremony and the Citizen: The Communal Year at Coventry, 1450–1550' in *Crisis and Order in English Towns, 1500–1700: Essays in Urban History*, Ed. P. Clark and P. Slack (London, 1972), is a fascinating account of urban government and habits.

For the state of the **law** the following should be consulted: W. Holdsworth, *The History of the English Law*, vol. 4 (3rd ed., 1945); M. Hastings, *The Court of Common Pleas in Fifteenth-Century England* (Cornell, 1947); C. Ogilvie, *The King's Government and the Common Law, 1471–1641* (Oxford, 1958); T. F. T. Plucknett, *Early English Legal Literature* (Cambridge, 1958); *Edward I and Criminal Law* (Cambridge, 1960); K. B. McFarlane, 'The Investment of Sir John Fastolf's Profits of War', *T.R. Hist. S.*, 5 ser., vol. 7 (1957); J. Bellamy, *Crime and Public Order in England in the Later Middle Ages* (London, Toronto, 1973), is the only modern book which deals comprehensively with this important topic. D. Sutherland, *The Assize of Novel Disseisin* (1973).

Index